C000193374

From
Stone

A BR Life -
Engine Cleaner to
Stone Projects Manager

Volume One:
The Footplate Years

by
David Butcher

THE OAKWOOD PRESS

British Library Cataloguing in Publication Data
A Record for this book is available from the British Library
ISBN 0 85361 623 X

Typeset by Oakwood Graphics.
Repro by Ford Graphics, Ringwood, Hants.
Printed by Pims Print Ltd, Yeovil, Somerset.

Dedication

***In memory of my life long friend
Peter Ian Paton ('Pip')
1934-2002
who started it all.***

Front cover: 'N2/2' class 0-6-2T No. 69538, complete with condensing apparatus, at King's Cross shed on 16th September, 1961. To the left is 'L1' class 2-6-4T No. 67793.
R.C. Riley

Rear cover, top: 'B12' class 4-6-0 No. 61572 in the shed yard at Ipswich on 27th April, 1958.
R.C. Riley

Rear cover, bottom: 'E4' class 2-4-0 No. 62785, in immaculate condition, at Cambridge station with a Cambridge University Railway Club special on 27th April, 1958.
R.C. Riley

Published by The Oakwood Press (Usk), P.O. Box 13, Usk, Mon., NP15 1YS.
E-mail: oakwood-press@dial.pipex.com
Website: www.oakwood-press.dial.pipex.com

Contents

The author sits on the footplating near the smokebox of 'B1' class 4-6-0 No. 61335 at Southend Victoria shed in 1956.   *Author's Collection*

Preface

This volume is the first of two that together describe my first career with British Railways (BR) from 1951 to 1968. It is a memoir of recollections that divide naturally into three phases covering, respectively, the footplate, office, and management years. Described is a career that was considered most unusual - some even suggest, unique - related to the times in which it occurred. Never, in the few fanciful dreams occasionally indulged in as it progressed, was it ever remotely imagined it would ultimately take the course that occurred.

References are made to current railway matters, comparing these with the period being described, as appropriate. Opinions are expressed with which not everyone may feel able to agree - responsibility for them is mine alone. The use of railway language and jargon is kept to a minimum - explanations are given, when used, to put them into context. This is above all a story with the barest minimum of statistical or technical data.

I have been a railwayman, or involved closely with railways, for most of my life in both BR and non-BR employment. With final retirement in 1996, a second career, summarized only briefly, was completed with BR and its successor, Railtrack. Like so much else in my lifelong relationship with the industry, this was never intended! By pure chance, my final day in 1996, found me standing at the exact location where it had all began in 1951 - the wheel had indeed come full circle.

To Paul Goldsmith, long time editor of the *Great Eastern Railway Society Journal* must go the credit for this narrative being written. He enquired over a 20 year period for articles and eventually I relented to begin writing for the 'Journal'. Once started, it became a natural step to continue recording the fuller progression of my working life in a bygone age.

Sincere thanks must be expressed to two lifelong friends - Fred Rich, and the late Leo Gibbs. Both served engineering apprenticeships in railway workshops, before developing their respective professional careers elsewhere. Their positive support has been an invaluable inspiration. To Bob Cartwright, a career railwayman, go my thanks for reading the completed manuscript, and to Gary Sanford a special 'thank you' for his considerable help with scanning many of the photographic images used.

Very special thanks must go to my publisher, Mrs Jane Kennedy, of Oakwood. She has had even greater patience than Paul, having been gently asking for over 25 years. Writing now, rather than then, has allowed a more complete story to be the outcome. It is maybe symbolic that when she first suggested the idea, we were standing on a railway station platform!

To Richard Hardy goes my appreciation and special thanks. He retired from a senior position at the BRB after a career that embraced many aspects of the industry. He is a well known author and speaker about railways in general and of the human impact in particular that working for the railways created upon employees' lives. He has a rare gift for being able to recall with remarkable clarity of detail, events and the names of people he has worked with, from the humblest to the highest, covering the entire period of his railway career. I am especially grateful to him for offering many useful comments giving fuller background details to some of the events described. As the narrative reveals he has been my manager, and hence the references to him in the text. These were written long before we unexpectedly met again when he very kindly agreed to contribute the Foreword. I had no wish to amend any remarks made about him (and of which he had no prior knowledge) and they remain as originally written, except for the additional facts he has suggested, now included.

Foreword *by R.H.N. Hardy*

This book could well be titled 'David Butcher, Railwayman', for it describes his working life in fascinating detail. Although he left British Railways many years ago, I never think of him as anything else but a BR man and I doubt very much if he does. I knew him first as an excellent fireman who once baled me out on his own 'B1', No. 1335. I fancied myself as a fireman but not that night at the end of Southend steam in December 1956.

Redundant, he was moved to King's Cross where he experienced the antipathy so often directed against 'foreigners' since the Grouping in 1923 when there was an influx of ex-GCR men on promotion. Booked with a certain difficult ex-GN driver, David triumphantly overcame this virulent ill-feeling in the only way open to him, a sign of things to come. By 1958, the diesels had arrived and David felt the job would lose the challenge of steam work that he treasured: so he decided to leave the footplate and, having had a good general education, had no difficulty in passing the clerical examination.

He had to be persuaded to apply from the clerical grades for a BR Traffic Apprenticeship on the Eastern Region. After a testing and somewhat argumentative interview (for he was an outspoken young gent) he was selected as a potential manager. His training is graphically described, the pitfalls and high-peaks, the flowering of his ability to become a manager, never forgetting the men he worked with to whom he soon realised that he owed so much. His first spell as a junior manager was at King's Cross Goods, a very rough shop. And so to July 1964 and my first visit to New England as the newly appointed Divisional Manager, King's Cross where I found that same young David Butcher appointed as Yardmaster with an excellent reputation in Great Northern House as well as on the job. And so he should have, for he had had a practical upbringing and a fair understanding of human nature. David had a splendid assistant in Harry Goodchild who had loyally served successive young men promoted over his head and the two men complemented each other. But there were signs that David wanted to move on when he applied for an apparently more prestigious post as Area Manager at Westbury, on the Western Region. He was recommended for interview and was appointed: good for him, so I thought, for my spell on the Southern was an unforgettable experience so why should I oppose a bright young man's chances of well-earned promotion.

It was a bad move to a rapidly changing Region with great opportunities for those in the right place at the right time. In the end, David decided to leave BR for the nearby and flourishing private sector. He did what I thought of doing in 1958 when my morale was at a low ebb. Being quicker on the draw than I, David took his chance to go whereas another door opened to give me the promotion that I had never dreamed possible. Railway life is inevitably one of peaks and troughs and I am sure had David been better advised as to his future, he would have stayed and, sooner or later, that door would have opened for he had the ability and character to have become a BR Senior Officer.

So I read parts of the book with a touch of sadness but there is much to enjoy, to study and on which to reflect. Above all, the reader will learn what our treasured way of life was really like.

Super power in the form of ex-MR 0-10-0 'Big Bertha' No. 58100 and ex-LNER Beyer Garratt 2-8-8-2T on banking duties on the Lickey Incline.   *P. Ransome-Wallis*

A portrait view of 'Big Bertha' at rest at Bromsgrove.   *D. Penney*

Prologue

It is the late afternoon of a warm day in August 1949. On the platform of Bromsgrove station, at the foot of the famous Lickey Incline, on the Bristol to Birmingham main line, the sun is shining and all around is a scene of interesting railway activity.

The equally famous ten-coupled banking engine, built by the Midland Railway (MR) at its Derby works in 1919, and for so long known by her nickname of 'Big Bertha', is quietly simmering nearby to await her next call to push a northbound train up the hill. She has recently been re-numbered from 22290 to display her new British Railways number of 58100, but her tender still displays the letters 'LMS', just discernible under the coating of grime, denoting her late owners, the London Midland & Scottish Railway.

Beyond the low brick wall dividing the downside platform from the adjacent engine shed, is the almost equally famous large Beyer-Garratt engine No. 69999, likewise displaying her new number, taking a short break between duties. She was previously known as No. 9999, and before that more famously as No. 2395, when owned by the London & North Eastern Railway (LNER), and had not long been transferred to Bromsgrove from her duties for many years of pushing heavy coal trains up the Worsborough Incline, near Wath, in Yorkshire. She arrived at Bromsgrove earlier in the year for extended trials on the hill to decide her future use, being scheduled for replacement on the Yorkshire duties by electric traction. Throughout her working life she has been the largest and most powerful unit of steam motive power ever to be provided for use in the British Isles, built by Beyer, Peacock Ltd of Manchester, in 1925. Her enormous tractive power is provided through two eight-coupled chassis power units that act like bogies supporting the intermediate main boiler frame.

To see and then hear these two impressive machines pounding away up the incline creates memories that are not forgotten - their raw aggressive might is truly awesome as they are opened out to full power to blast their way upwards to the top of the hill.

In addition to these two large and unique engines, working alongside each other for the first time, are the fleet of standard former LMS six-coupled side-tank shunting engines to supplement the efforts of the two big engines which are unable to meet the full demand for trains requiring banking assistance.

This impressive array of engines, all allocated to Bromsgrove shed, are used specifically for banking work round the clock, seven days a week. With a steep ruling gradient of almost 1 in 37 commencing immediately off the end of the Bromsgrove station platforms, the Lickey Incline runs in a straight line up to Blackwell, two miles away in the Lickey Hills. To view it looking upwards from Bromsgrove station is an impressive sight.

With two school friends, we are spending the day observing all these engines on their normal duties. The sights and sounds, watching and listening to the trains being worked, is quite unlike anything we have seen or heard anywhere within our already wide experience of observing trains in action. We are staying at Rugby with the relations of one of my friends. Our four week holiday out and about almost every day has been spent visiting places of railway interest, using the many local train services that radiate from Rugby. This trip to Bromsgrove is our final highlight, saved as a special treat, before having reluctantly to return

Six o'clock in the morning! Two of the Lickey bankers, class '3F' tanks Nos. 47303 and 47435, get into their stride as the early morning sun is just peeping over the horizon at Bromsgrove station.
Author

Class '3F' No. 47308 at Bromsgrove shed, taken at 6.00 am. A poor image, but the only one I have of the engine upon which my first footplate trip took place.   *Author*

home to Essex in a couple of days time. Little do I realise how special it will become.

We are armed with the inevitable sandwiches, bottles of pop, chocolate bars and engine spotting notebooks. The station master, whom we have seen at intervals, had stopped to talk with us earlier. He wanted to know where we came from, how long were we staying on the platform, what service were we returning on, and similar questions during the course of a long and very friendly conversation. He is an oldish man - at least he seems so to us 14 year-olds - who has shown a very kindly interest in answering our many questions about the train workings through his station. This afternoon, he again stopped for a shorter talk this time, and again queried our return service home.

Meanwhile, the sun continues to shine as the trains come and go in a steady procession. All those going up the hill stop, either in the station or in the sidings before the station, to attach banking engines, ready for the slow upward journey. Particularly impressive is the working of the many goods trains that come to a stand in the sidings, their engines usually taking water, while the banking engines buffer up ready for the big push. By the time the whole ensemble comes past us through the platform, they are getting into their stride, producing a simply deafening crescendo of noise as they thunder by. It makes the hairs down the back of our necks stand on end on every occasion. The station vibrates as they pound past, working absolutely flat out. We have spent about five hours semi-spellbound by the entire spectacle of the action we have been witnessing. Altogether, a very memorable day out that we are reluctant to take our leave of.

As our train home up the bank to Birmingham is signalled, shoulder bags are packed ready. Imagine therefore our complete surprise, with the train approaching hauled by one of the 'Jubilee' class engines, to be asked, 'Would we like to ride on the banking engines?', by the station master who has appeared by us, smiling broadly. The answer is a foregone conclusion! Before we can fully absorb what he has just said, he is explaining, 'There are three engines banking this train. Give your bags to the guard to look after. One of you can ride on the footplate of each engine. The train will stop at Blackwell, where the guard will look out for you.' We cannot believe our good fortune!

As the engines come out of the sidings to buffer up to the train, we remember to thank the station master. He explains he has enjoyed having us on his station, without having to worry about what we might have got up to, meaning mischief of some sort or other. This was our reward for our 'exemplary behaviour' - not my words, but his. This particular phrase is clearly remembered.

Quickly climbing up into the cab of No. 47308, the middle one of the three engines, we are soon under way. The chimney of the engine behind is barely six feet away. The sheer power and noise that is coming from that chimney is deafening. At the same time, 47308 is pounding away and vibrating under my feet. A once-in-a-lifetime pleasure! The all too few minutes spent on this engine, in a previously unknown world, will have a profound influence upon my future life - although this is not immediately realised!

The rest, as will be revealed, is history . . !

The author on the footplate of 'A4' class Pacific No. 60022 *Mallard*.

Chapter One

Introduction

Throughout the 1950s the steam footplate not only claimed my interest, but also enabled me to earn a living. This concluded with a year on main line express workings as the final era of full steam operations on the East Coast route was dawning. A memorable trip to Newcastle on *Mallard*, the 126 mph world speed record holder for steam traction, and the introduction of main line diesel power, became two defining events to prompt a decision to alter the planned course of my career. I became a willing victim of unplanned decisions thereafter!

The 1960s encompassed a career in management. This was the direct result of a social evening in a local pub - not the usual way to develop one's ambitions! The outcome was a progress way, way, beyond the most optimistic of aspirations that were hoped for at the time. Even now, writing these words, it is still difficult to appreciate how improbable it all was. Hence, the long standing suggestions that it should be written about. With final retirement came the opportunity to do so.

This is a story of the realities of railway life, of daily challenges met and usually overcome, related in a factual and honest way to describe how it really was, not how others today sometimes imagine it was. We will meet some of the personalities who had an influence on my career, and hopefully a genuine picture will emerge of what it was like to be a railwayman - and woman - in an era that has long since disappeared. No business should ever stand still as to do so creates staleness and stagnation. The railway system of today has altered out of all recognition compared to my early years, which is as it should be, to reflect the differing circumstances obtaining today. Equally, this should not mean past practices - related to the eras in which they occurred - were wrong or inefficient, simply because they belonged to a bygone age. If they had been, the industry could not have developed as it has to encompass the needs of today. In 1994 it was a pleasant surprise to discover my long experience of the former ways was still very relevant and helpful to the younger generation, far more so than anticipated.

So, what was the older BR like?

Speaking to people interested in today's age of steam preservation suggests a strengthening opinion of how marvellous it must have been to work on the steam footplate 'in the old days'. I am finding it is being increasingly romanticised by my listeners when talking about it. This does not just apply to the younger fraternity, either. The truth is that many of us had other thoughts to describe it. It was a challenging, and more often than not, very rewarding job in terms of the satisfaction you derived from doing it. But, and it is a big but, this does not justify it being described in the glowing terms sometimes heard today.

Today, there is an ever widening variety of published material catering for people interested in railways and the rail industry. This includes the development and performance of the steam engine. It is good this should be so.

Usually, these tend to highlight the designer and the achievements of his engines. Sometimes, suitable recognition is given to the footplate crews responsible. Sometimes, the driver will be named, but not his fireman. Occasionally, writers are scrupulously fair by including full information. Many writers appear to have only a minimal appreciation of the true conditions that footplate crews frequently worked under, day in and day out. When writings do appear in print about footplate work, some written by former enginemen, these usually record the positive aspects of the work. The less attractive features are only rarely chronicled in other than superficial terms - a quite understandable human trait. This biased emphasis explains, in part at least, why unfairly favourable perceptions of life on the footplate are gaining greater credibility. If allowed to continue in similar vein, such emphasis could come to be accepted as the correct picture and thereby distort the genuine realities of what life in the footplate grades was really like. This would be unfortunate. For want of an adequate description, there is a kind of 'Murphy's Law of Inverse Ratio' at work to suggest this possibility might increase as the number of us who actually did it continue steadily to decrease. Particularly, as the years progress further beyond 1968 when everyday main line steam traction finally ceased on our national network.

Railway work out on the ground was always a hazardous, and potentially dangerous job. Some of the circumstances to be related will explain why. A momentary lapse of attention could incur fearful results, if insufficient concentration was given to a task being undertaken. Within the footplate grades in particular, most enginemen can recall serious incidents that occurred either to them personally, or to their colleagues. In all operating grades, especially in areas of close contact with moving vehicles, danger was always close at hand. Marshalling yard and permanent way staff were especially vulnerable. Personal accident statistics always made salutary reading. The high level of personal safety awareness instilled into all of us by the example of others, and by management, successfully curtailed the ever present daily risk to life and limb to which our duties exposed us. Measured against the normal safety disciplines of the time, to look back now in retrospect with the knowledge of modern approaches to such situations, it was remarkable to achieve the very low level of serious accidents relative to the high level of risk that existed.

I enjoyed my years as an engineman - most of us did. It would have been almost impossible to have continued doing it if we did not. A tiny minority had the odd moment of public acclaim as I was to very briefly experience on one occasion only, to be referred to in Chapter Five. The very considerable majority had no public mention whatsoever. We were simply doing a job, for which we were paid.

It is essential to separate the circumstances we worked in and our experiences then, from the totally different environment that exists now in the era of steam preservation. This narrative will attempt to explain both the positive and negative aspects of our working environment, as well as recalling some of the humour we enjoyed. Today's steam crews receive more public attention, adulation even, because of the circumstances surrounding the operation of preserved engines. This is inevitable and proper for it to occur when and where appropriate. It did not happen to us, apart from the rare isolated occurrence. Herein lies one of the fundamental differences between yesteryear and today. If, in a discussion, my former background is mentioned, a noticeable change will often occur in my listeners. It is an understandable reaction from people, who through no fault of their own, are unaware of the facts. Many are too young to remember BR steam workings - by now nearly half the population of Britain.

These observations stem principally from the considerable interest generated by our preserved railways and main line steam workings, and also as reflected by writings on the subject. To cite two examples - (i) it is taken for granted today, that engines will be clean and in top mechanical order - how nice it would have been for us to have always enjoyed such benefits!; and, (ii) the privatised train operating company crews who handle steam on the main line today, quite rightly have back up support crews travelling with the train to assist them in their duties. Such support was totally unknown when steam power ran the railway system, even on special train workings. We were on our own and survived entirely out on the road (i.e., the track) with very little external help or guidance - banking or pilot assistance excluded - provided for operating reasons to keep traffic moving. A special working might justify an inspector travelling with us, particularly if with an unusual engine, but even this would not necessarily happen. Very occasionally there would be detailed special preparations made, such as for a Royal Train. Otherwise, apart from a visual 'spruce-up' of the engine, most were just another working to be undertaken as a pleasant diversion from the usual routine, with minimal special attention being given or offered to the engine crew.

Please, clearly understand, I am not in the remotest way, complaining. It is how it was done, it was the normal routine, and we did not expect it otherwise. The very progressive and positive steam scene today is excellent, and long may it remain so. For entirely justifiable reasons matters are handled differently now, and furthermore, it is proper for this to be so. My concern is to see these differences explained and placed into a more balanced perspective, by recounting the realities experienced by the average railwayman, and woman, prior to 1968. By creating this record, it is hoped to assist future students of the subject to gain a more realistic appreciation of it.

The earlier chapters describe my experiences as a steam engineman under the working conditions of the post-World War II era and afterwards. These generally applied until almost the final demise of everyday working steam on our main lines. I say almost, because the final months were different. Then, a very considerable interest mushroomed as the wider population, particularly that element concerned for our industrial heritage, woke up to the reality that this section of it would soon be just a memory. We thought at the time this would be for ever. Only the world famous *Flying Scotsman* engine had a signed contract allowing it to continue running on the main line. All other main line steam working was said by the authorities to be totally finished, for good. Fortunately, later events were to reverse this policy, but nobody could foresee this when main line steam finally ended on 11th August, 1968.

I am a great admirer of the progress and achievements of the preservation era. The major re-construction and re-birth from a decimated scrapyard hulk of the only BR-designed express engine to be built, the *Duke of Gloucester*, is a truly magnificent feat by the preservation movement. Likewise, the building from new, currently being undertaken, of the class 'A1' engine, *Tornado*, to the ex-LNER design by A.H. Peppercorn. These truly monumental achievements demonstrate there is now little that cannot be undertaken in the future, so long as the finance is forthcoming and the skills required remain available. Long may it be so.

Today's steam movement owes a considerable debt to the late Dai Woodham, MBE, for running a scrap metal business at Barry Island in South Wales. He did not condemn the last surviving withdrawn BR engines, that fate had put into his ownership, to extinction from his cutting torches. The modern preservation era would have been largely still-born but for this much respected man whose actions allowed over 200 condemned main line engines to survive that should not have done so. Mr Woodham's decision not to cut them up, when he could have done this, has resulted in many people enjoying the pleasure of seeing a lot of them at work today. He was the only person, from among those who purchased the thousands of engines disposed of by BR, who did not ruthlessly reduce them to scrap. He chose instead to earn his financial returns more slowly by offering a lasting legacy to the nation. He gave to the preservation world the priceless gift of time, extending to well over 20 years in total. This allowed the required finance to be slowly raised progressively to purchase all except a very small number of the engines that he had obtained.

To see them in action again is good, but it must be kept in perspective. The many preservation activities do an excellent job in re-creating the ambience of steam. They are supported by untold voluntary hours of effort and finance to keep it alive for present and future generations. But, to suggest doing it for real as we did, would be an extremely difficult, if not impossible, aim to achieve.

Under the 1921 Railways Act, over 100 separate railway companies were grouped into four main companies. These were the Great Western Railway (GWR) - already existing, which absorbed several smaller railways - and three totally new ones: the LMS, the LNER, and, the Southern Railway (SR), companies. Prior to this grouping one company had realised the need for a structured scheme to train young men for management responsibilities. This was the North Eastern Railway (NER). This was soon to be of greater significance to the new and much larger organisations being created under the Act.

Designated as traffic apprentices, these men were selected and trained by the NER which had the commendable foresight to realise the positive benefits of such a scheme. The three year training curriculum was to remain substantially unaltered until the mid-1960s. The scheme was inherited by the LNER who immediately grasped its potential benefit. It stood the test of time very well and produced many worthy managers. These included Sir Henry Johnson, who reached the very pinnacle of the industry to become Chairman of the British Railways Board, thereby completing a long and successful career that had started when he became one of the earliest LNER apprentices. He was to have a key role in my selection into the scheme. I have always understood that only two former steam enginemen, with significant footplate service behind them, were accepted for training throughout the 40 years that the original NER/LNER/BR Eastern Region (BR/ER) scheme remained in existence. I became the second. The first, according to advice received at the time, had served as a commissioned officer with HM Forces after graduating from university. Upon return to civilian life, he opted to join the railway as an engine cleaner 'to get away from it all' until at a later stage, having achieved his purpose, decided to try, successfully, to develop a management career. I had no such ambitions when beginning my employment, nor the educational background to aspire to such an apparently far-fetched idea. Indeed, until the entirely unexpected possibility of it began to emerge, it was not even considered!

At intervals after 1923, the three other companies saw the benefit of the LNER approach. Each was to introduce broadly similar schemes. Inevitably, each scheme was managed differently, but the principle was the same. BR inherited and continued to develop each of them. The training structure for the BR/ER scheme (as the direct successor to the original NER/LNER one) was reviewed in 1963, and subsequently revised to incorporate developing training needs. This review was influenced by observations submitted by our 1961 intake of trainees, on the scope and relevance of the training we were receiving. From the mid-1960s onwards, BR progressively harmonised the differing schemes. Of far greater significance, was the widening spectrum given to potential trainee's background history. This was a long overdue development to improve the opportunities for existing employees like I had been, to gain selection for training. Prior to this, people from a wages grades background were only rarely considered. I had left school just after reaching age 16, to start work in the (lower status) wages grades (retirement at 65), before entering the (better status) salaried staff grades (retirement at 60). To be selected for traffic apprenticeship training (potentially higher status) under the existing (pre-middle 1960s) appointment procedures was a notable achievement. My father was a self-employed builder and my mother a dressmaker, before they married. My success proved that greater consideration should be given to such candidates to supplement the more normal selection criteria. Like so much else at the time, opinions were beginning to be re-appraised, which was a most welcome change. I think my circumstances, together with our group's recommended review of future training needs, played a part.

Initially, even after my selection, such thoughts and attitudes were alien, not appreciating the full significance of my achievement. A long time elapsed before the inevitable pressures of social change that steadily developed after the last war, began more fully to exert their influence. A more level 'playing field' was to emerge in the selection of apprentices, with increasing emphasis on ability and less on social background, although this was still considered. These observations must not in any way be interpreted as a condemnatory social statement. They simply attempt to explain the changing social patterns of society that occurred, as reflected within the rail industry in the era of my selection. The process was to gain a wider momentum through the 1970s and onwards.

By the early 1960s so much of the existing procedural way of managing a railway system, originating from the 'pen and quill' age, had become totally inadequate. The era of information technology was in its infancy and beginning to impact on the old manual ways of running and managing the business. An early main frame computer had started to grapple with train timing. Mechanised accounting centres were being expanded. The traditionalists did not like it, but it was unstoppable, although slow to get going. Management and the training of future managers had to adapt, and hence the developing need for an updated training scheme.

Using the description 'grapple with train timing' is correct as this is precisely what occurred. Mainframe computers in 1961 were enormously huge and very heavy pieces of equipment. Very few firms could afford them, and equally few thought they might need them. The monster installed on the ground floor of Great Northern House in the Euston Road, London (because the total weight precluded a higher level in the building) was obtained by BR because authority hoped it would speed up and simplify the twice-yearly preparation of the seasonal timetables for winter and summer. In those days computers were very much cruder than is the norm today. The micro-chip, as we now know it, had yet to be invented and the total processing power was minuscule compared to that considered normal now. Eventually, the programming was given up as being too difficult. One of the main problems was the then inability of a computer to calculate 'backwards', which is a necessary requirement for special train working. To illustrate this difficulty - party organisers will specify arrival times to meet their purpose and expect the railways to decide the departure time to achieve this. The train timer would 'back path' such trains from the destination point to calculate this: the mainframe computer could not, and thus the expected manpower savings were partially negated and with it the justification for the huge costs involved became diluted. This, of course, was far from being the only problem, but simply one of many that emerged. The concept was correct, the technology was not yet equal to it. Today, all has long since been resolved and computers are an integral component of the industry.

I came to realise, progressing through the training schedule, that my background of wide practical experience was of inestimable value. This was discussed with my senior officers, which factor may have been a contributory influence in their decision to review the scheme. The curriculum was based upon a three year course of training and study for the various exams to be taken. *Except for myself.* So far as can be ascertained, I have been the only apprentice (including the aforementioned other person from the footplate) throughout the long history of the older NER/LNER/BR ER scheme, and the later developments of it covering more recent years, who completed the full syllabus *in half the usual timescale*. This meant my training was completed ahead of the previous year's intake. It caused many flutterings in the organisational dovecot!

In (total) fairness, with their more traditional backgrounds, my fellow apprentices could not initially understand my shortened training. There was no desire on my part to prove a point. From the very first day all my efforts were concentrated entirely upon working and studying hard to succeed. There was neither the time nor inclination to become involved in the reasons for my selection or why my training programme was so dramatically reduced. I knew how it occurred (as will be explained) but this was irrelevant to my contemporaries. My primary aim was to vindicate the faith of the senior officers who had offered me this unique opportunity, and to gain the maximum possible benefit from it. It was very hard going, but eventually successful, particularly as the scope of the training scheme was considered to be equivalent to a full three year degree course, comparable to a typical university curriculum in the intensity of the studying and of the wide depth of knowledge to be assimilated.

The revised training scheme from the mid-1960s onwards, offered a two year curriculum which then led into the pre-existing use of supernumerary appointments offering more practical 'hands on' experience under guidance in the third year. The new trainees did not have to struggle to the same extent through the acres of manual accounting procedures covering goods and passenger train revenues and the like, as these were in process of being altered. Much effort was expended learning the old fashioned procedures, to be of only limited use to me afterwards! Like so much else in the industry, the pace of change was beginning to gain momentum.

A brief experience of working in one of those very old style offices, still complete with inkwells and a row of tall stools at sloping desk tops, had offered a taste of older style conditions. The chief clerk sat at his - level topped - desk on a raised platform in charge of us all. It came as a culture shock to my generally open approach to life to realise such attitudes were not welcome. The atmosphere was one of strict status and seniority and of speaking when spoken to - and this was in 1959! As a probationary clerk, I quickly realised I was the lowest of the low. It was a far cry from the open camaraderie of the footplate, or of office life as it came to be known subsequently. The probability of suffering it for very long would have been unlikely, had events not soon moved forward!

Starting out upon my management career, the drawbacks to operating a system dependent upon steam haulage became ever more glaringly obvious. As the 1960s unfolded, the industry was struggling to retain a viable foothold in the commercial market place. The economic arguments that underwrote the decision to eliminate steam were irrefutable. The emotional case to retain it caused private sorrow to see it disappear so quickly into the history books, but it had to be. For 130 years, from the opening of the Stockton & Darlington Railway in 1825, until 1955 when the modernisation plans to improve the industry were formulated, our railway system had developed and survived on the strength and rugged reliability of the steam engine. But, and it was a very big 'but', it was always very labour intensive. The fuel it used was becoming less reliable and increasingly more expensive. Opposition (mainly against smoke emissions) from environmental interests was growing. Problems of recruiting and retaining sufficient staff to operate and maintain it were proving difficult to resolve. More attractive employment conditions elsewhere took their toll on labour availability.

The possible option of oil firing to improve the economics was not realistic when compared to full scale dieselisation. Limited trials using oil firing during the coal shortages in the late-1940s had not been conclusive. The underlying maintenance drawbacks - highly labour intensive; frequent boiler washouts;

track hammer blow (through the coupled wheels), to name some of the problems - would not be removed by conversion to oil firing. Government legislation to help the growing road haulage industry had begun to offer it greater freedom, by relaxing the previous full state control. Road haulage was becoming a serious competitor in the market place. The emerging commercial realities of life had to be faced up to. Dieselisation offered greater train unit haulage capacity at beneficially lower unit costs per ton/mile. So much so, that steam had to go - and quickly. The final 'Indian Summer' in mainland Britain, when 999 steam engines built to new standardised designs were put into traffic by BR during the 1950s, could not be sustained any longer than absolutely necessary. Very sad, but essential for the future of the industry.

The existing BR commercial attitudes, with which it was necessary to contend as a manager, required urgent review. I tried to advocate a different marketing approach formulated to listen to the needs of customers, rather than to tell them in a somewhat arbitrary manner what the industry could do for them. My attempts to query these attitudes with my peers, was a frustrating experience. Especially so, were the blinkered attitudes towards the smaller, but still potentially significant, customer. It became a considerable challenge. It also became apparent my suggestions were not welcome in the routine HQ decision making levels of the industry. That it was to eventually play a part in my decision to leave BR employment was not foreseen. Some support was received for the main principles of my proposals, but for far too long, empirical attitudes prevailed. I lacked the seniority to make any impact. The chance to make progress was unnecessarily delayed by long established practices and BR suffered in consequence. Road hauliers did not stand around twiddling their thumbs before speaking to potential customers, they got on with establishing their requirements. The established BR technique was to explain what we could offer, not to ask a potential customer what their needs might be. Sales representatives called and went through the motions, but their hands were tied by the disciplines of the system. Creative thinking, certainly prior to the Beeching era, was a rare commodity within my experience - it did happen, but far too often it did not. Even, post-Beeching, it took some years for the new ethos he had proposed to become accepted.

The decision to part company with BR came unexpectedly from reading a newspaper. By chance, there was an advert for a senior post with a company struggling to develop a rail operation. My growing frustration had created increasing restlessness. Battling with an organisation that could always produce reasons for not doing something, and only rarely said, 'Yes, we will do it', had become demoralising. Perhaps a greater patience should have been exercised and the battle to improve matters continued, but there comes a time in any situation when a decision has to be made. After serious thought, it seemed better to progress matters from without, instead of from within, BR. It proved to be a good decision, although a few colleagues saw it as a betrayal. I did not.

The decision 'to go private' was just in time to forestall a real danger of road transport being used instead of rail for a new traffic flow that was under development. The commercial pressures that finally made the use of rail possible drove BR to move forward very dramatically, once the dam of traditionalism was broken. They were given little choice - and the blame came my way for a large element of this! A major reason for the change of policy was the development potential of the particular traffic on offer. The decision to use rail, rather than road, had been a close run contest. Without doubt the impetus generated in favour of rail, following my appointment, played an important role in the decision by my new employer to persevere with developing a rail operation during the final era of the older style BR commercial response to his proposals.

The move into private industry was vindicated. Increasing help was received from my former colleagues on BR, most of whom came to appreciate the reasoning behind the decision to 'change sides'. Regrettably, a small number continued to think otherwise, but this is life. Every effort was made to treat them with complete courtesy, on the basis that everyone is entitled to hold their own opinions. There was one exception to this standpoint - that they did not try to obstruct our rail developments because they were dealing with me. When the message penetrated that our demand for ever more trains was for real, as our plans quickly turned into solid reality and revenue income, this concern gradually disappeared. Our joint efforts laid the foundations for a success story that continues today. Some years later another unplanned challenge, again in the private rail industry, arose to open a second rail operation. Not many people can make such a claim at any time, and certainly not in the era when closing, not opening, was the established trend.

These later developments from after leaving BR in 1968 are outside the scope of this narrative. They are summarised here to explain the motivation to leave. It was pure co-incidence, that both steam and I finished with BR in 1968. Believe it, or believe it not, these two events had not been consciously connected until the writing of this narrative. Remarkable!

A very considerable debt of gratitude is due to BR for their investment in my training. Hopefully, this has been repaid many times over through my subsequent actions to encourage rail traffics. In the years after leaving, and, again more recently in the 1990s, I always endeavoured to remember this. The offer, in early 1994, of a second career with them to help ease a little of the organisational stress of the privatisation process was, yet again, totally unexpected. All of which just goes to prove how unwise it can be to anticipate the future!

To return now to the theme of this narrative. It is appropriate first of all to expand the general background of my career, before developing the details of it. This will hopefully provide the canvas against which the individual parts may be progressively related to the whole as the story unfolds.

A view looking east at Stratford Central Junction in 1949. In the foreground can be seen material lying alongside the track from the recently replaced semaphore signalling. To the left of the signal box is an ex-LMS 'Jinty' 0-6-0T on a goods train. The lines to the left are for Temple Mills, Cambridge, Chingford and Ongar, those straight on are for Shenfield, Colchester and beyond.
British Railways

A view from the top of the water softening plant at Stratford on 19th May, 1956. In the left background an ex-SR 'Q1' class 0-6-0 is taking the line to High Meads at Loughton branch junction with a Temple Mills-Feltham trip freight. In the centre is a transfer goods bound for Temple Mills. On the extreme right is Chobham Farm Junction signal box. On the extreme left part of High Meads carriage & wagon shed can be seen and in the right foreground are the outlet roads for the running shed.
R.E. Vincent

Chapter Two

Setting the Scene

It is a fundamental fact that steam footplate work was a job, no more, no less. In the early post-war years, industries in the larger conurbations were competing to recruit sufficient staff. This fact is often overlooked by people who regret the loss of the so called 'steam years' without acknowledging this major problem. It is important always to remember this when lamenting the loss of ordinary main line steam traction on BR. The long history of dominance by steam power on our national system had to be re-assessed and this was one of the key reasons why, despite the final flourish of new construction in the 1950s, the problems of operating a large fleet were becoming ever more serious in magnitude, particularly the difficulty of staff recruitment. There were also other reasons, to be discussed as our journey together proceeds.

Job vacancies in many industries in the post-war 1940s and 1950s, and to a lesser extent the 1960s, exceeded the ability to fill them. This was largely due to the manpower attrition caused by the war, coupled with the upsurge in demand for trade and industry to meet the demands of the post-war recovery. Plus, a war-weary nation was ill-equipped to cope with these pressures as the country struggled to re-establish a more normal life again. With completion of schooling in 1951 came the possible choice of several potential jobs, had I wished to commute daily to London. This was before any serious attempt to seek employment! I suffered as a youngster from claustrophobia - a legacy of a childhood accident which had caused severe concussion with the after-effects causing the loss of several weeks away from school. This limited my ability to consider available indoor office jobs and influenced a preferred desire to work outdoors. The choice of a footplate career happened also to accommodate my keen interest in railways - an interest that had steadily developed ever since the trip up the Lickey Incline. My initial ambition had been to enter a railway drawing office, but such ideas had to be re-considered as my educational progress faltered after the accident.

All careers have to start somewhere - mine happened to be at the Stratford engine sheds in East London. It has been suggested this was one of the roughest and toughest of any shed in the country. Maybe it was. The wide scope for employment openings meant the shed management had a never-ending battle to recruit sufficient staff. That is, except for drivers, appointed by promotion from being a fireman, but the former were of limited value unless you had sufficient of the latter. Employers, including BR, were being encouraged by new government schemes to begin looking elsewhere, such as to the West Indies, for example. By such means was it hoped to reduce the shortfall in labour availability, so serious had the situation become. These schemes may not seem so remarkable today, but they were a revolutionary concept then. It also introduced the social pressures that developed while different cultures and spoken dialects learned to work together. Listening to a real broad Geordie driver from Gateshead shed alongside the River Tyne in the North-East, and a

A general view of Stratford shed in July 1951. The locomotives on view are , *from left to right,* 'B12/3' class 4-6-0 No. 61572, BR Standard 'Britannia' class 4-6-0 No. 70002 *Geoffrey Chaucer,* 'K1' class 2-6-0 No. 62019 and an unidentified 'B1' class 4-6-0.

This image is included to show the engine upon which I had my very first firing turn at Stratford in 1951. Seen here at Yarmouth Town is class 'J65' No. 68214, destined to be the lone survivor of this class for another three years. It had been an unexpected reprieve when she had her final general overhaul in 1951.   *Author*

likewise broadly spoken West Indian fireman, now domiciled in London, speaking with his quite different Caribbean accent, discussing engine valve gears on one occasion in the mess room was pure entertainment for the rest of us. They were both speaking the English language, but anybody not familiar with hearing both dialects could be forgiven for thinking otherwise! We soon got used to the various dialects and understanding the different cultural backgrounds of fellow workmates and came to think little of it. It was bad enough for all new recruits into the industry, irrespective of national or regional origin, to learn the strange railway language in the first place. Many words and phrases are used that can be incomprehensible to the layman. Official publications would instruct us, for example, 'to run round the train' and yet you never saw anybody doing it! The phrase meant 'take your engine to the opposite end of the train', but that is not how it was written. We all suffered, irrespective of background, until the technical language - both the official written word and the unofficial spoken jargon - was learned and understood. It certainly had its many lighter moments!

At some sheds, particularly those away from the larger city areas, recruitment problems were less difficult. The main flows of commerce are between the main areas of population. It therefore follows that the main demand for employment arises within these areas, and hence the associated labour availability problems that occurred. These were not confined to London, being applicable to nearly all of the larger conurbation areas. There is a limit to how far it is economically possible to move work from a larger to a smaller area of population in the need to mitigate staff shortfalls. A smaller shed might offer less difficult labour availability, subject to its size and facilities being able to cope. Herein lay one of the problems facing the BR management - to move or not to move the workload around, and if the former, within what physical and financial constraints could it be achieved? Another real difficulty was how could they continue to operate and maintain a large fleet of steam engines in often adverse surroundings? In areas of denser population, air pollution in particular, was a difficult and recurring problem that was constantly monitored. Local authorities were becoming ever more particular and less tolerant. The social pressures of environmental awareness were beginning to manifest themselves to a degree previously unheard of. In its wake came ever more stringent regulation. A very few large sheds, such as that at March in Cambridgeshire, were sited away from nearby sizeable areas of housing, but to introduce this as a policy would have been prohibitively expensive.

The irregular shift patterns were a serious drawback that deterred many potential job seekers. The hard physical nature of the work and generally unsociable conditions were further drawbacks when compared to the cleaner working environments available elsewhere. Subsidised canteen facilities in other work places became a factor in discouraging many youngsters from following a railway career. We still had war-time food rationing in the early 1950s. Parents actively encouraged their offspring to seek employment that eased the domestic pressures at home by being able to eat cheaply at work.

There are numerous published descriptions of footplate work. Descriptions of the sometimes sordid reality of the dirt and grime we tolerated in our daily lives

Class 'J19/2' 0-6-0 No. 64668 at Stratford shed.   *Author*

Class 'N7' 0-6-2T No. 69621 at Stratford Low Level having just arrived with the 5.10 pm North Woolwich-Palace Gates service on 1st June, 1962.   *Leslie Sandler*

that were accepted as normal, if referred to at all, are usually discussed only in the most general of terms. Neither am I am aware, for example, of a factual description of footplate employment conditions of service that has appeared in print available to the general reader - the major aspects of these will be discussed. Footplate life created a stubbornness in our determination to succeed. This in turn created a breed of men, the like of whom have now almost disappeared. Looking back with the benefit of hindsight, I was fortunate to share my formative working days alongside so many of them. It was a unique training ground that taught a tough discipline and deep respect for one's fellow human beings. It was to be very useful in my later management career. It also created within me the strength to defend my corner when occasion required. It was an attribute that unwittingly helped my selection as a traffic apprentice. Not by any pre-conceived forethought - it happened through the absorbed instinct acquired in the rough and tumble of my earlier working days.

The average steam engine driver was essentially a simply educated, but intelligent, ordinary working man. Some even aspired to high public office in their local community, as for example, did Southend driver Bert Davies who became Mayor of the County Borough of Southend-on-Sea, and King's Cross driver Charlie Simmons who achieved this honour representing the Borough of Finsbury, in North London. A public recognition achieved by very few of us. I wonder how many of my readers realise that drivers had no formal indentured apprenticeship or the associated official papers to underpin their professional skills, and that they did not receive any official training, other than acquired by their own efforts on the job over many years? In lieu of this gross failure by those in charge, men created in their own unpaid time and often at their own expense, their own organisation of self help that came to be called the Mutual Improvement Classes. These were run on a purely voluntary basis to learn the required knowledge for promotion exams. Such formal instruction would be a usual pre-requisite in any other type of manual labour employment requiring such a high skill level of ability and knowledge - even in those days. In fairness, management gradually began to help the classes indirectly by providing some basic facilities, such as an outdated vehicle for a classroom, and supported inter-shed class competitions, but they did not officially educate or pay staff to learn the required skills that they employed them to use - a staggering situation, judged by the standards of today! Other industries offered formal recognition for comparable skills. All other grades within the public vision had, as a minimum, badges identifying that they were a Porter, Guard, Inspector, Station Master, or whatever. Drivers' and firemen's hat badges simply said 'British Railways' which said nothing to the customer. (In later post-steam years this was to be corrected with embroidered titles stitched on hat headbands.) I cannot think of any other public transport where such an omission was tolerated or legally allowed. Bus drivers and conductors were, and are, required by law to display special badges affixed to their uniforms to confirm their status as authorised Public Service Vehicle employees, for example. Airline and maritime crews display insignia of rank. Taxi drivers must display a local authority licence on their vehicles. Footplate staff neither displayed nor carried any official indication at all of being qualified to be responsible for the safety of the

BRITISH RAILWAYS

B.R. 87257

MOTIVE POWER DEPARTMENT,

Cambridge

9 . 1. 19*53*

Will you please note that you ~~will be~~ *were* *promoted*

from *Passed Cleaner* to *Fireman*

with effect as from 29 . 12 . 52 19

For the purpose of your next firing advance you will be credited with

34 weeks Passed Firing service

C. N. MORRIS
~~Dist. Motive Power Supt~~ Signature
per *R.S.*

To *D. Butcher (394)*
Cambridge

Letter of appointment to the post of fireman at Cambridge on 29th December, 1952.

The little class 'E4' 2-4-0 No. 62781 on which I had my first rostered firing turn at Cambridge in the shunting pilot link. She had spent time in the 1930s working over the Pennines on the Darlington-Penrith/Tebay lines and also a two year spell allocated to Tweedmouth shed from 1940. The severe weather conditions that could occur required a side window cab to be provided, which she retained for the rest of her days. She is seen here at Cambridge shed in 1953.

Author

public. They received a routine letter, sometimes just a duplicated pro-forma style advice, depending upon which area of BR they worked in, to confirm they had been appointed. Sometimes these letters did not even say the requisite exams had been successfully passed! My letter of appointment promoting me to fireman, was written on a pro-forma printed advice dated 11 days after this was effective! I had moved home and arrived for duty at my new shed on the basis of a general instruction to do so! No reference to my successful exam tests or any complimentary remark at having passed these. I even received the carbon copy, not the original, as my 'letter' (*see page opposite*). We were forced to rely on 'in-house' knowledge of our achieved levels of proficiency. Small wonder that many staff had limited pride in the job and looked upon it as just that - a job. Likewise, there were those with great pride in their work who were the happier for it. They were of a type who would have taken similar pride in any work they did. I count myself among this latter group.

In France, for example, aspiring engine drivers underwent a comprehensive technical training and had the satisfaction of knowing the effort of studying was formally recognised. They had the option to retire earlier than allowed in Britain, once they had reached age 50. Such career prospects were attractive and helped employee recruitment. In this country some enginemen did receive a better recognition by their employers, but these were the exception. For example, footplate staff recruited by the former Great Northern Railway (of England) prior to 1923, were eligible to join that railway's Superannuation Fund which offered a worthwhile pension. They could also retire at age 60 - a right they retained throughout their subsequent employment after 1923. Few railways in Britain treated their enginemen so favourably. The new LNER Company soon withdrew such conditions for new recruits, including at the former GNR sheds, who had to work to age 65 with no comparable pension scheme. Small wonder then, that LNER-recruited GN section enginemen were not as happy in their work as they might have been - it created a very understandable resentment working alongside superannuated staff who could retire earlier, although doing the same job.

Drivers accept very heavy responsibilities in their normal everyday work. They have total responsibility for the potential safety of, maybe, many hundreds of people in a train, every single one of whom places their complete trust in them, and similarly, with a valuable train of goods traffic, petrol, chemicals, etc., under their care and control. They were, throughout their working lives, only rarely supervised with no manager nearby to turn to in an emergency. Drivers take continual decisions every few minutes when out on the running lines controlling trains and reading signals. Any one decision taken wrongly, especially if travelling at speed, can lead to absolute disaster. The tragedy at Ladbroke Grove, Paddington in 1999, very sadly demonstrated an extreme case of the enormous damage that can occur when something goes wrong. The very high record of safety in the industry is a silent testimony to the operating skills and dedication displayed every day by railway staff of all grades. Do not forget the numerous times, particularly in the war and earlier post-war years, when badly leaking steam glands could impair forward visibility as well - a circumstance unknown today. Trains not only ran, the most important requirement after safety being that they ran to time. Prompt explanations were required from a driver when they did not, if any of the time lost was booked to the engine. Fifty years ago explanations for just a very few minutes' delay would be called for. Inadequate answers could mean disciplinary action.

Sadly, today, Britain's trains are more generally perceived as being less reliable for timekeeping than once they were. It is questionable to claim punctuality is better or worse than formerly, particularly if the present growth in total passenger numbers since privatisation is considered, together with the many service accelerations compared to the steam years. It is all too easy to be persuaded by relentless media focus on claimed poor performance. Under Railtrack, enormous clerical effort was expended to collate and analyse train delays for the purpose of allocating responsibility. A weakness in present day management is the absence of impartial traffic inspectors out on the ground to chase up the delays and generally impose their authority to put matters to rights. Meanwhile, the organisational mountain created to operate the penalty payment provision clauses in the franchise contracts continues to thrive. It is always the customer who ultimately suffers.

We were regularly aware of traffic inspectors monitoring train workings, but only very rarely did we have a motive power inspector ride with us. Maybe for a single trip, or at most, for a day, but more probably, for part of a single trip only. Other than for promotion exams, men could go through their career as a fireman or as a driver and never have an inspector or manager ride with them in this time. Reflecting on this now, it seems incredible that this was so. In steam days footplate staff were not re-examined in knowledge of the rules once they had qualified in them for each new grade. Drivers could work, say, for 30 years and never have another rules examination. By comparison, most other key operating grades, guards and signalmen, for example, were re-examined every two years. Today, different criteria apply, and standards of direct supervision have been updated. We were left very much to manage on our own and were expected to do so. It was a tough but successful discipline to work under, but it is important also to realise drivers could not be recruited direct into the industry as happens today. This is not a criticism of today's practices, merely a comment to explain the circumstances that now exist.

Today, it is not necessary to know, let alone to understand, the limits to which it is possible to operate a badly run-down steam engine; or, of how to manage such an engine in adverse working conditions; or, likewise, of the skills necessary to coax such a machine to produce a good solid day's revenue earning work. You have had to experience how badly worn engines sound and feel like to work on, to understand what this statement means. Such engines would never be allowed anywhere near a main line today, let alone on one. Here again, this is how it should be for today's engine crews. It doesn't remove the fact that the knowledge and experience required to handle seriously run-down machines in the effort to maintain a booked schedule was once very necessary. To suffer the vibration and heavy knocking from badly worn axleboxes without wedges to compensate for the wear, was not for the faint-hearted. The lumping from badly worn big end bearings with each turn of the wheel would frighten today's crews with no previous experience of it, running at the speeds which were expected, hopefully to keep time. Such severe circumstances could be frightening until the limits beyond which it became potentially dangerous to continue were understood. We tolerated it, but we did not approve of it. As my footplate career progressed, matters did improve as the post-war maintenance arrears were progressively overcome, but many engines could still be lively performers in terms of their poor riding qualities. Our class 'B17' 4-6-0s, for example, were notorious for the rough treatment they could dish out, when becoming due for their next overhaul. Some other classes were little better in this respect, either.

I would never wish to see such former working conditions return. The inherent dirt and grime we had to put up with through engines not being cleaned regularly enough, was always a source of discontent. Equally, it is most important to understand it was not all doom and gloom. We generally enjoyed our work, even if we did not always show it. We could not have stuck with it otherwise. Given my working life over again, in similar circumstances, I would still opt to do it all again if such were possible and I could wind back the body clock to do so, mainly because I learned so much about genuine railway work, and life in particular. It made me grow up and develop mentally, very quickly. It was a far cry from being romantic or glamourous, when measured against our normal experiences, as some writers have attempted to suggest. Let nobody think it was. Challenging? This it certainly was! Herein lay the secret - the challenge to succeed. If we are honest, most of us like to face a challenge, but there are limits to this. More often than not, sheer hard graft in trying circumstances would more accurately describe our working lives. Not always, but too frequently for such difficulties to be considered unusual. The British climate cannot be controlled, but it regularly added its share to our daily lot. Preparing and then working an engine in pouring rain was something we accepted as being beyond our control. The newer BR Standard engines with their tender cab design style did ease the discomfort, but these were in the minority as a percentage of the total steam fleet. Fortunately, for the steam crews of today, most of these circumstances, the weather apart, no longer exist. The world, and with it our expectations from life, has moved on. The excess of dirt and grime has gone - and a good job too! Managed nearly, but not quite, out of existence by today's health and safety at work legislation and practices.

Some will argue such legislation has now gone too far the other way, where such matters are concerned. I disagree, just so long as the more extreme proposals one hears of from time to time are not enacted. Preserved steam workings cannot be fully compared in all respects to general factory-style legislation. Common sense has to prevail, and most times, so far, it has. The problem is that the 'jobsworths' (in Brussels and elsewhere) continue to make their presence felt whenever fresh ideas on how the steam preservation scene should be managed are proposed. It is important that any proposals be kept in a proper perspective. British steam preservation has a very good safety record. This is not accidental. It is because it is conducted in a responsible and disciplined manner.

In ordinary times to work with steam was challenging enough. Imagine what it must have been like, for example, in wartime. Imagine trying to stop

'B17' class 4-6-0 61610 *Honingham Hall* heads the 2.50 pm Liverpool Street-Southend out of Brentwood on 11th April, 1953.   *A.R. Carpenter*

accurately in darkness at stations and maintain a scheduled service in the poorest of lighting conditions. Cabs enclosed to prevent glare from the firehole, quite apart from the ever present worry of bombing raids. Being at school during the war years I was spared such extreme experiences. I have enough memories of the bombs and Hitler's 'V1' flying bomb 'doodle-bugs' and 'V2' rockets, as it is. Full wartime conditions working on the footplate must have been unmitigated misery, judged by some of the descriptions heard from men who lived through it, on those occasions when it was possible to persuade them to discuss it. Working in the aftermath of such conditions when our railways were still struggling to recover from the huge arrears of maintenance and lack of capital investment was salutary enough. It is impossible to refute the considerable difficulties - environmental, economic, and physical - that the operation of a national fleet of main line steam engines used to create. Legislation and social conditions have changed considerably in the intervening years since their demise from 1968 in normal everyday use.

This can be better illustrated by taking an extreme example. Stratford shed was, in its heyday, the largest steam shed in Europe. (I am not sure, it may even have been so in the world.) In December 1922 the full allocation on the roster totalled 555 engines! When I commenced work there in 1951, this vast steam fleet was being reduced, replaced by electric trains, but there were still somewhere about 350 engines on the roster - which still qualified it as the largest steam shed, etc., as just described. Allowing for engines included in these totals under overhaul at any one time and for those out-stationed at the sub-sheds (maybe about 30 per cent overall), this still left an awesome figure of machines physically working out of the shed each weekday. It was an experience to see the place in action and to be a part of it. I regularly was when stationed at both Cambridge and Southend sheds after moving away from working there.

With the working practices then taken for normal, Stratford would today be shut down by official agencies. They would require the many working hazards to be rectified. Always assuming, (i) that they could be, and, (ii) the air pollution control authorities had not beaten them to it. In practice, of course, under today's procedures had they been in existence then, the inspectors would have consulted and initially issued improvement notices. It would have been prohibitively expensive, if not impossible, to have complied with such requirements. It would be impossible to re-create that establishment today, even on a limited scale, hoping to operate it in a similar manner, with the working practices that were followed and accepted as normal and which enabled the place to function in a practical manner. These had developed over time, based on the cheapest or most convenient, i.e., usually the quickest way, to do a task and which, in turn created the flexibility essential to operate the shed. To handle the truly massive volume of daily engine movements required slick operating practices, with time being of the essence.

Safety and the application of safe working practices was always important, but not necessarily as the over-riding priority. This may seem a surprising comment to make - let me explain. Staff grew up with the practices that existed, and understood them. This did not automatically mean they were the safest possible way to perform a task, but it created its own degree of built-in safety. Safety often meant time, which created physical constraints, which created cost. All costs were strictly controlled - they had to be. This is not a criticism, but, yet again, a plain statement of the facts as they then existed. BR was little different in this respect from most other large employers of the time. Indeed, the industry was probably better than most in respect of its ongoing diligence to achieve the highest safety standards. Safety of staff in the working environment was taken very seriously, but not to the extent it would be today under modern legislation. This is inevitable, because the development and application of safer working methods, like so much else in life, is a continually evolving function.

As an easily understood example to illustrate the point being made, there was a lapse of several years between the introduction of overhead electrification and the eventual provision of safety warning signs affixed to engines to remind us about the existence of the overhead catenary. This is the kind of safety consideration that was lacking for so long, as I had reason to know. When these signs were first suggested, their provision was queried on grounds of cost. Eventually, came the day when there was the inevitable fatality. Then, and only then, was the decision finally taken to provide them. It is difficult to envisage such a failure today to highlight an obvious potential hazard for so long from after it was created.

Steam sheds in normal BR days were potentially very dangerous places, the larger ones especially so. Steam sheds in preservation can still be so, if due respect and precautions are not observed. Generally today, the railway preservation establishments are well organised and managed. They are usually much smaller than the average, even the smaller, BR shed was, and therefore easier to organise and control.

In writing a narrative of this kind, it is difficult to entirely avoid the use of the everyday technical terms that we used. As examples, I will refer to 'link' and 'diagram' workings which are an integral part of any description of footplate work. The former is not a piece of metal, but a group of staff allocated to a particular segment of the work roster undertaken by a shed. The latter is not a drawing, but a daily duty roster of work instructing the engine crew as to what they are required to do during their shift on duty. The daily diagram duties will be described in plain language rather than use the presentation style we read in tabulated form each day, which to a non-railway person might be confusing to understand. Should a particular term not be explained, please accept my apology in advance. It can be a delicate task to tread a middle path between clear description and tedium caused by over simplification.

One fundamental description must be explained - to footplate staff, steam power was always an engine, not a locomotive; diesel power was - and is - normally a locomotive and not an engine. This is because diesels can be powered by more than one engine within the one locomotive structure. I know it is confusing, but this is how it was, and remains so to this day. You never asked a steam crew, 'What locomotive number have you got?', you simply asked 'What's your engine?' Today's diesel drivers are usually asked for their 'loco. number'. In both steam and diesel parlance we rarely referred to the class description, only the number, when answering this sort of enquiry.

Initially, after forsaking the footplate, office life was not easy. Fortunately, the earlier problems with working indoors had partially receded, but not entirely. Life in the RAF had helped in this respect. My first clerical grade appointments offered the opportunity to go walk-about, which 'broke me in' gently to my new lifestyle. The fear of being trapped in an enclosed space has never left me. Working in smaller sized offices was always stressful if unable to escape for a short break.

My six month probationary period as a clerk was undertaken working shifts at King's Cross passenger station on the parcels section. It was difficult mentally, to adjust to this new environment, after the varied life of the footplate. Securing my first permanent post at the Hornsey engine sheds in North London was helpful. This offered the chance to again be involved with the everyday life of such an establishment. The primary purpose of the shed was to provide power for the cross-London goods trip workings, and for the slower main line goods trains between the London, Ferme Park, and Peterborough, New England, yards. Variety was provided by the earliest series of main line diesels, then entering service. These were housed alongside the steam engine shed roads, which was far from being ideal. Eventually more modern facilities were provided at the new Clarence Yard Depot built two miles north of King's Cross station. This occurred after I had moved to pastures new, in the Liverpool St offices.

At Liverpool St, although this was a promotion move, my duties were to be the junior clerk in the office. This was a compact and completely new section. From this office we planned for the major recasting of the Great Eastern (GE) section timetable workings introduced during the 1959/1962 era. It was a very interesting phase of railway work with which to be associated. The knowledge gained complemented my earlier 'outside' working experience. It became a key foundation upon which to build my subsequent career and proved very useful.

My final clerical appointment found me working in the King's Cross Line Traffic Manager's Office HQ as the editor of a key safety document issued each week to operating staff. It was a demanding task requiring total accuracy of detail. The need to achieve prompt distribution to every single person requiring it in connection with their normal operating duties, was always a challenge. It required the weekly printing schedule to be managed to precise time deadlines at each stage of the production sequence. We had the occasional problem, but during the few months I was doing the job, the system never failed. The major problem was the intense level of concentration required while working in a cramped office. I just had to escape every lunch hour into the wide open spaces. The job was good, the small office was not!

This demanding and strict discipline with such a critical safety implication taught me a very fundamental lesson that was to help in guiding me as a manager. My manager, Jack Watson, trusted me completely. He never once interfered in this very important task, but emphasised he was always available to help if needed. In my turn, I was to remember this trust and never forgot the professionalism of my staff. You have to trust your staff and learn not to interfere except when they expected this or sought guidance or a decision. When one is the boss it is not always easy to do this. To ignore such a fundamental consideration is to invite problems. Many managers just have to interfere - they are often wrong to do so. This goes hand in hand with

The prototype 'Deltic' speeds through Hornsey with the 12.20 pm Hull to King's Cross express on 12th April, 1960.   *M. Edwards*

Hornsey shed scene on 15th June 1959. On shed awaiting their next call to duty are 'J50' class 0-6-0Ts Nos. 68979, 68960, 'N2' class 0-6-2T No. 69524, and 'J50s' Nos. 68894, 68983, 68968, 68926 and 68970.   *Author*

encouraging pride in a job properly and safely done, sometimes in difficult circumstances.

Staff in each and every department make a contribution by being a part of the whole. Few, if any, do their particular job for long without back up support from one or more of the other functions involved. My footplate background and subsequent management training gave me this essential insight. It is important to appreciate how a company is structured and organised, from the ground level upwards to the higher levels. Then, hopefully, your own decisions harmonise more readily with the larger overall objectives. If your staff can appreciate this, their support will increase. By encouraging them to develop their own professional skills and delegating authority downwards as far as possible, you liberate their thinking. Job satisfaction is a tremendously positive attitude if it can be attained. A manager must help this to happen. All managers have their own philosophies. Mine was to practice trust, delegation, and encouragement, as the three key issues. You will find the other aspects of managing any activity, such as technical competence, responsibility, and self-discipline, for example, will usually emerge naturally, once you have set your staff mentally free of needless restrictions. If you doubt these offered words of advice - go try it. You may be surprised!

To summarise my career progression - August 1951 to January 1959 was on the footplate (less two years national service); thence to September 1961 as a clerk; thence traffic apprenticeship training until spring 1963. My management career spanned the remaining years to resignation in December 1968. The chapters progress in chronological sequence to reflect this.

Having thus set the scene, let us begin. We have prepared the engine - the content of the story has been outlined. We must ensure the cylinder drain cocks are open to avoid possible damage before the cylinders have warmed up. (To cause damage in this way was a disciplinary offence.) We will put the engine in the correct gear for the movement to be made - in our case forwards, because this is the direction we are taking as the story unfolds. Next, after making a check all round that it is clear and safe to move, and that our power brakes (as distinct from the hand brake) are working correctly, we will 'pop' the whistle, release the hand brake, take a second quick visual check around to make sure nothing is in our way, and gently ease open the regulator . . .

But . . . before doing so - are we going to obey Rule 0 in the Rule Book? (This officially non-existent, but very important requirement, will be referred to again - you are warned!) You mean to say that as my companion on this journey back into a bygone age, you haven't made the tea? A railway runs on tea - it is most important to understand the vital contribution made by this humble ingredient to a successful operation! Management had their failings, but they never, ever, failed to provide the basic equipment of water, kettle and a source of heat, wherever it was needed. They well knew the value of doing so - it was more than their job was worth to overlook it. The staff provided the ingredients, authority provided the where-with-all to create it. Today, we describe such simple equipment as the 'infrastructure' - how times they have a-changed, with the use of modern jargon! Describe it how you wish, the important point is to remember what you mean, and to make sure the other party likewise also understands you. Another essential skill - clear unambiguous communication.

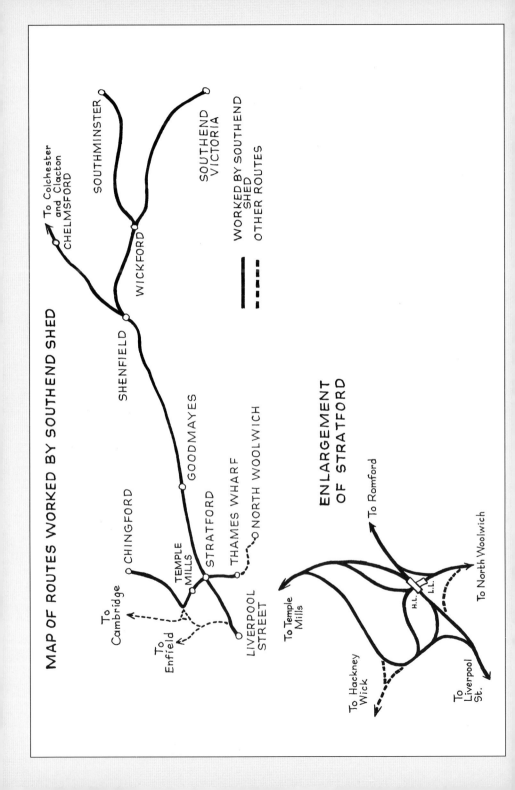

MAP OF ROUTES WORKED BY SOUTHEND SHED

SOUTHMINSTER

CHELMSFORD
To Colchester and Clacton

WICKFORD

SOUTHEND VICTORIA

WORKED BY SOUTHEND SHED

OTHER ROUTES

SHENFIELD

GOODMAYES

CHINGFORD

TEMPLE MILLS

STRATFORD

THAMES WHARF

NORTH WOOLWICH

To Cambridge

To Enfield

LIVERPOOL STREET

ENLARGEMENT OF STRATFORD

To Romford

To North Woolwich

To Temple Mills

To Hackney Wick

To Liverpool St.

H.L.

L.L.

Chapter Three

The Footplate Years - Southend

The detailed diary notes of my footplate career covering 30A Stratford shed (1951), 30D Southend Victoria shed (1951/52), 31A Cambridge shed (1953), and 30D again (1955/56), and, finally, 34A King's Cross shed (1957/59), make very interesting reading today. (1953/55 were spent with the RAF.) All now just memories supported by detailed notes written up each day to record my duties. It is a long time ago, but which readily returns to life again, when re-reading the diaries!

Before leaving school in July 1951 an application was submitted to become an engine cleaner. In due course back came instructions (accompanied with a free travel pass) to report for interview at the Stratford shed offices. My application form had mentioned my grammar school education. Become a humble engine cleaner? No way, I was told, 'We wish to recruit you as a clerk'!

The superintendent in charge of the Stratford District was T.C.B. Miller. I think it was his chief staff clerk, Mr Cox, who interviewed me, with the declared desire of recruiting me as a clerk, not an engine cleaner. And so started the first of many contrary incidents that were to occur at intervals throughout my career. To the chief clerk's considerable surprise, he learned my humble ambition was to be an engine cleaner or not at all. We had quite a tussle! People who tried to dictate my life usually received short shrift, often much to their surprise. Ask? - yes; dictate - very difficult!

My instinct has rarely let me down in my desires from life. Two, in particular, predominated over all others. To be happy in my work, and to retire at age 60, earlier if possible. The first was always followed, sometimes to the detriment of my income. We are granted one journey and one journey only through life. To enjoy and gain fulfilment from it, has always been the overriding objective, subject only to one primary consideration - always to be aware of the effect of any actions taken upon those around me. The second was an ambition to achieve, although unsure as to how it would happen. In the event it happened at age 58, only for BR to then spoil it! But, as already mentioned, this is another story, beyond the scope of this narrative.

Pressure was then applied to say I should work at Stratford. Wrong approach! My desire was to be at Southend; where there was a vacancy.

Another tussle, resolved by me finally asking, 'Is there, or is there not, such a vacancy?'

The answer was a reluctant, 'Yes'.

So it came to pass that my interviewer's wishes were thwarted, not once, but twice. Much later one learned such things were not done. Unfortunately, Mr Cox had a small problem - he did not yet employ me. In complete innocence my own wishes took precedence, not his. It did me no harm, but it might have done. At age 16 you have a lot to learn! In retrospect, his expressed wishes were entirely understandable; as a manager I would have had similar views towards a suitable job applicant.

The great adventure started by reporting for two weeks classroom training in the 'Instruction School' at Stratford shed. This had been specially set up to help ease the acute footplate staff shortages. To have such a facility at a large engine shed was not unknown. To be paid to learn was totally unheard of in those days. It proved, if proof were needed, of how serious the need to recruit additional manpower had become. It showed the positive steps being taken to overcome the problems. Normally, youngsters like myself were taken on and expected to acquire the requisite knowledge through voluntary study in our own time during many months of cleaning engines. This system had broken down at Stratford in the post-war era. A 'fast track' training scheme became essential to reduce firing vacancies by curtailing the time taken to the barest minimum between initial recruitment and getting us to work out on the job. This served a twofold purpose - firstly, it met the need to get new recruits qualified as quickly as possible, and secondly, it ensured they quickly earned the higher rates of pay to discourage any desire to seek higher paid work elsewhere, related to cleaner's pay rates. Both important factors at a shed like Stratford.

All new cleaner boys had to suffer initiation ceremonies - in my case a thick, gooey, cylinder oil poured over me - and to suffer our legs being pulled unmercifully. We all went through it. I remember being sent to get pink paraffin for the red tail lights. 'Remember to keep it separate from the blue paraffin for the purple head lights and the clear paraffin for the white headlights' was the stern instruction given.

Paraffins in these three colours denote different burning characteristics. In a new and strange environment, changing from childhood school to adult working place, what might you have done? (GE section engines carried a route code display system comprising different combinations of purple and white circular enamel discs by day, with similar coloured headlights by night, to assist signalmen in correct train routing over the intensively worked London area lines. See picture on page 30 for an engine exhibiting the London-Southend headcode.) The Stratford storemen and most other staff throughout the shed were, clearly, very familiar with the routine. We thus learned our way around this vast establishment being sent on from one building to the next, in a quite fruitless search looking for the pink paraffin stores! It was a prank that gave a good laugh and served a very useful purpose. We sensed it to be a prank, and yet had our doubts, so convincing were the perpetrators of it. Being unsure, we had not the courage to disbelieve it. Thus, we hung ourselves in the eyes of our peers, but early on learned our way around that vast sprawling complex. It was all good innocent fun! We soon learned, and were not slow to inveigle our successors into the same trap.

After just 9½ days of closely detailed instruction (we worked Saturday mornings) we were examined in our newly acquired knowledge and sent out firing as part of the qualification procedure. We learned the fireman's duties for preparing and disposing of engines; the main rudiments of the passage of steam round the engine; the automatic braking systems - both the Westinghouse compressed air and the vacuum; steam heating; boiler injectors; how to break and trim coal; personal safety; rules and regulations; principles of signalling and the different types; wrong line orders (used in emergency train working arrangements); train protection; hand shunting signals; coupling and uncoupling procedures; engine management; assisting the driver and working to his instructions; and much, much, more. Looking back, the senior driver who took the class worked very hard to achieve all this, and was a good instructor. There were about a dozen of us in the class. His clarity of explanation, in no nonsense language, was excellent. One rapidly learned a new vocabulary, both official, and unofficial, not always in the Oxford Dictionary - this latter filling gaps left out from the school education! Sadly, his surname cannot be recalled, although being able still to clearly recall his round, ruddy complexioned face, even after all these years. His first name was Sidney - 'Sid' to all and sundry. He well and truly earned his wages during that fortnight. He earned 1s. per day extra on his basic pay for his labours, forfeiting the chances to earn normal overtime money, which was a dubious reward for such enthusiasm and dedication. He pushed us hard and we learned, we had little choice! On my last day at Stratford after being successfully passed out by the inspector as competent to undertake firing duties, it is nice to recall the thanks due to him were remembered and returned with a genuine handshake by him to wish me good luck. As events turned out, our paths were never to cross again, which in a way was a great pity. The basic disciplines and respect for authority that he endeavoured to instill in us at the very start of our careers have, for me, stood the test of time very well.

My first footplate trip was very nearly the last - on a class 'F5', 2-4-2 'Gobbler' tank No. 67208 (so called because they allegedly gobbled the coal quicker than other engines) from Stratford Low Level to North Woolwich and return. (*Appendix One* explains the engine wheel arrangements and ex-LNER engine class designations.) I had still to acquire my 'footplate legs' and in Silvertown tunnel there was a slight kink in the track. Well known to all, except myself who was suddenly overbalancing and on the way out of the cab. The very alert driver grabbed me just in time. He apologised and was upset for not warning me in good time to hold on. This was the first of the mythical nine 'lives' said to be granted, to be used up during my railway career. The inherent dangers of railway work have been mentioned - in my career, over half of the lives were to be used up by potentially serious events. The fact of becoming directly responsible for the maintenance standards of this very self same stretch of line, over 40 years later, provides an ironic twist to this particular incident. I would regularly inspect this tunnel and it never failed to recall the experience, such was the impression it had made!

My first firing turn, after passing the required oral and written examinations was with another fireman, but my first 'proper' turn without someone to assist my efforts, was on an old design of shunting tank engine built in 1893, the small class 'J65' 0-6-0T No. 68214. This had just been out-shopped after overhaul and was being run-in before returning to its own shed. It somehow seemed appropriate for the newest fireman to be on one of the oldest engines. She had been unexpectedly granted a reprieve to work one final spell before scrapping when she next returned to the works. (Like ships, railway engines are normally referred to in the feminine gender - I have no idea why.) The following week found me firing to driver Arthur Peters who became my first regular mate,

An aerial view of Southend shed taken from the top of the coaling tower. The curved track to the top left of the turntable was called the Half Moon road; the next road to the right was known as the disposal pit road and beyond it in the further distance is the 100 Foot road. The small concrete building, centre right, was the store for oil and paraffin. Southend Victoria station is to the top right. Top centre is the water tank over the staff accommodation and the water softening plant. The wooden buildings on the left are temporary structures erected for the 1,500v dc electrification works. *Author*

albeit for only six days. We worked on more ex-works engines, of classes 'N7', 0-6-2, and 'L1' class 2-6-4 tank types. After just eight firing turns, I was passed out for firing duties following a practical examination by the inspector as being sufficiently competent to take up duties at Southend, and my official grade description became 'passed cleaner', the first promotion had been achieved from being a 'cleaner'. There was a final attempt to change my mind, hoping to keep me at Stratford, so pressing was their need to try! (A 'turn' is a work duty - it can be of any duration, not necessarily a full shift. A firing turn might be to cover just one job of work such as disposing of an engine, in between normal cleaning duties.)

Reporting to Southend with just three weeks seniority to my credit, soon had me allocated into one of the cleaning gangs as the junior hand. The full complement of cleaners at the shed was 24. Being a seaside town with limited full year-round employment opportunities, it was a little easier usually to have, although not always, a full staff complement. We were divided into four gangs of six, booking on duty in a four weekly rotation at 8.00 am, 2.00 pm, 4.00 am and 10.00 pm. The 24 hour clock was not used then, this was to come later on. Each shift was for eight hours. As a 16-year-old my pay commenced at 1s. per hour. We worked a 88 hour, 11 day fortnight of 6 days and 5 days per week alternately. The twelfth day was a rostered 'Rest Day'. These rotated each fortnight beginning on Tuesday in fortnight one, Wednesday in fortnight two, and so on, to give us a long weekend (Saturday/Monday) off duty in each 12 weekly cycle, which was rostered between the 2.00 pm and 4.00 am weeks. This gave us just a minimum long weekend off. A request to have this altered to fall between the 4.00 am and 10.00 pm weeks to give us a really long period off was refused as this interfered with our potential availability for Sunday rostering! (It was almost impossible to have been available between finishing at 10.00 pm Saturday and booking on again at 4.00 am Monday, and hence why this weekend was chosen.) We had rostered Sunday duties, paid at overtime rates. On average, we had one Sunday duty per 4 weeks. On a basic weekly wage of 48s., for a 6 day, 48 hour week, income tax was deducted at 2s. 10d. Being qualified as a passed cleaner, my pay was increased when on firing duties. When on cleaning duties, the pay for both cleaners and passed cleaners was the same. A full week of firing turns could equate to as much as £5 15s. 0d. before stoppages. These rates of pay were increased after October 1952. The basic weekly rate at age 16 then became 56s. although by that time, being age 17, my basic pay had increased to 63s. 6d.

After handing over a share to contribute towards the household expenses and my keep, this was real money compared to the 3s. per week that had previously sufficed! (This had been 6d. pocket money for doing odd jobs , plus 2s. 6d. earned by helping the local milkman every Saturday. For many years it was expected for my 6d. to be divided into - 2d. for saving in the Post Office bank; 2d. for sweets [still rationed]; and 2d. to spend as I wished). Although now in regular work, my father's signature was still needed as guarantor for the hire purchase agreement to buy a new bicycle for work, being under age 18 - this is one of the very few aspects of life covered in this narrative that has not altered during the intervening half-century!

An aerial view of the approaches to Southend Victoria station looking towards Prittlewell. On the left are the upside carriage sidings (with the coal train); then the up and down main lines with downside carriage sidings partially obscured by the concrete coaling plant hopper.

Author

Ex-Great Central Railway class 'A5' 4-6-2T No. 69826 at Norwich shed. In 1951 several members of this class were sent on loan to Southend shed for several weeks while the Liverpool Street station turntable was rebuilt. This engine, with others of the same class, were long term residents at Norwich shed in the 1950s and often worked the Cromer line services. While at Southend they generally gave a good account of themselves and were accepted by the crews, although being totally different to their familiar ex-GER classes.   *Author*

Higher grade duty was very strictly governed by seniority. The senior cleaner not already out firing on each shift had first claim for firing duties, within the hours covered by that shift. A turn of duty could start up to a maximum of 4 hours either way of the rostered booking on time (2 hours for drivers and fireman). This was subject to having a minimum 12 hour rest period between duties when out firing. When cleaning we could be brought back into work on a shorter rest period. If it was known in advance that a vacancy existed for a full week of firing duty then this was allocated on a total shed seniority basis. This was irrespective of the particular shift we would have been on. This ensured the most senior hand had first claim for the work, and so on in descending seniority order. The daily vacancies were allocated to the nearest shift, again in descending order of seniority, but within that shift. We used to watch the posted roster sheet amendments like hawks to ensure correct allocation of duties. Our duty roster clerk, Tom Jackson, rarely slipped up!

Daytime hours, worked between 6.00 am to 10.00 pm, were paid at flat rate. Overtime hours between the same times were at time and one quarter. Night time basic hours, 10.00 pm to 6.00 am, were likewise at time and one quarter. Night overtime was at time and one half. Sunday duty, midnight Saturday to midnight Sunday, was paid at time and three-quarters throughout between these hours. On weekdays, the moment we signed on (at anytime between 0.00 am and 11.59 pm) we were guaranteed 8 hours pay, unless becoming incapacitated for work during the shift, or for disciplinary reasons. On a Sunday turn (i.e., booking on between 0.00 am and 11.59 pm) we were paid for actual hours worked, which might be for as little as 4 hours only. It would occasionally occur that we booked on early am Monday, then again late pm Monday to Saturday, thus doing seven shifts within the same calendar weekday week, although a rest day would be rostered, if possible, to avoid this. At sheds were staff shortages caused rest days to be worked, then up to eight turns might be worked, if a Sunday duty was also rostered. Higher grade work was paid at pro-rata rates per hour for the hours on each type of work. We could be on cleaning duties for, say, seven hours, at cleaners' rate of pay, then do one hour on firing duties at the appropriate firing rate of pay. If we did a minimum of two hours during our shift as a fireman, we qualified to be paid for the full shift at the firing rate of pay. Similar arrangements applied for a passed fireman on driving duty. It could be a nightmare for the wages office to calculate our timesheet, particularly if, in addition, we had undertaken shed staff duties, as well. Firing and driving rates of pay progressed upwards each year over a six-yearly graduated pay scale related to qualifying experience, to achieve the highest pay rates. Cleaners and passed cleaners pay scales were related to age, with an increase at each birthday, when the highest pay rate was reached at age 20. We commenced in the scale according to our age when starting in the job. This, again, was a six-year scale, with the lowest level for those aged 15 - in those days the permitted school leaving age.

We could not undertake firing duties below age 16, even if already passed out to do them, which might be arranged ready for reaching 16 years of age. Officially, we were not supposed to fire on running line duties until age 18, but due to the acute staff shortages, dispensation had been given to relax this to age 16. We were regularly firing on the main line at this age and I was appointed as a permanent fireman at age 17. Similarly, drivers retired at age 65, but special dispensation was permitted up to age 70 in rare circumstances, but not on running line duties. Stratford was a 'rare' circumstance for drivers, Southend was not, but both sheds had age 16 dispensations. In due course these dispensations were withdrawn, first for age 70, and much later, for age 16. At the outset of my schooling the minimum leaving age was 14, subsequently raised to age 15. If my birthday had been in August, and I had left school in July at nominal age 15, it would have been possible to have commenced at age 14. Thus, it was still possible, just, to achieve a full 50 years' service with retirement at age 65 for a youngster starting work in my era. Several instances are recalled of staff retiring after 50 and more years' service on the footplate. New entrants have been unable to achieve this length of service since the minimum school leaving age became age 16.

Firemen and drivers progressed up their respective pay scales, related to their length of qualifying service in the grade. Progression in these grades was not age related, although we had to be at least age 21 (normally it was age 24), to be passed for driving duties as a passed fireman. Again, age 21 was a special dispensation. As a cleaner we were credited with a firing turn on each occasion we did the higher grade duty, which qualified us to count these up. When we reached 287 turns credited, we became entitled to permanent pay at the 1st year firing scale rate even if on cleaning duties. Likewise, if we were still not appointed a permanent fireman, and achieved another 287 turns we then qualified for the second year rate, and so on. To reach the all important first 287 turns credited could take up to three years at Southend; at other sheds this timescale would vary considerably. The same procedure applied for firemen qualified for driving duties, so that when they reached the first 287 driving turns, they received the 1st year driving scale rate, and so on. Before the introduction of Rest Days the qualifying number had been 313 turns, i.e., 365 days, less 52 Sundays equalled one working year. When the 26 Rest Days per year were agreed, i.e., one per fortnight, then 287 days became a working year. In later years, after my time on the footplate, as additional days off were agreed to achieve eventually a regular 5 day working week, so the annual number of qualifying turns for the permanent higher grade pay were reduced pro-rata to compensate. Footplate pay scales were complicated to understand - this description covers the main essentials only. Mileage pay rates will be explained in a later chapter.

All higher grade duty was allocated in strict seniority order, because of the above procedure to qualify for the extra payments. If a junior man was accidentally given higher grade duties, then the most senior man wrongly passed over could claim and receive a credit for the firing or driving turn (and the pay) that had been lost, to go towards the critical 287 total. The junior man in this circumstance received the higher pay for the turn worked but lost the credit for it, not having been entitled to it in the first place. This explains why the junior hand normally worked the night shift at Southminster (to be described), as the chance of a firing turn was unlikely. The risk of losing a firing turn was ruled to be of greater importance, because of the longer term permanent benefit to our on-going pay rates. The enhanced pay earned when working 12 hour night shifts was ruled to be less important, compared to the possibility of losing a firing turn. As each new hand was recruited on each shift, so they took over the Southminster duty.

After arrival at Southend in September 1951, as the junior hand qualified for firing duties, it became my turn to be rostered for weekly turns, every fourth week, at Southminster shed overnight. We booked on duty at Southend each evening and off duty the next morning, doing a 12 hour shift to coal up and look after the class 'N7' engine out-stabled there in steam. This was a regular duty to work at night alone on shift work. At age 16 this would be strictly prohibited today in these so called enlightened times, for someone so young. It did us no harm whatsoever, indeed it did us good, whatever the 'experts' may claim today. We learned at the outset of our careers to accept responsibility and to use common sense. Yes, of course there were risks in working alone, but it made you more careful. No mishap ever occurred to anyone in my time. We had been instructed on the exercise of 'due care' in our duties, during the Stratford training classes.

On the first night the incoming junior hand was accompanied by the outgoing hand who was being displaced. We learned the 'what, when, where, and why', to ensure our competency. In due course my turn came to do the same for my successor. The weather could be dreadful and cold, it made no difference. The job had to be done, otherwise the branch lost its first local train to Wickford in the morning. This would never do. Up to three tons of coal had to be shovelled into the 'N7's' coal bunker each night. Shovel? - well, yes, this was possible, after the first two tons or so had been thrown by hand out of the corner in order to reach the floor if you had a fresh truck. This happened always once, sometimes twice in the week. We could have dropped the truck side door, but we had further to throw it into the bunker. Moving the same ton, two, maybe, three times to get it there, was a pointless pastime. Plus, the coal spillage to the ground when the door was initially opened had then to be shovelled back up onto the coal stage. Moving it once was hard enough, without playing with it. It was always a soul destroying moment when the noise of the first lumps hitting the metal floor of the empty engine bunker echoed back in the darkness of the night! We did have basic lighting that was barely adequate. A paraffin flare lamp balanced precariously on the top edge of the truck side was always helpful to supplement the gaslit lantern, unless too windy to risk doing this.

The perk for us youngsters when looking after the engine overnight, was to be allowed to do the driving over the branch between Wickford and Southminster. In return we did our bit to prepare the engine ready for the morning crew. These early experiences in gaining valuable knowledge of the skills and art of handling engines (as we used to say, 'having hold' of the engine) were invaluable. It took time and practice to learn smooth braking into stations. As a teenager not long out of school, instruction was absorbed very quickly. We were, of course, under the eagle eye of the driver who watched very closely. The train formation over the branch was always four non-corridor, Thompson, or Gresley design, outer-suburban coaches. These included a first composite with toilets for each class - first and third, and an all-third brake with a 'ladies only' compartment next to the guard's brakevan, i.e., half a normal

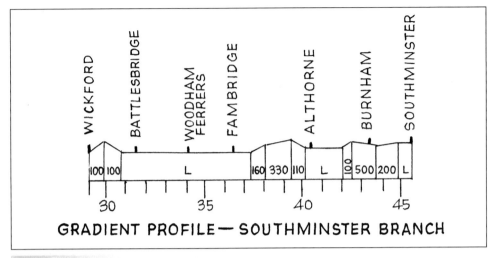

GRADIENT PROFILE — SOUTHMINSTER BRANCH

The basic engine shed facilities at Wickford - hand coaling stage on the right, having a single electric lamp, with older style shallow servicing pit in front of the 50 ft diameter hand-pushed turntable (on which I often sweated to turn our class 'B12' engines) with a grounded ex-GER wooden inner suburban four-wheel coach body beyond doing duty as the messroom-cum small non-inflammable stores, and a short siding beyond the turntable long enough to stable one engine on. The messroom had a single cold water tap with sink and open soak-away as drainage, an enclosed coal-fired stove for heating water on in a heavy cast-iron kettle and for cooking 'fry ups' in a frying pan. Out of sight to the left of the picture was a small brick-built flammable stores building for paraffin, etc., which also had a single toilet; and behind the photographer off the bottom right of the picture, the headshunt spur off the inlet road, long enough to stable one engine and two or three wagons. With the exception of the turntable, shed facilities did not come any more basic than this! Such crude conditions and facilities would not be allowed, let alone tolerated, today. *Author*

Southend eight-car set. (Third class was to survive for many more years yet, but a curiosity on the GE section was the rare survival of second class on the Harwich boat trains to match the continental railway classes, long after general withdrawal of this category in Britain. It always looked odd seeing the cars with the figure '2' displayed on the exterior door panels.)

In milder weather a stroll around Southminster village in the 'wee small hours' was sometimes taken. On one occasion the local bobby was - unusually - out and about. Neither of us was expecting to meet the other. A toss of a coin might have settled who was the more surprised! He regained his composure first.

'Who are you, why, and where are you going?', was his opening enquiry asked in a very suspicious tone of voice.

'Just having a wander round, Officer', sounded a rather lame reply.

Well, you imagine meeting someone in overalls at 3.00 am in the street in a remote rural village as Southminster still then was 50 years ago, who is not purposefully striding along and obviously not intent on heading somewhere specific! A natural conclusion - particularly for a naturally suspicious constable - would be to assume a suitable premises were being sought to enter illegally, seeing me in no obvious hurry strolling along, hands in pockets. It was a bright moonlit night and having paused to admire someone's front garden flower display - how do you explain to a police officer you were not 'eyeing up' the place?!

Then I was asked, 'What is your name and where do you come from?'

When you give an address from 20 miles away the plot has all the scope to get completely out of control! It was a nerve racking few minutes until eventually and somewhat reluctantly, he conceded he was convinced. Possibly, my invitation to call by 'to share a "cuppa" in half an hour's time' (when the kettle would be organised), maybe solved the problem and allayed his suspicions. We chatted amicably for probably half an hour, including a visit to the engine cab as part of his tour round the premises. The peculiar thing was that he did not know the shed was staffed during the night. The coal shovelling must have made a noise audible from the roadway, and the shed lights were lit. Perhaps he was a holiday relief not familiar with the area. We never met again - maybe the strong footplate style tea was not to his liking!

In those days Southminster was a small sleepy Essex village located not too far from the edge of the marshes that fringe the River Crouch thereabouts. There were still commercial sea-going craft using the tidal river to the mills at Battlesbridge, the head of navigation. These included some of the last remaining Thames barges to be seen trading under sail if we were lucky.

Today, the regular commercial river traffic has long since ceased. The Thames barges still sail, but no longer in commercial use. Southminster has grown out of all recognition, populated more by city commuters than folk working locally. The Bradwell nuclear power station has been built a few miles away along the coast. This requires rail-borne nuclear flasks to be handled through the dedicated railhead loading facility in the former station goods yard. This is the only non-passenger revenue-earning traffic along the branch. As elsewhere, most of the old goods yards are car parks for the ever-growing commuter business.

Wickford station from the up platform looking towards Shenfield and London on 15th March, 1955. The up Southminster bay is on the extreme left and the down Southminster bay on the right behind the nameboard. This tranquil scene was soon to be disfigured with electrification overhead wires and masts.   *H.C. Casserley*

'B12' class 4-6-0 No. 61550 at Liverpool Street with a Southend train in October 1955.
Michael H.C. Baker

Southminster had two regular sets of enginemen allocated to this little outpost of Southend shed, comprising two drivers and two firemen, both passed for driving - Chittendon was one of the passed firemen, known to all and sundry as 'Chitto'. He took an interest in helping us youngsters to get on, if we were prepared to listen. The Southminster branch is 16½ miles long from Wickford Junction and it must have been a bit boring just trundling to and fro all day. 'Chitto' helped us and eased his own fairly monotonous routine by doing so. He was a decent sort of chap who, so it was said, 'Had other rural interests' when off duty. What these were, remained shrouded in mystery! Maybe poaching, or it might have been tending his allotment - it was not discussed.

The first up service of the day at 5.48 am was the only weekday through train from Southminster to Liverpool St. It was always worked by Southend men who arrived with the eight-car empty set for it from Southend Sidings, from where they had departed at 4.22 am. It was usual practice on this turn to work engine first to Wickford and then tender first to Southminster with a tarpaulin sheet rigged up to offer a limited protection from the elements. In the summer not too bad, but in the winter it could be a very uncomfortable trip, although there were ways to ease this. The usual ploy was to give the fire a good charge of coal before leaving Wickford sufficient to get to Southminster. To do this we planned ahead to arrive at Wickford with a good body of fire to ensure you didn't accidentally 'black' it out when building it up again ready for the branch journey. This we did while taking water from the platform water crane (column) to top up the tender tank using the platform lights. This avoided the need to use the crane at Southminster where the shed lighting, as already mentioned, was meagre. As we set off along the branch the tender coal opening slide was dropped shut to keep out the dust. The next ploy was to huddle up in the corner on the long wooden bench seat alongside the boiler with the side window closed. We always had a class 'B12' 4-6-0 on this working, known as '1500s' from their original GER numbers when first built. Sitting alongside the boiler was a bit warmer, except on No. 61546 which had a lubricator in the way in the fireman's corner - most uncharitable! In the winter, it being dark, little purpose was served in looking out continuously to see where we were going. The warmer corner of the cab was most welcome. In the summer in daylight it was necessary to keep a good lookout in case an early morning walker was taking an illicit shortcut along the track. The early start from Southminster gave an arrival in London before 8.00 am thereby qualifying for the cheap rate workmen's fares available in those days, long since abolished. There was no return through working to Southminster in the evening, as passengers' return journeys were more spread out over the late afternoon/early evening period, unlike the up train. Stopping at all stations, we would have a decent loading aboard by the time we left Battlesbridge, the last station on the branch. Nobody then could have imagined the hourly electric timetable of through trains to London that is the normal basic service today!

It was the usual practice at the Wickford sub-shed to stable their two class 'N7s' overnight, one in the engine headshunt, the other beyond the turntable

Southminster station and signal box on 19th March, 1955 shortly before diesel multiple units replaced the steam workings. Class 'B12/3' No. 61546 is waiting to depart from the shed outlet after turning on the hand-operated turntable. The engine shed structure immediately left of the box has been nearly demolished, although the basic facilities survived for another few years until goods workings were dieselised.   *H.C. Casserley*

Althorne station showing the oil lit platform lamps still in use on 2nd April, 1955.
H.C. Casserley

to leave a clear access to it. Some drivers declined to run tender first on the branch, opting instead to turn the engine at Wickford and again at Southminster on the 4.22 am cars working. This meant scrambling about with the tight timing margins, if a late departure from Southminster was to be avoided. It also required a full tender tank and the fireman not to have too much water in the boiler, as otherwise it was difficult to get a good balance on the small turntables provided at each shed. A real struggle could result to turn the engine, if the fireman got it wrong. Turning was done the old fashioned way by hand - this could be pure misery on a frosty morning!

Most platelayers' huts (to use the correct job description of the time for track maintenance staff) along the branch had engine firehole smoke scoop deflector plates standing upright on the top of their chimney stack. This was to protect the chimney pot from the depredations of our attempts to shy coal at them as we ran tender first to Southminster. Naughty really, but it was a different kind of railway in those more relaxed times. Such antics were only possible in the daylight summer period. Likewise, we would also try our luck at rabbits disturbed by our early journey, the 4.22 am cars being the first working of the day along the branch. In the winter time it was a regular practice when working this train to drop the larger coal lumps off adjacent to the platelayers' huts. We filled our tenders from the mechanical coaling plant, and it required less effort for us to do this than for the hand-coaled branch engines to do so. All very irregular but a frequent practice to help one's fellow workmates. Occasionally, a 'thank you' would be received in the form of a rabbit passed via a station master for 'services rendered'. This gentleman was prepared to oblige as it meant he was able to keep back a little more coal from the annual allowance for his station fireplaces, in lieu of supplying the huts.

In darkness, Althorne was the worst station to stop at. It had oil lamps providing only a weak light. There were few reference 'markers' to locate our position as we approached it. Althorne, in those far off days, was a bleak place at which to stop if there was no moon. Today, it is much easier, with modern lighting, and front view train cabs. In those days it was just 'wall to wall' grass between the fence boundaries. There were few markers outside the fences to help us at this remote location. At all the other stations along the branch - Battlesbridge, Woodham Ferrers, Fambridge, and Burnham on Crouch - there were easily identified markers that could be used for reference points when braking as we approached them.

Wickford shed had five sets of enginemen. A shedman coaled the engines by hand similar to the arrangement at Southminster - direct from a loco-coal truck. There was no engine shed building, and the site was very cramped for space. All duties were carried out in the open, with a small coaling stage, ash pit, water crane, manual turntable, and a small brick-built hut (for fire risk prevention) provided the oil/tool store and toilet, as the 'infrastructure'. An old GER grounded wooden coach body, with minimal headroom, provided the meagre creature comforts. All very basic and never updated. The coaling stages at both Southminster and Wickford were in regular use, but generally it was easier to shovel the coal direct, truck to engine bunker.

Southminster shed building in April 1954 with the roof structure still largely intact. It was demolished soon afterwards.   *R.M. Casserley Collection*

Class 'N7/3' 0-6-2T No. 69721 at the back of Southend shed in 1953. This engine was a regular visitor to the shed, for working the Shenfield local trains and on the Southminster branch, being only rarely seen working in the inner London area throughout the 1950s.   *Author*

Southminster had one, Wickford two, engines, always class 'N7s', as the normal allocation, rotated at regular intervals to and from Southend for periodic boiler washouts, and routine maintenance. By contrast to Wickford, Southminster had a substantial two-road brick-built engine shed comparable to Southend (but without the same provision for fitters accommodation), built on a site with potential for further expansion. When first built in the 1880s, both the Southminster and Southend branches were single track with passing loops. It was presumably hoped the Southminster line would develop in a similar way to the Southend line, and hence the facilities. In the event it did not and remains single line to this day. The Southend line soon needed to be doubled and quickly became the busier of the two. Hence, why Wickford's facilities were inferior to Southminster's, although the busier shed in the later years of steam working.

We had a light engine (LE) turn at Southend known as the 'Billericay Shunt' which, on its return trip from Billericay, shunted at Wickford. We sometimes had the detested task of propelling trucks of fertilizer up the heavy gradient at the start of the Southminster branch. These went to a factory siding located near the top of the gradient. The factory was located within the apex of the former railway triangle that bordered the site. (There was a junction hereabouts with the lifted Fanton curve originally installed to allow direct running of trains from Southend to Southminster, and to Maldon via Woodham Ferrers, which was taken out of use before World War I.) On a warm day the obnoxious aroma from the trucks, tarpaulin sheeted which further increased the temperature within and the smell without, had to be experienced to be believed. The smells from the old style sewage works were pure bliss by comparison. The scent emanating from the trucks was powerful and can be better understood when it is explained the product was called 'Humanure'! It was clearly identified by paper stickers pasted to the wagon sides to advertise it - please believe me, this is true. Why anyone would choose to give a product a name like this and to then advertise it was a real conundrum. Wickford men also shunted Wickford yard on an 'as required' basis, but avoided the fertilizer trip, given half a chance - and who could blame them! In the winter time, the odour was tolerable, but on a hot summer day . . !

The Thompson-designed class 'L1' tanks very occasionally worked over the branch to Southminster. On 8th March, 1952 we had No. 67728 on Saturday Diagram 13. We worked the 12.31 pm passenger Southend to Shenfield, returned with the empty cars to Wickford to work a down passenger to Southminster, before returning with the 3.37 pm up passenger to Wickford, and finally work LE to Southend. 'L1s' were rare on the branch as they were not authorised on it. Old working publications for 1952 confirm this, perhaps special authority had been given for our trip. The branch was route restriction category RA6, the class 'L1s' were RA7 which therefore prohibited them from travelling over the branch. The only regular dispensation allowed was for the Gresley-designed class 'V3' 2-6-2 tank engines. These, having three cylinders, would be better balanced and therefore have a lighter hammer blow on the track compared to the 2-cylinder class 'L1s'.

All ex-LNER lines were given a route category number between '0' and '9', known as the 'RA' - route availability coding. '0' was the most restrictive and '9' the least in terms of the size of engine allowed to work over the route in question. All engines were allocated a similar code related to their total weight in working order, loading gauge profile (i.e., the air space occupied by the engine superstructure), and their highest individual axle weight. The higher the RA number allocated, the more limited were the routes over which the engine could work. Engines were barred from working over routes with a lower number category than that allocated to them. Special dispensations were authorised in the working publications, such as just mentioned for the class 'V3' tanks. It was a very easy to understand classification system. Other BR areas had different methods. The former GWR system used coloured circles painted on the cab side in place of the 'RA' coding. Whichever system was used, all were designed to ensure the safe working of trains over each individual section of the railway system.

My last trip over the branch before moving away to Cambridge, was on 8th December, 1952 firing to a well known Southend driver, one Alfred Ottley. He was known to all and sundry as 'Alf'. We were on class 'B12' No. 61573, I think it was his regular engine. At that time, Alf was one of the junior hands as a full driver. He was a very jovial person with, shall we say, a comfortable deportment. He usually had a pipe in his mouth emerging under a neatly trimmed moustache. He exuded a very casual air that belied a very careful and professional competence. He was not above a practical joke at the right time and place, and could produce a really wicked glint in his eyes on such occasions.

This recalls another trip with him, this time on No. 61572 when, having a particularly good day, the cardinal error was made of saying so. Shortly afterwards, it all began to go wrong. Alf had quietly notched the reverser up to bring it back nearer to mid-gear far more than was usual, without any comment. This had the effect of softening the exhaust and therefore lessening the strength of the draught on the fire. This, your humble scribe initially failed to notice, as the steam pressure began to fall back, through too heavy firing. And there it remained for the next section while Alf looked as serene as you like, enjoying the situation! Having eventually let the fire become thinner to compensate for his softer driving style, during which time we had lost the odd minute or two, he then 'opened her up', as we would say, on the next section to regain the lost time. This then required rapid action to keep up with him, due to the stronger draught on the (thinner) fire! It was all harmless fun, but it taught you to be alert to what was happening, as it happened. A useful lesson learned. An even more important lesson came later in the shift on how to 'chat-up the guard to square his journal' so as not to show the time lost and then regained. Such wrinkles were the bread and butter content of 'railway work' as it was called. How to keep the job running with apparent smoothness when it wasn't, and yourself out of trouble at the same time!

Today, it is less easy to indulge these little 'tricks of the trade'. Increasingly, everything is automatically recorded by computer, and your sins cannot be hidden or denied. Train speeds can be accurately calculated at any location controlled by a modern IECC type signal centre (Integrated Electronic Control Centre). This is done by re-running the tapes that record the precise times of each track circuit occupation. One driver on a Norwich express, who must remain nameless, discovered this when he inadvertently went through a particular crossover above the authorised speed limit. He denied his action until shown the tape re-run of his train working. This confirmed his otherwise scrupulous observance of all speed limits. He subsequently conceded he was not expecting to be routed through the crossover in question. Such is the capability of modern technology, totally unknown in my footplate era.

The tapes record the 'strike' time of the first set of wheels to activate each track circuit. The exact physical length of each circuit is known. Thus, as the first wheels 'strike' the next circuit the occupation time of the previous circuit is recorded and by reference to the known length of it the train speed can be calculated. Track circuits are the basis upon which the entire safety system of signalling trains within these modern signalling areas operates. The occupation of a track circuit electronically 'locks' up that piece of track and others related to it, to prevent points and signals from being set to create a possible conflicting train movement.

The engine working diagram Alf and I were working together on 8th December was one of those oddities that made for an interesting change to the normal routine. We booked on duty at Southend at 4.00 am for diagram 10 (typical of the demands of working unsociable shifts, requiring a 3.00 am awakening, when all sane persons are sound asleep!), prepared our engine, booked off shed at 5.00 am to work tender first LE to Wickford, 13 miles away, prior to working the 6.34 am passenger to Southminster. If the weather was bad, we could have gone engine first to turn on Wickford's turntable, not a popular action, when you do not have to do it, as already explained. We turned at Southminster before working the 7.54 am passenger to Wickford, where we again turned before working the 8.51 am passenger back to Southend. After this the engine was disposed (i.e., fire cleaned, etc.) and prepared again for the next set of men to work the 11.54 am passenger to Liverpool St. (It was always necessary to have a tender engine correctly facing forward when working passenger trains, if the facilities to do this were provided.)

The balancing diagram for the cars (coaches) off the 8.51 am was covered by diagram 12. These men booked on duty at 5.45 am, walked to relieve their early turn crew at the station, then worked the 6.03 am passenger to Shenfield, returning with the 7.30 am Pcls/Fish to Southend, then to work the 9.50 am cars to Wickford (with the coaches off the 8.51 am from Wickford), before going LE to Billericay to shunt the yard there as required and then LE on to Shenfield to work the 12.30 pm passenger back to Southend with the set taken up on the 6.03 am working.

When working on diagram 12 it was my usual practice, while we waited in platform 1 at Shenfield for the parcels and boxes of fish to be loaded, to sterilise the firing shovel over a white hot fire and cook our breakfasts on it. This often amused any passengers standing nearby who, having smelt the aroma, then watched fascinated. This was one of those rare occasions of 'playing to the gallery' doing something we often did away from public view. It was the only few minutes available on this turn in which to have our breakfast. It took no more than five minutes at most to produce two excellent fry-ups, complete with crispy fried bread - it was all too easy to overcook the meals if you were not quick enough!

(A note of explanation: empty coaching stock trains were officially designated as 'ECS' in our working publications, but on the GE section we always referred to working 'cars', not ECS. Each area of BR had [and to a lesser extent today, still has] its own jargon, or shorthand language, which makes for the fascination of it all. Some areas, described ECS as 'stock' and so it went on, each word or phrase having its respective origins in the practices and language developed by the former pre-1923 private railway companies, going back, in some cases, to the very earliest days of railways. Just as the computer industry has spawned a whole new language to describe itself, so this happened when the new railway industry came into being.)

Visiting Southminster again for the first time in many years, shortly before final retirement (from my second shorter BR career in 1996 with Railtrack), revealed a station that was but a shadow of what it once was. The yard area was derelict apart from the Bradwell nuclear flask operation. All engine servicing facilities - the shed building, turntable, coal stage, inspection pits, etc. - had long gone, with the total shed site overgrown and unrecognisable. The entire station area looked a sad scene of neglect. One could not help recalling when a winter fire burned in the waiting room, the platform was swept and cared for, the small station gardens were attended, toilet facilities with nicely polished pipework existed without being vandalised, all station buildings and adjacent cottages were *in situ* and looked after, and everywhere looked so much more tidy and inviting than is the case today. All along the branch, station facilities have been reduced to a basic minimum, signal boxes swept away, goods yards are now car parks, track operating flexibility reduced, and so on. It is a sign of the times and reflects the changing circumstances in which the railway operates today. The vital factor, of course, being that it is still there, unlike many other once busy branch lines elsewhere. We worked hard and earned relatively less wages for our efforts, compared to potential earnings outside the industry, but generally had a much greater pride in our jobs. This last factor was frequently missing in many of the better paid jobs, say in a factory or office, judged from talking to my former school contemporaries at the time. They envied my variety of work and lack of repetitive tedium, compared to their fixed environments - an interesting commentary about life and what we expect of it!

Today, pride in the job is more likely to be absent, despite the proportionately higher wages relative to work done, and not forgetting the generally cleaner working conditions. Perhaps there is a moral to be drawn somewhere between the two contrasting circumstances. My opinion is to think there is. Without doubt former railwaymen - and women - were happier in their work than their more modern counterparts suggest today, based upon my own experience and observations of both eras. Yes, of course there are exceptions to this opinion, but not from the general impression seen in my normal work then, and more recently. Many employees today are increasingly frustrated with the frequent changes in the industry. The greater perception of railway managements being a political target when things go wrong, is sadly evidenced by the willingness of politicians and similar agencies to make strong pronouncements when silence would serve a more constructive purpose. The various political influences, each with their own agenda as to how the industry should be regulated and managed, cause tension in what is an already complicated inter-locking business operation. They shouldn't, they needn't, but all too often, they do. Is it any wonder that strains develop in staff loyalties and commitments, against such a scenario? The bureaucrats can huff and puff as much as they choose, but it is a fact that each change of emphasis propagates the next change, because of the resultant on-going uncertainty. Stability is desperately required - the problem is how?

On a much more constructive note - the one huge plus factor on the Southminster branch, from when I first knew the line, is the electric service. This is encouraging commuter travel. It has triggered a significant residential development all along the line. Somehow it is out of context to see Althorne station with this superb service. Apart from a rank of old railway cottages, there is, relatively speaking compared to the other stations on the branch, not the same density of houses to be seen nearby on the north side of the line. To the south, the open views towards the River Crouch familiar to me from 50 years ago still survive. For how much longer, since my last visit in 1996, this will remain so is unknown. It must be one of the best served 'greenfield' country station locations anywhere with a direct hourly electric service within one hour's travelling time to London. To live along this pretty, and still mainly rural, branch line with the tidal River Crouch never far away must have its attractions. The excellent train service for the growing dormitory conurbations around each of the old villages must offer a more relaxed lifestyle, compared to living in suburbia nearer to London.

The branch to Southend Victoria from Shenfield (on the Ipswich main line) is just over 21 miles long - but what a fascinating stretch it could be to work over! Many Stratford firemen hated it, because they found the road hard going. ('Lines', in this context, routes, are usually called 'roads' which derives from the early railway term of 'rail-road', i.e., a road using rails, described thus to distinguish it from an ordinary road or cart-way.) If you didn't work it regularly this was easy to understand. There is little level track. Even the Victoria station terminus is on a slight down gradient towards London. To us who traversed it daily, and knew all its little foibles, it was a joy to work over, once you had mastered the many changes of gradient. This is where the loose-coupled goods train workings proved their worth to me as a young fireman. We learned the gradients very thoroughly. Careful engine management by the driver working in close harmony with the guard, was vital if a breakaway through a broken coupling was to be avoided. These workings were entirely handled by Southend traincrews - footplate and guards.

The goods train workings were interesting. As a general comment, a lesser volume of goods traffic for the Southend area arrived via the London, Tilbury & Southend (LT&S) route. The LT&S had some goods traffic, but not to the extent of the GE route. We operated each weekday, Mondays to Saturdays (50 years ago a normal working railway week for goods trains was six, not five, days as now), four inwards loaded trains, predominately coal traffic, and three outwards trains, for general goods and empty coal trucks. We also had one outwards express class 'D' vacuum braked service direct to Thames Wharf on the North Woolwich line, to convey perishable and export traffics via the

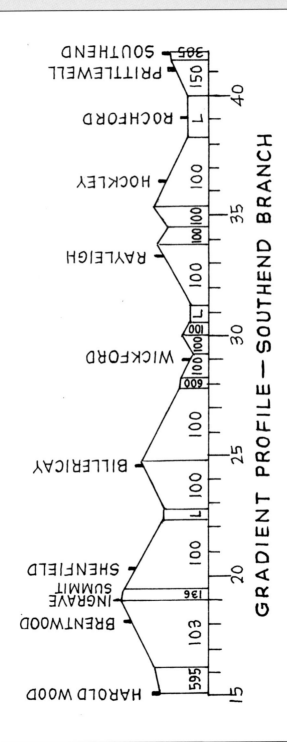

GRADIENT PROFILE—SOUTHEND BRANCH

London Docks complex. This departed in the early evening at 5.40 pm usually with no more than 10 vehicles, often as few as five, but which attached additional traffic *en route*. On this turn we worked back to Goodmayes, either direct or via Victoria Dock or via Temple Mills Yards. The other up road workings, all to Goodmayes, departed from Southend at 2.10 am, 9.15 am and 10.55 pm, and the return down road workings from Goodmayes were at 12.15 am, 3.15 am, 6.00 am and 2.25 pm. These timings varied slightly over the years, but this was the pattern that operated during the steam era.

All our ordinary goods trains normally ran over the up and down electric lines between Shenfield and Chadwell Heath. Up trains crossed over at the Chadwell Heath Jn from the electric to the main lines and then onto the up goods line to enter the Goodmayes up yard reception roads - all under the control of the Chadwell Heath box. The exception to this was the Thames Wharf working. This usually ran on the up main line throughout from Shenfield to Ilford, then 'round the back' as we called it, alongside the Ilford flyover and onto the up goods line behind Manor Park station to join the up electric line at Forest Gate Jn. Today, the once extensive down and up yards at Goodmayes are just a memory, now commercially re-developed. The dreadful connecting line between the two yards, crossing four main running lines, that gave the Goodmayes box signalmen so many problems to get a clear path between trains to use it, has likewise long gone. The permanent way gang had difficulty in maintaining it. There are some features of the old railway that few will lament the disappearance of, and this crossing was one of them!

Talking of signal boxes, at the time of writing, just two signal centres, at Liverpool St and Colchester, control the entire route, Liverpool St to Norwich, including most branch lines. (The East Suffolk route between Ipswich and Lowestoft is an exception, having a dedicated self-contained radio-controlled system.) This includes the Southminster and Southend lines, now controlled from Liverpool St. Between them these two centres replaced approaching 100 former signal boxes. This total included 16 boxes which had themselves replaced nearly 50 boxes as part of the original Liverpool St to Shenfield electrification scheme finalised after the last war. Such is the rate of progress, reflecting the high level of investment in the industry in this one area alone, some 150 boxes replaced by just two power installations! The human arithmetic equated to about 60 signallers replacing around 500 signalmen, including box lads, plus proportionate reductions in maintenance fitting staff.

The Thames Wharf working was booked in at Gidea Park to wait on the up goods line alongside the wagon sheet works (the former Eastern Counties Railway engine factory prior to the old Stratford [Polygon] works being built). Sometimes, we would watch the heavy shunt horse doing his thing with the trucks in the sidings. This was one of the last locations on the entire BR national network where such a once common sight could still be seen on BR-owned tracks alongside a main running line. Later, it was claimed this was the penultimate horse shunting operation anywhere on BR. There was an item about the last few surviving shunting horses in the monthly staff magazine at the time. This method of shunting survived here for so long because of the nature of the track layout within the works area. There was also the risk of

Class 'N7/3' 0-6-2T No. 69711 leaves Victoria Dock station with a North Woolwich-Palace Gates train in March 1959. *C.J. Sarah*

Horse shunting at Gidea Park wagon sheet factory in 1956. It is believed this was the final location anywhere on BR where such a daily sight could still be seen in operation immediately alongside a main line, with trains passing just a few feet away at 70 mph. It is believed to have been the penultimate use of shunting horses on BR. It had survived into the diesel and electric era because of the high risk associated with freshly repainted tarpaulin sheets. The factory had been built as the original Eastern Counties Railway engine works before this activity was transferred to Stratford works. *Author*

sparks from engines not being welcome in a works producing freshly weather-proofed wagon sheets.

After regaining the up main line at the country end of Gidea Park station opposite the signal box, we ran to Ilford Milk Sidings, calling at Romford yard *en route*, before being turned onto the up goods line at Ilford Car Sheds box. Here we would pick up more traffic from the Ilford goods yard before resuming our journey as already described above, via the Manor Park up goods line. We turned off the main route to London at Stratford to take the Eastern Jn Curve down past the Low Level station platforms to Stratford Southern Jn - a route long since lifted. It is sad to recall the intensive goods workings that once required a four track main line southwards from the Southern Jn to Thames Wharf and onto Silvertown (if one included the high level over the docks, and low level through the tunnel, routes). All this traffic gradually ceased with the demise of the London Docks. The restrictive working practices by the London dockers helped to influence shipping company decisions to invest large sums developing containerisation and taking their traffic elsewhere. The inevitable terminal decline of the once mighty docks thereafter became a foregone outcome. The new Jubilee Line tube trains now run where the old goods lines were. The only non-passenger trains on the remaining passenger lines to North Woolwich today are the occasional engineering train at night time, plus the high speed track recording train to check track profiles.

The local goods yards along the Southend branch were served by a variety of workings. Prittlewell was shunted in the early morning by a main line goods engine sent for the purpose from Southend; in the mid-morning by the Southend yard shunting pilot engine; and, later in the day, by a shunt trip that also covered Rochford, Hockley and Rayleigh as required. Rochford was shunted by the mid-day 'Hockley Shunt' trip engine including Rayleigh if required. Finally, the 'Billericay Shunt' trip engine, already mentioned, shunted there in the early afternoon, and at Hockley and Rayleigh outwards, and at Wickford inwards. Wickford engines additionally shunted Wickford as required throughout the day. All these shunt trips (except the Prittlewell mid-morning one) were usually worked with our main line goods engines. This meant the driver required plenty of 'elbow grease' winding the reversing wheel to and fro with the shunting. Opportunities for the older drivers to suggest to their young firemen, once they had come to know and trust you, 'that you might like to do the driving' were not unknown! This was how we gained our experience. The 6.03 am passenger diagram included a shunt at Billericay late morning, as already described. Billericay also had an early morning shunt by a Stratford-manned diagram, that ran LE to and from Shenfield in between other workings - this was the only goods train activity not covered by Southend branch men and engines. Thus, all the yards had a good service for their traders, with each shunted at least three times per day. The Goodmayes trains called at each station in both directions (except at Prittlewell and Billericay in the up direction, the former because it was not necessary to do so, the latter because the track layout made it awkward to do so), to attach and detach trucks as required.

Today, all this traffic has long since gone. The former station goods yards are now car parks. The final decline commenced with the footplate strike in 1955. In

E.D. Bruton

Class 'N7/3' 0-6-2T No. 69635 at the head of a short down milk train approaching Forest Gate on 24th March, 1951.

my firm opinion this was the worst decision ever taken by the Associated Society of Locomotive Engineers & Firemen (ASLEF) Union, who, unfortunately, played right into the hands of a Government desperate to get the fledgling post-war road haulage industry better established. Goods traffic never recovered from this set back. It returned for a time, but the loyalty was broken and traders, once bitten soon became twice shy, as the saying goes. It was to do considerable and irreparable damage to the industry. Trying to travel home on leave from the RAF during the strike was a nightmare.

As already mentioned, Prittlewell was shunted each morning by the Southend goods yard pilot. This duty gave it a daily chance to slip its leash from humdrum shunting duties - usually the resident class 'J67' or 'J69' 0-6-0 tank engine. Class 'J67' No. 68534 was the normal prime mover in the early 1950s. She had the GE pattern wooden-planked shallow-roofed cab which required a six-footer like me to be ducking my head all the time - not pleasant. Later, another class 'J67', No. 68529, arrived in the mid-1950s - another low-roofed machine. Our 'Buckjumper' (derived from the term 'Bucking Bronco' because they used to be lively riding engines in the days when they worked the inner-London area suburban passenger trains), class 'J69' No. 68636, had a higher arched metal roof - much more convenient! She was the regular station passenger pilot, from May 1956. In 1955/56 one of the three regular drivers on the goods yard job was Wally Alderman who had been a GER driver before 1923. He was a real character. When I first fired to him in 1951/52 he was working the Shenfield locals. When his eye sight deteriorated further he became confined to the yard link, but was allowed his 'main line' run to Prittlewell - his official main line working ban being 'overlooked' for this short trip! In those days official instructions were more likely to be 'interpreted' in practical terms, not slavishly adhered to, to the exact letter as is the requirement today. It all reflects the differing values of society today with people being increasingly influenced by the possible reaction of litigation - a sad commentary about the ever increasing regulation of our actions, not only at work but throughout our lives generally.

To work our goods trains we had five main line tender engines. Four class 'J20' 0-6-0, all steam and vacuum brake fitted for fast goods workings (oddly, Westinghouse brake - or 'Westo' as we called it, was never fitted to these ex-GER-built main line engines). These were known as the 'Long Box Knockos' as they had long fireboxes and had a regular knocking noise from the axle boxes. They were called 'Long Box' to distinguish them from the similar, but smaller sized class 'J19' 0-6-0s - the 'Short Box Knockos'. During 1951/52 the fifth engine was class 'J39' 0-6-0, No. 64783, which was both vacuum and 'Westo' fitted (a 'Standard' because the 'J39s' were a Gresley LNER standard design). This engine had the traditional ex-NER style 'fish and chip' firehole screen, so called as the top screen arrangement was a curved two piece hinged shutter we lifted up to fire the box. After firing we then lowered it back onto the two top-curved shaped side sheets to protect ourselves from the heat and glare of the fire. It looked similar to the curved lids once common in fried fish shops - not an ideal arrangement compared to our more popular GE designs, but it had been most useful in the wartime to curtail the glare from the firehole. The four regular

Class 'J20/1' 0-6-0 No. 64677 near Shenfield on a down Southend freight in May 1952, traversing the down loop line (today bi-directional) built to ease traffic confliction over the flat double track junction for the Southend line at the country end of Shenfield station. This single line was also known as 'the avoiding line' or the 'dive-under'. It ran beneath the Ipswich main line (*out of sight behind the train*) through this cutting to rejoin the main route to Southend Victoria at Mountnessing Junction approximately a ½ mile further on.

Brian Morrison

'J20s' were Nos. 64675/6/7/81; 64676 still had its original square-shaped Belpaire-type boiler and was the last of the class to be rebuilt with the later design of round-topped boiler. All four 'J20s' were good strong engines that steamed well and were immensely powerful. Until the advent of the SR Bulleid class 'Q1' utility engines designed and built during the last war, they were the strongest 0-6-0 engines in the country for over 20 years. The round top engines had the standard-sized twin boiler water gauge glasses fitted. The Belpaire example had a truly enormous single water gauge glass plus three manually-worked water cocks for use if the glass should shatter. This engine would run for miles on a glass full of water - very useful if you were, unusually, short of steam, maybe with the poor coal we sometimes had. The 'J39' was a good engine but not so comfortable as the class 'J20s' fitted with the GE-style wide side bench shelving to sit on. The piano-style stools on the 'Standard' were a miserly perch by comparison. She was a free-steaming machine well able to take her turn with the 'J20s', although not so powerful and having a slightly lighter gross weight. She was not quite so good when it came to braking the heavy coal trains down the Billericay Bank using techniques unknown to today's younger footplate staff, which it is interesting to describe.

It was the regular working practice with down road loaded goods trains (unless we were, unusually, not up to a full loading) to come to a stand in Billericay station with the engine and front of the train on the downhill gradient just past the crown of the uphill gradient. Then, with the engine steam brake hard on, the train was allowed to roll back away from us down the gradient behind, to get all the couplings fully stretched out. The fireman might drop a few handbrakes on the leading wagons if the driver required this. Before beginning the descent of the bank the fireman screwed the tender handbrake hard on then eased it back off just enough for the driver to start the train against it. The guard would be doing likewise with his van brake to help keep the couplings stretched out tight. We then pulled forward onto the full down gradient with the fireman tightening the tender hand brake as required by the driver to maintain control in conjunction with the guard doing the same with his van handbrake. By this means the forward half of the train then gradually buffered up to the engine, while the guard's brake held the rear half in check to prevent the full weight of the train pushing the engine beyond its preferred braking power. The steam brake would be used as little as possible during the descent so as to keep the engine brake blocks (as distinct from the tender blocks) cold for back up use if needed. In this manner we would slowly descend the bank at about 10-15 mph, taking up to 25 minutes or so for the 4½ miles, depending upon the weather. Completely dry or thoroughly wet rails caused less problems. It was the in-between conditions, particularly if the rails had an early morning dew on them in the long cutting or were only partially wet after a shower, when extra vigilance was needed. Very rarely did matters become problematical, but the occasional slide with all the engine wheels locked up for a short distance was not unknown in greasy rail conditions. We could tell when this happened, the engine suddenly became much quieter as the regular knocking from the axleboxes ceased and we would hear the 'hissing' noise made by the sliding wheels.

Had we not stopped in Billericay station first, there was the risk of the train parting in two. Surmounting the steep gradient change from up to down (that occurred in the platform: see the attached gradient diagrams) the wagons would be trying to move in opposite directions within the middle of the train as the weight was transferred progressively from stretched-out to buffered-up couplings in the front portion of the train. If this wasn't done smoothly a nasty snatch could occur and one of the ordinary three-link couplings might break, dividing the train into separate sections. The coupling strain transfer from the wagons behind the engine to the wagons in front of the brake van as the guard applied his handbrake would not be fully controlled. Bringing the train to a stand transferred the drawbar strain from the front to the rear of the train in a controlled manner. We got no thanks for a runaway rear part of the train. This could then either run back towards Shenfield to become derailed at the catch points on the upward gradient behind us, or retain sufficient momentum to breast the summit to follow us down the bank to catch us up, with potentially serious results. Working fully loaded loose-coupled trains over the Southend road required a very good knowledge of the many changes of gradient, particularly in darkness. Billericay was the only place where we regularly stopped, owing to the severity of the gradient change with the long downhill gradient to the busy Wickford Jn station at the bottom. At other gradient changes along the line, the driver and guard managed the train control on the move as the gradient changes were generally less severe. We did not go rushing around! No incident of a breakaway train occurring on the Southend road goods services can be recalled. No doubt it had happened at some time in the history of the line.

One of the head shunters in the Southend goods yard was a real character, 'Sailor' Milan. Their duties included shunting the sand wagons into and out of the engine shed. 'Sailor' ran his yard like a military operation, sometimes much to the amusement and occasional frustration of others. His powerful voice to call someone's attention away down in the yard could be heard without too much difficulty! He had a very proud, upright bearing (a legacy of his naval service) and would stand erect with his shunting pole (the 'toothpick') leaning onto his shoulder at about 20 degrees from the vertical while discussing the next moves to be made. Breaks for meals were scrupulously observed when he was in charge. He was a bit of a firebrand in his own way, but quite a jovial personality, who knew how to get on with the job. He always positioned himself so his hand signals could be seen very clearly. At night his nicely polished oil handlamp was always easy to see. It was kept in immaculate condition and a joy to behold. It has to be said the other head shunters in the yard went about their work with similar efficiency to 'Sailor', but with less hustle and bustle.

Shunting a yard could be strenuous work and very dangerous if we failed to keep our wits about us. A driver relied entirely upon the shunter for accurate instructions. When we had the occasional sea mist, shunting would be carried out 'blind' using whistle codes blown by the shunter as authorised in the rule book for such circumstances. Woe betide the fireman who let the engine safety valves blow off or who turned on the boiler injectors at the wrong time so the noise prevented the whistles being heard! The driver would be concentrating solely on listening for the shunter and had to rely entirely on his fireman to work unsupervised by him. Not always easy if he had a young junior hand as a fireman, not yet fully experienced in the finer arts of engine management.

An occasional task that came our way when engine cleaning, would be washing off the coal dust that accumulated on the red-painted ex-GE six-wheeled wooden coach adapted for use as a toolvan for re-railing and breakdown duties. This ancient vehicle was stabled on a short spur line off the turntable next to the coaling tower. We would scrounge, beg, borrow, or if 'push came to shove', steal, a long-handled carriage washing brush and oval bucket for the purpose. The important point being to ensure the large rubber washer was on the brush handle near the head. This stopped the water from running back down it - we only forgot to check this once! This venerable vehicle saw only rare usage, but was a very vital piece of equipment when it did venture out on the main line. The interior had been adapted to provide a small basic mess compartment at one end with a cooker ring operated from a calor gas bottle. The main compartment housed numerous baulks of thick timber, planks, blocks, chain tackle, manual lifting jacks, and re-railing ramps. I cannot recall hydraulic jacks - these I think may have come later. It had cutting gear and all sorts of spanners and general tools, oil, grease, etc.

The class 'L1' engines were not only dirty, but also noisy to work on, and not very popular machines. The metal cabs resonated to the banging from the rear coupled wheel axleboxes. The first Westo-braked series, Nos. 67701-30, had side tanks built of wartime quality sheet metal. These gave trouble with water leaking, even squirting out a fine spray over passengers, as we ran into stations. Very soon most sported repair patches welded over the cracks, caused by the surge of water as we stopped when the tanks were partially empty. If we had one on a London diagram (strenuously avoided, if possible) it was essential to top up the tanks at Shenfield during the 'leaky tank' era, before they were all eventually repaired. Shenfield was one of the very few locations where we could fill up with water directly underneath the dc electric overhead wires. These were strung above the tracks at their maximum height in the station area. The electric trains looked a little comical with their diamond profile pantographs fully extended above the train.

In the days before red electric warning flashes on a white background plate were affixed to engines to remind us of the overhead catenary, I did a very stupid thing in Platform 11 at Liverpool St. The centrally-located tender tank filler lid had been inadvertently left open after we had taken water in the turntable yard. I had just been distracted by a defective rubber vacuum pipe ring while coupling onto the train, having fitted the spare ring always carried in my overall pocket for just such a contingency. On the GE section we coupled and uncoupled our own trains; on other sections shunters were provided to do these duties. After coupling up and climbing back on the platform, the open filler lid was noticed. Without thinking, I climbed up the tender footsteps to close it! Returning to the platform the enormity of my action dawned, causing momentarily trembling with the shock of it. Looking up at the catenary it was obvious how fortunate my escape had been. Catenary is staggered from side to

'L1' class 2-6-4T No. 67729 leaves Lea Bridge on the 4.46 pm North Woolwich-Palace Gates train on 1st June, 1962.   *Leslie Sandler*

'L1' class No. 67724 runs into Custom House bunker first with the 12.40 pm (Saturdays only) North Woolwich-Palace Gates service on 2nd June, 1962. The signal bracket by the box is an original ex-GER example, becoming an increasingly rare survivor by this date.   *G.D. King*

side between each supporting mast to even the wear on the pantograph carbon collection strips. At the critical location the stagger was furthest away - had it been the reverse there is little doubt this book would not have been written. I came within a hairsbreadth of receiving 1,500 volts direct current. The station catenary was strung at the lowest permitted height because of the overbridges, so to say it was fortunate to get away with my stupidity, puts it very mildly! It never happened again! Neither did I tell my driver, as it might have distracted him from his driving duties, thinking about how narrowly his mate had come to killing himself. Such is the inherent danger of footplate work. This was the only 'loss of a life' from the mythical nine, attributable to my own thoughtless negligence. Eventually, warning flash plates to remind us of the dangerous hazard began to appear following a fatality to a footplateman on the Clacton branch.

The third 'life' to be lost occurred in the Southend shed while emptying a smokebox of ash. Another engine accidentally ran very heavily into the rear of us. This knocked me forward off the footplating and the engine then ran for several feet over the top of me, even though the tender handbrake was applied. By good fortune we were on a pit and I feel clear into it, although landing very heavily as the drop was several feet, fortunately onto a soft heap of still hot ashes that cushioned my heavy fall. Again, I could have been killed, or at best, seriously injured, but instead badly singed my overalls and suffered burns on one hand. The other driver thought the points were set for a different line, and realised his mistake too late to stop in time. His subsequent apologies were distressingly offered with sincere regret for his error. To avoid any disciplinary inquiry no note of my injuries appeared in the accident book. No real harm had been done and a 'Nelsonian blind eye' was agreed to. Nobody deliberately intends to hurt somebody else, particularly the driver concerned, who was known as a steady and normally careful man.

We had another former GER driver at the depot - Harry Saville, who had started as a lad 'knocker-up' in 1907. Until his retirement he continued to wear a GER engineman's cap - at least this is what he claimed, although it was barely recognisable as such and definitely showing its age. He resolutely declined to wear the modern shiny plastic greaseproof-top style cap, saying they made his head sweat. He was another man who was a pleasure to work with, never rushing, quietly going about his work and a delight to fire to. He had opted to remain on the Shenfield locals in his final years. 'Had enough of London', he would say. It was difficult to persuade Harry to talk about his early GER years, but he was less than pleased with 'modern day practices' as he called them. (Not much alters over the years does it? Today's enginemen can be heard making similar remarks about our former practices!) He talked of the GER with a grudging affection, but never failed to refer to the long hours and stern discipline that applied. All for very low wages - 'blatant exploitation' he would say! Wally Allen ('B1' link on No. 61363), Ken Tweed (Goods link) and Charlie Archer (Shed turning link) were other men I can recall who declined the grease tops. All preferred to wear their LNER issue soft top serge type material hats.

Mention of Ken recalls the only occasion of a game of snooker in the company's time. We had worked the 10.55 pm goods to Goodmayes with the

A close-up view of 'J20' class 0-6-0 at Southend shed in 1955, showing useful modelling details.
Author

This close-up view shows the valve gear detail of class 'B17/6' 4-6-0 No. 61610 *Honingham Hall*. The knuckle joint of the Gresley Holcroft gear 2-to-1 combination/rocking lever can be clearly identified behind the piston valve crosshead above the piston slide bar. This gear eliminated the need for three full sets of valve gear by using the two outside sets to drive the middle cylinder piston valve. *Author*

Belpaire-boilered 'J20' No. 64676, and were booked to return with the 3.25 am working on the Sunday morning, 26th October, 1952. BST finished at 3.00 am so we had an extra hour to kill while the clock went back to 2.00 am to come round again to 3.00 am. We used this extra time in the London Transport Seven Kings bus garage canteen situated very conveniently just along the Romford Road from the Goodmayes yard. We were allowed to use the LT staff facilities by invitation, if our overalls and boots were clean. We always asked first and were rarely refused unless they were very busy, which at 2.00 am they certainly were not - and the snooker table was not being played on! It provided an amusing interlude to the normal routine.

Southend shed was responsible for working the Shenfield to Chelmsford local services. This brings to mind the fun some of the junior drivers indulged in. They competed for the unofficial 'blue riband' for the fastest non-stop time over the generally favourable grades from Shenfield to Chelmsford. In those days the lower speed restriction of more recent years on the long viaduct into Chelmsford was still in the future. With a long travel valve class 'N7' 0-6-2 tank engine, or a class 'B17' 4-6-0 tender engine on the job, we would fly! Par for the course, start to stop (verified by the guards who acted as unofficial umpires) was generally about 13-14 minutes for the class 'N7s' and about 10-11 minutes for the class 'B17s'. The distance was just over 9½ miles with start to stop booked timings of either 17 or 18 mins, depending upon pathing margins, usually the latter time. The absolute record was claimed as just inside 'even time' with a class 'B17'. The grapevine said it was achieved by No. 61648 *Arsenal*, but such a claim has to be suspect. She did have a reputation of being a strong engine and certainly one of the better members of the class in 1952. She was not so rough riding as some could be at that time, so such a claim could just be possible. To achieve such a time, the train would have departed from No. 3 down main line platform at Shenfield. (Trains from No. 1 platform had a crossing to negotiate which took longer to gain the down main line.) Mention of rough riding engines recalls class 'B17/6' No. 61613 *Woodbastwick Hall*, which was a very notorious machine, clearly remembered from bitter experiences, and which will feature again in this narrative. She was definitely not one used for the higher speed exploits! They kept her off the London turns because she was so bad, confining her to the local Southend to Shenfield and Chelmsford workings. Normal loading was four Thompson or Gresley design outer suburban coaches, weighing somewhere about 110 tons tare, on these workings. The high speed runs were only indulged in with the 'B17' engine (and bogie) leading, and the 'N7' bunker (and pony truck) leading, to ensure a safe ride. Speeds through Ingatestone would be up into the 60s with the 'N7s' and well into the 80s with the 'B17s', with such a light loading. If running tender first, or engine first with the 'N7s', speeds would be kept down just to maintain the booked schedule. We didn't indulge in these little delights with the class 'B12s' - there wasn't the same challenge as getting an 'N7' swinging along, or the thrill the higher speeds gave with the 'B17s'! Such antics were of course strictly unofficial, but nobody ever complained, nor was any crew ever asked to explain why they were gaining so much time on the schedule. The guards 'squared' their journals to hide the higher excesses of time gained. Guards' journals were hardly ever checked against signal box register entries that recorded the actual times. Journals were the normal basis of any running time queries booked to the engine and hence if the guard performed 'correctly', authority was rarely the wiser!

Two of the main protagonists, I recall, were Ron Meeson and Reg Salmon, who usually shared the honours. One or two others, such as Bill Stevens, were not far behind. Ron, today, as these words are being written, enjoys a well earned retirement and still lives, so far as I know, in Southend. Reg lived at Rayleigh in those days. Ron's dad, Phil, was a senior driver at the shed, so we had both father and son as drivers. Phil was more gentle with the regulator than Ron who could, and did, make the sparks fly when required (and sometimes when it wasn't!). He could be depended upon to turn in an energetic performance. It was unknown for Ron to ever have lost time booked to him. Both men were a real pleasure to fire to, although with totally different driving techniques.

Firing to Phil one day in 1952, we had class 'L1' No. 67738 on an unusual working for Southend men. We booked on duty at 8.50 am to work diagram 16. We relieved the early shift men at the station to work the 9.10 am passenger to Liverpool St, and then to work the 11.39 am cars to Temple Mills - this was in the days before the modern marshalling yard was built there. After returning LE to Stratford we took the 2.42 pm cars to Liverpool St before working the 3.54 pm passenger to Southend. We were relieved on arrival by the third shift of men. It was an unusual working as passenger train crews only rarely went to Temple Mills, plus this was the only turn when crews changed over at the station at both the start and end of the shift. We liked it with no preparation or disposal of the engine to do, even if on this occasion it was on a class 'L1'!

As already mentioned, tender engines had to work engine first when on passenger workings, unless this was not possible, when the safest option had to be adopted. On the Shenfield-Chelmsford workings, we would work engine first down to Chelmsford after turning on the manually-operated Shenfield turntable. Pushing these tables round certainly kept you fit. This was located on the upside of the main line at the country end of the goods yard, now covered by the inevitable car park. We always worked back tender first on the slightly slower schedule for the return, mainly uphill, journey to Shenfield. Normal timing margins allowed non-stop, were two minutes longer on the up road. By doing it this way round, rather than going tender first to Chelmsford, we minimised any potential risk, because of the slower schedule. Firing a class 'K2' 2-6-0 No. 61737, on the 6.13 pm Shenfield to Southend with Reg Salmon in 1951, we worked tender first because these engines were too long to turn at Shenfield. It was rare for any engine which couldn't be turned at Shenfield to be used on these workings, because of the 20-odd mile trip involved. We had a very uncomfortable ride against a strong side wind. Coal dust blew everywhere, despite regular soaking with the slacker hosepipe. These engines still retained their ex-GNR design lever reverse and were the only class so fitted that I worked with on main line duties. The driver needed a strong arm to handle them.

The 'K2s' were known as 'Ragtimers'. They first entered traffic before World War I at about the time this dance was popular. They could give you a very lively trip when it came to riding qualities, and hence their nickname, reflecting the energetic dance steps. They also had the unpopular horizontal pull out and push in regulator (rather than the more normal quadrant operated design) which always required extra care. These regulators had a dangerous habit of re-opening themselves if not fully and firmly closed, that could catch an unsuspecting crew unawares. Some drivers would additionally wedge them closed with a lump of coal as well as tightening down the butterfly nut provided to lock the regulator when leaving the engine screwed down and unattended. It was also absolutely vital to make doubly sure the cylinder drain cocks were fully open and the reversing lever in mid-gear. This was the normal procedure at all times, but ignored at your peril with these engines. Likewise, any failure to check the boiler water level before opening the regulator to move one when the pressure was low. They would 'pick-up the water' (this is, over-carry the water from the boiler into the main steam pipe to the cylinders) very easily if the boiler was full, with the need to open the regulator wider than you would normally if the pressure was higher. A class 'K2' engine took a swim to finish up at a steep angle tender first in the River Lea at the rear of Stratford shed caused by this very circumstance. It didn't help that the engine (one of three to be specially prepared, so it was said) had just been out-shopped freshly re-painted in apple green livery for inspection by the LNER Board of Directors at Liverpool St! Joe (I never learned his surname) who had the misfortune to be the driver of this unplanned dip in the waters spent the rest of his days demoted to working the turntable at Liverpool St. This was management's retribution for upsetting such an auspicious event. He it was, who told me the story and of his part in it.

An unplanned dip in the waters! Class 'K2/2' 2-6-0 No. 1734 repainted in post-war LNER lined green livery sampling the murky depths of the river alongside Stratford shed in 1948, with the distinctive signal gantry of Channelsea Junction in the background.
Author's Collection

By 1951 and maybe earlier, Southend men were working to Clacton, on a three-shift diagram. The first shift worked up to Liverpool St and back to Shenfield, to be relieved by the second shift who worked Shenfield to Clacton and back to Shenfield, to be in their turn relieved by the third shift who worked Shenfield to Liverpool St and back to Southend. Each shift travelled passenger to and from Shenfield 'on the cushions'. This turn was worked with a class 'B1' engine. I believe the trains worked - all passenger - were the 5.51 am Southend to Liverpool St, 8.36 am to Clacton and 1.00 pm back, and the 5.33 pm Liverpool St to Southend. The Clacton portion of the diagram had definitely ceased by the winter 1955/56 timetable, but possibly earlier than this. The story behind why this unusual working came about is an interesting one.

From 1948 (or maybe1949), Southend men had a similar three-shift diagram to Ipswich, working a fast express each way between Liverpool St and Ipswich. I believe the 8.30 am down, but do not know which up working. This came about because Stratford men were regularly losing time on the diagram. 'Authority' had ruled that Southend men should be given the work instead. 'They' wanted to allocate the then new class 'B1' 4-6-0 tender engines, to the job. Instead, Southend men requested, and were allowed to keep, their regular 'B12s'; Nos. 61571/72/73/74 were allocated with No. 61575 as the spare for the link. It was said each went into the works for a valve and piston examination. While there the valves were re-set. It was also said one of the drivers in the link knew the valve setter in the works and asked him to do 'a special job' on the four regular engines. I can clearly recall being told the story, but cannot confirm the factual accuracy of it, but it does have credibility. Ted Woods was one of the firemen in the link, I think on No. 61571, firing to the same Wally Alderman mentioned earlier. Wally was always a very light driver. Ted described to me how, with this engine, they would run up from Ipswich with a 10-car formation of main line buckeye stock, probably weighing about 300 tons tare. He was able to run with a very hot, thin, fire that needed firing once round the box only, i.e., about 12 shovelfuls - 6 down each side, just 12 times for the complete trip, once the fire had been initially built up prior to departure. This was witnessed by the Stratford footplate inspectors who would express surprise, thinking it could not be done. Stratford men were sore at losing the work and laughed when they heard about the request for the old fashioned '1500s', by this time just over 20 years old and built to a design originating back another 15 years before that. They claimed the task was an impossible one for these engines to manage, and then sulked once the high standard of punctuality achieved by the Southend men became a fact!

Eventually 'authority' relented, and let Stratford have the work back, on the strict condition that any lost time and Southend would keep it for good! I believe the impending arrival of the new BR Standard class 4-6-2 Pacifics - the 'Britannias' - may have had something to do with this decision. The probability is that with the major alterations being proposed for the Norwich services, Southend men would have lost the work anyway. The quid-pro-quo was the substitution of Clacton for Ipswich, which was the working in operation, as above described, at the time of my arrival at the shed in 1951. To work on the Clacton diagram was a pleasure that never came my way. I have always understood that the legendary Leslie Preston Parker, formerly the Stratford district motive power superintendent, and then the Eastern Section locomotive running superintendent from the early war years onwards, was responsible for the Ipswich working coming to Southend. If this was the case, such a decision would have been typical of him to take in the circumstances explained.

'B1s' did come to the shed. Our fleet throughout the 1950s era of steam comprised Nos. 61335/6, 61360/1/2/3, mostly delivered to the shed when still nearly new. The spare engine, often as not, would be No. 61370 or sometimes the first member of the class, No. 61000 *Springbok*, allocated to cover for boiler washouts, etc. The first six engines were each manned by two regular crews to create the top passenger link of 12 sets of men. I was to have No. 61335 in 1955/56 as my regular mount for 15 months. One small detail of interest on this engine was the LNER apple green paint that could be seen in areas where the later BR lined black livery had worn away, as likewise on No. 61336. On the remaining four, Nos. 61360-63, there were no such traces of green, so they were presumably painted in the BR lined black livery from new.

The standard 8-car trains that maintained services throughout the day to London, also some of the 4-car Shenfield to Chelmsford services, were covered by two links of 12 sets of men. They had four regular-manned class 'B12s' for each link with three sets of men per engine. This required eight class 'B12s' for the basic roster. These were Nos. 61546/49/71/72/73/74/76/78 with, usually, No. 61575/80 as the spares for routine maintenance. Stratford would rotate other engines in the class to the shed as required. These included Nos. 61512/16/19/50/54/55 and 79 at different times. For a short period in 1953 after returning to Southend from Cambridge, No. 61578 became my regular engine with Harry Loker as my mate. We had hardly got to know each other before Her Majesty required my services for the next two years, which was a great pity as Harry was an excellent mate to be booked with. He had a very pleasant, placid disposition, rarely complained about anything, and enjoyed smoking his pipe - as likewise myself - and was good fun to be with. He had the happy knack of not saying overmuch and yet always generated a 'presence'. He was a good engineman who helped to make his fireman's work as easy as he could. We had one tough trip together on a very rough engine (to be described in Chapter Five) with poor coal and he used his intimate knowledge of the gradients to help me. On the few trips we had together on No. 61578, it was a pleasure to be at work.

Class 'B1s' were known to us as 'Bongos' (in some other areas as 'Antelopes' although this wasn't very commonly used) because the first members of the class were named after various species of deer. On the GE section they were always known as 'Bongos', which rather suited them as they could bounce around. The ribald cockney humour of Stratford more usually described them as 'Bleedin' Bongos'. They were good, strong, versatile engines, usually very reliable and free steaming machines, that could be lively runners when required. They could also be very rough riders when approaching the time for their next overhaul!

The six regular-manned 'B1s' and likewise the eight regular-manned 'B12s', with the odd exception, all carried Southend code '30D' shedplates, as did some of our four class 'J20s' - the 'Long Box Knockos', and our regular shunting pilot engines. All were nominally allocated to Stratford shed as 30A engines in the official engine record lists issued to detail transfer movements. There were no issued transfers which listed 30D as a shed in its own right. For some peculiar reason engines allocated to 30B Hertford, 30C Bishops Stortford, and 30D were always regarded as Stratford engines for allocation purposes. Engines allocated to 30E Colchester, and 30F Parkeston, although both in the Stratford '30' District like us, had separate engine transfer allocations issued. Why this distinction existed remains a puzzle.

Additionally, in the earlier 1950s in particular, we always had a good sprinkling of the class 'B17s'. These were usually known to us as '2800s' after their original LNER numbering when introduced in 1928. The small GE tender ones were also called 'Sandies' - referring to the first one built, named *Sandringham* - and the large LNER tender ones 'Footballers' - referring to the many named after football clubs. The ones we had at the shed, of both types were mainly Westo, but a few were non-Westo fitted. We also had regular visits by the 'K3' 2-6-0, class, known as 'Jazzers' because they entered traffic after World War I when this dance was popular and like the earlier 'K2s' could be lively riding machines - all 'K3s' were non-Westo engines. The class 'K2' 'Ragtimer's', already mentioned, that were Stratford allocated engines, were nearly all Westo-fitted. These classes provided back up for engines in main works, stopped for repairs, etc. We also had various Stratford 'L1' tanks, most of which were Westo-fitted. These were usually kept on the Shenfield services, being only occasionally used to London, and only when 'push came to shove', as already mentioned. We had a rotating allocation of class 'N7s' (all Westo-fitted) for the Wickford and Southminster out-station sheds, and some Shenfield to Chelmsford services. Regular class 'N7s' - but not regularly manned, except Nos. 9618/45, included Nos. 9616/18/45, 9701/03/14/18/21/32. Nos. 9618/45 were at separate times the passenger station pilots with regular crews until displaced by an ex-Midland 'Tilbury' 4-4-2 class '3P' tank No. 41936, which covered this duty for quite a long period up to May 1956. The final regular engine on this job was the 'J69' 'Buckjumper' No. 68636, until Christmas Eve 1956, when she was sent LE to Stratford. This commenced the planned programme to transfer the, soon to be surplus, engines away from the shed. These transfers were completed a week later, with the full dc electric services starting from 31st December, 1956, to be discussed more fully in Chapter Five.

It should be explained that all the main line engines, irrespective of type, that worked from Southend were equipped to work vacuum-braked trains. The former GER system had worked its passenger trains with the Westinghouse compressed air braking equipment. Many of our engines still had this equipment fitted and in use for their own brakes. Most passenger rolling stock had over the years since the 1923 Grouping been fitted with the vacuum equipment which was standardised by the LNER throughout its system. The inner suburban 'Jazz' trains working out of Liverpool St remained air braked to the end of steam on these services in late 1960, as explained in *Appendix Two*. There were also ex-GER main line coaches still in use with air brake equipment fitted. At Southend we would still occasionally find ourselves working air braked stock in the early 1950s. This became almost unknown in the final run-up to the demise of our Southend steam services. It was most likely to occur on the evening special excursions for the Southend illuminations that used to be very popular in the post-war years. We were rather like people who are fluent in two languages - we were equally at home using either braking system, as the Stratford District was one of the few surviving steam areas on BR still regularly using air brake equipment and the only mainland one still regularly working steam trains using this system. A few areas retained the Westo system for use on their engines, but no longer used it for train working. The Isle of Wight network used Westo only, and, with the surviving Liverpool St area services, these remained the only pure air brake-operated steam-hauled passenger trains in the final steam years. (A different form of air braking was to become the new standard braking equipment for BR in its later years, being introduced as steam workings were drawing to a close.)

We had two running foremen, Albert Avery and Bill Wren, whose official shifts week and week about were 4.00 pm to midnight and midnight to 8.00 am. They always changed over at 11.00 pm, as it was easier to go home and come to work with the street lights on, which in Southend were turned off before midnight in those days. No all-night street lighting as we have today. Even the main roads and the High Street were in darkness. Cycling to work required good headlamps. Bill came to work on a beautifully maintained pre-war green Raleigh bicycle of the type with the chain fully enclosed. It was his pride and joy and a regular item to be cleaned by us as an unofficial part of our work. In those days one rarely queried the foreman's instructions. After we had given it the standard 'cleaning treatment' Bill would give it a final wipe over with a soft rag. It always looked like a new machine, even though it must have been nearly 20 years old. He loved that bicycle.

Albert was a very placid man who would allocate our duties for the shift, then leave us to get on with it. We organised our mealbreaks to suit the work and generally he ran a happy ship. It took something out of the way to get him worked up at all. Bill, on the other hand, was more restive and less relaxed, although equally good to us youngsters. He would not trust us, as Albert would. He regularly checked our work and would not allocate duties for a full shift. We never knew what was to be done, until instructed. This could be very frustrating. On occasion when something had upset him, he would vent his frustration by wanting engines in out of the way places to be cleaned. This might mean the buckets of cleaning oil and rags being carried a quarter of a mile to the far end of the shed roads. This area was called 'The Field' - with ample justification! Normally we cleaned engines stabled in the shed building under cover. On one well remembered occasion Bill had been more irritable to us than usual. It was raining, and this he did not like. He had a fair decent fire stoked up in his office stove. The chimney flue pipe ran up the side of the water tank that sat over the complete top of the building. This also included our messroom. Waiting until he left the office we climbed the long ladder to the tank top with a bucket, dipped it in the tank and gently poured the contents down the pipe. Someone even suggested a detonator was more appropriate, but common sense prevailed! He returned to his office to find a puddle and a fire that was nearly out. He made no comment, not so much as a whisper. But, for the rest of the week we had the dirtiest engines to clean that he could find - and in the worst locations. And - the weather was not too warm either! It was worth the prank, even though it was game, set, and match, to Bill! Possibly someone had seen us and told him - we never found out.

One of our regular duties, particularly on the night shift, was to keep the engine disposal pit clean and clear of ashes. This was a miserable job at the best of times, but an even worse task if it was raining. If we wore a mac, we sweated profusely and got wet. If we forewent the mac, we didn't sweat so much, but still got soaked through just the same. As we shovelled the still very hot ash and clinker out of the pit we got covered with a fine grey dust. If it was dry we got covered, if it was wet we still did once the damp crust was broken - we couldn't win! As with other jobs we just had to grin and bear it. These were essential duties to keep the shed working. It was a particularly hated job if a strong wind was blowing.

Other dirty jobs that came our way might be to help Harold, the boilersmith. This would be cleaning tubes and brushing the accumulated 'fur' that developed on the tube ends over the brick-arch. We would carry, and, under his supervision, replace brick arches and firebars, or maybe sweeping out the insides of smokeboxes. Cleaners were general 'dogsbodies' to be used wherever required. Shovelling spilt coal off the backs of tenders and from the tender fire-iron compartments was another job that often came our way, working 10 ft above the ground, with no safety protection if we slipped. We regularly worked perched up on boiler handrails, up to 9 ft above ground level and used ladders for cleaning the upper areas of tenders - today such antics would probably require proper scaffolding or someone standing on the bottom rung of the ladder, if it was still deemed safe to use it. We would walk around footplating and along the tops of boilers without even thinking about it. Like so much else to do with the normal daily tasks when working with steam, it was all part of the accepted duties and taken for granted as just a part of the job. Such dangerous working hazards were normal. We very rarely, if ever, had any mishaps. I cannot recall a single instance of anyone falling off an engine from the heights we worked at. We quickly developed very safety conscious attitudes which stood us in good stead for our later careers, and which is still instinctively with me today in whatever task is being undertaken.

The shedmaster's clerk and general solver of all problems was Tom Jackson. Tom was one of those endearing persons who was everybody's friend. He was always most helpful, no matter who you were. One of his main jobs was to prepare the weekly and daily work rosters for all the footplate grades staff, comprising about 150 of us. This could be an absolute minefield for anybody unfamiliar with it. His duties embraced far more than this, though. He collated all the drivers' daily work tickets, kept the seniority records and details of duties worked, the higher grade duty records, maintained the frequent diagram working amendments posted in our glass-fronted notice cases, kept staff records of sickness, etc., up-to-date, dealt with the routine paperwork on behalf of the shedmaster, daily engine availability returns, handled all requests for free and privilege ticket travel, kept details of uniform clothing issues, ordered the oil and general stores required to keep the shed fully operational, issued the brass pay checks each week, and did almost anything else that was needed. He was the essential administrative lubricant that kept the many conflicting demands of the shed operation well oiled. He achieved a good degree of compatible harmony, which was not always easy. Our shedmasters relied on him absolutely. He was the soul of discretion and people trusted him. He shared the same office as the shedmaster. My first shedmaster was Mr Donald, succeeded by Mr Micklethwaite and finally, Les Thorn. Tom had a very neat and clear handwriting that immediately identified any notice he had issued. All his writing was done using an inkwell and pen-nib pen and blotting paper - ball point pens not yet having become a standard issue item and he declined to use a fountain pen. He rarely became angry, in my experience, although when he did, it was wiser to keep one's distance! In his unassuming way, he was one of the real strengths of the place. A real character hidden behind his prominent thick pebble lens glasses. These made his eyes seem to peer at you from afar - he was very short sighted. He wore a running foreman's blue dust coat and included these duties in amongst his normal work, helped in this by the shedmaster, when available. He worked a regular daytime shift, and his job was certainly no sinecure. A kindly man who would help anybody if he reasonably could.

The storemen who ran the oil and tool store also kept their eye on the footplate staff booking-on window to check the arrival of staff reporting for duty and would alert the running foremen to any problems, such as someone late for work. The signing-on lobby, as it was called, displayed the staff rosters, late notices, e.g., new speed restrictions, line closures for engineering work, diversions, etc., general notices, the master seniority list, union notices, minutes of union meetings with the management, and other information. Many of us were members of the Provident Mutual Life Assurance Company, the Great Eastern Sick & Orphan Funds, the Hospital Savings Association (HSA), Railway Convalescence Homes (RCH), and of the Railway Employees Privilege Ticket Association (REPTA). Each had arrangements to post information in the notice cases.

Provident Mutual had an agent in most sheds and depots, always a working member of staff, who undertook these duties in his spare time. Policy contributions were deducted via our paybill. It meant we started saving at an early age, long before we might otherwise have considered the need to do so. Thus, when marriage loomed, I had a good policy record to offer for a mortgage. In those days building societies were more particular about granting them than is the case today. These were the sort of indirect benefits that being a railway worker could offer you. Railway employment was considered to be safe and secure. Our wages as manual workers may not have been as good as in many other industries, but we were usually considered as a safer risk, particularly if you could produce evidence of regular saving, when applying for a mortgage, for example.

The Great Eastern Sick & Orphan Fund was set up by the Great Eastern Railway to help staff when off work through injury and sickness. The RCH was an excellent organisation, which will be mentioned again later on. The HSA membership was very useful in helping partially to compensate us for lost wages when off sick for prolonged periods, as I was to be with two separate occasions in hospital.

REPTA issued a yearly handbook detailing many retail outlets which offered special discounts to members. We purchased all our furniture through the then well known Houndsditch Warehouse Co. near to Liverpool St station, with a hefty 10 to 15 per cent discount, using my REPTA card. It helped us considerably.

The signing-on lobby was like the local launderette. It was where you heard all the latest news and gossip, often amidst much hilarity, it has to be said.

Talking of hilarity, recalls two perfectly true stories that merit a mention in this record to give a little idea of the flavour of what could happen. Each reflect the vagaries of human nature, in a light hearted vein, but in totally contrasting ways. One levelling a score to be settled, the other a prank.

The first refers to an event on the last down passenger train of the day (always known as the 'Midnight') from Liverpool St, 12.15 am, first stop Shenfield. This train was a well known haunt of the 'ladies of the night' (as were several of the late evening services) who had season tickets to practise their 'profession'. On the night in question, 2nd July, 1952, I'm firing to Joe Thatcher, one of the younger hands at that time. Our engine was class 'B12' No. 61573. Joe was another of nature's gentlemen, with a habit of wrinkling his brow when talking to you. He was always a good mate with whom to share a day's work. He also enjoyed a good laugh if the circumstances were right. On arrival in London on the 8.54 pm up passenger, he said 'keep an eye open' and disappeared, I assumed, to the toilet.

Nothing more was said, until shortly before departure time, when he suggested 'a decent fire' should be built up. Most odd, because Joe never normally interfered with his fireman's working. On getting the 'Right away' we departed the terminus faster than was usual. Thereafter we crossed from down main to the down electric and vice versa at every available crossover at a nudge above the normal limit of 25 mph. Safe, but a bit faster than legal. Most of the signalmen were at their windows waving dusters. Joe hadn't let on what was afoot until the reason for this unusual routing began to emerge. At each signal box he gave a short 'pop' on the whistle to the signalman. In those days there were boxes at Liverpool St, Bethnal Green, Mile End, Bow Junction, Stratford, Forest Gate, Ilford Station, Ilford Car Sheds, Goodmayes, Chadwell Heath, Romford, Gidea Park, Brentwood and Shenfield, all of which controlled at least one, sometimes more, crossovers. The railway at this time of night was not busy. In between each set of crossings we 'fair motored' as some would say. The journey was lively to say the least! On stopping at Shenfield high bedlam was let lose. A couple of the 'ladies' rushed up to the engine to shout the most profane abuse. Joe calmly alighted onto the platform (we had run in well to time, despite the accumulated delays with the many crossings over) and said in quite plain language very calmly and not in any way rudely, 'Any more abuse and you get the same treatment every night for the rest of the week'. They had had the most serious difficulty in accommodating their customers, due to the less than smooth ride through the crossings! On the previous night (I was not firing to him) he had apparently been sworn at by one of these 'ladies' for running early into Shenfield. This of course had curtailed their 'business' time. (Knowing Joe, he'd probably done that deliberately as well, just for the fun of it!) He had organised with the Control in London - which explained his absence - to have our train routed through each crossover. Needless to say everybody obliged when they knew the reason! He later confirmed there had been no further trouble that week. Without doubt, one of life's less serious moments!

The second refers to a little prank that was indulged in for just a short time. The guard always rode in the front brake compartment on up road trains from Southend. This was because of the short up platform at Prittlewell. Normally, guards ride at the rear of the train. This meant, most unusually, they were always next to the engine. The 'ladies only' compartments (normal ladies this time!) were always immediately next to the guards compartment on the Thompson outer suburban stock that made up most of our carriage sets. Most older readers will, I'm sure, recall the tremendous furore that greeted the daring introduction of mini-skirts as worn by teenage girls in the 1950s. Initially, these were just loose fitting shorter versions of longer skirts. They soon became a very tight fitting garment of minimum length which closely hugged the upper thighs of the wearer as she walked. This was when the brighter sparks among our youthful drivers saw an opportunity too good to be missed!

The guard had to be next to the engine so he would be on hand to assist - very willingly it must be added. He was thus near to the driver to ensure no possible mishap could occur. Even when indulging in an innocent prank, it was instinctive to safeguard our passengers' safety at all times. The train was stopped very precisely with the 'ladies only' compartment positioned at the top of the platform ramp. The skill was to be just off the end of the normal height length of the platform. The guard had then to help the innocent victim up into her compartment, and revealing the maximum of shapely legs at the same time! Ladies with mini-skirts were, in the earliest days of the fashion, reluctant to sit in ordinary compartments facing strange men on busy trains. They were keen not to forego the relative privacy of travelling in the ladies compartment. Within a short while, as the style became more universal, their shyness soon disappeared. Before it did, the fun was in seeing just how far you could run the train past the level platform onto the ramp before the exercise of 'assistance' became a non-starter! Very soon some of the young ladies latched on to this prank and quickly got their own back by reverting to wearing the looser fitting style garment. It made for many a smile from our usually tolerant younger customers. Once the skirt became established fashion attire, the novelty wore off and the ladies were left in peace. It was all a bit of innocent fun while it lasted for a couple of weeks. Like all good pranks, it lost its humour if you didn't know when to stop.

As 1952 progressed, our promotion prospects to fireman were being thwarted by men from other sheds transferring in to take the vacancies. This they were entitled to do. But, we were not best pleased! A mini-council of war was held between a group of us cleaners to discuss how we could prevent it. The next chapter explains the outcome.

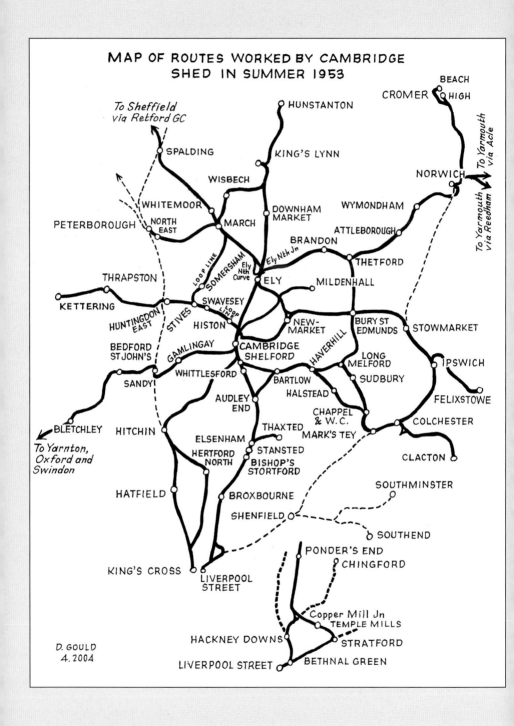

MAP OF ROUTES WORKED BY CAMBRIDGE
SHED IN SUMMER 1953

D. GOULD
4. 2004

Chapter Four

The Footplate Years - Cambridge

In late 1952 a successful application was made to secure a fireman's vacancy at Cambridge. How was it possible to move from one shed to another, indeed from one motive power area to another? (Stratford was No. 30 area, and Cambridge, No. 31 area, under the national BR coding scheme that was a direct development from the previous LMS one.) As with so much else in a large organisation there was a procedure - in this case one that had been negotiated at national level. This had been gradually developed between the unions and the former private companies up to 1947. From 1948, BR took over union negotiations, conducted in succession under the Railway Executive, the British Transport Commission, and finally, the British Railways Board organisations, within the steam era. Today, the wheel has again turned full circle with the unions once again negotiating with individual private companies. Since privatisation, 'tailor made' agreements are emerging with varying types of arrangements to reflect the altered traffic working commitments of each company. This in many ways is similar in principal to the circumstances that existed prior to 1923. The details then were considerably different to reflect the wider variety of traffic needs and thus motive power organisation arrangements that existed, but the principle of individual negotiations was very similar. After 1923, greater uniformity became possible through agreements negotiated by the unions with the four principal main line companies. After Nationalisation in 1948, almost universal conditions were introduced - the principal detail variances concerned the former GWR territory. It is the post-1948 arrangements governing footplate grade promotion in the 1950s that are summarised in the next paragraphs.

At regular intervals footplate vacancies at sheds within a designated territory, i.e., normally a Region, were advertised on a footplate grades vacancy list. This was circulated to each shed within the Region concerned. Regions did not circulate their lists to other Regions, as each one organised its own promotion arrangements independently of, and separate from, the others. The one exception to this statement was for sheds that had been transferred to another Region, who continued to receive vacancy details for their former Region in addition to their new one, for staff who had opted to seek promotion in their former Region. Our territory was the new Eastern Region of BR. This was basically the old Southern Area of the former LNER adjusted as necessary to reflect BR Regional boundary changes. Thus, for example, after mid-1949, the ER took over the former LMSR Tilbury section, transferred to it from London Midland Region control. Staff at these sheds retained certain options entitling them to apply for vacancies within their former Region, but they could opt also to move within their new Region instead. Likewise, at a much later date, the former Great Central section staff in the southern section of that company's former territory, found themselves being transferred from the ER to the LMR giving these staff the choice of remaining with the ER promotion ladder or opting for the LMR one.

An up class 'F' express freight train at Elsenham headed by 'K1' class 2-6-0 No. 62036 on 29th August, 1952.

'J15' class 0-6-0 No. 65473 is passed by 'B17/1' class 4-6-0 No. 61640 *Somerleyton Hall* as it leaves Cambridge on the 4.50 pm train for Liverpool Street on 10th May, 1953.　　　*B.I. Nathan*

The procedure to allow moves between sheds within each Region was included in a National Agreement titled the 'Scheme of Promotion, Transfer and Redundancy for Footplate Staff', known to all as the 'PTR Agreements'. You will by now realise that with railway work almost everything has an official designation and an unofficial one too! Most engine classes had nicknames, and likewise, most administrative procedures, acronyms or 'slang names' which everybody instantly understood. Confusing, until one learned the language. All National Agreements had been negotiated over time at national level under an overall 'umbrella' procedure called 'The Machinery of Negotiation'.

Some agreements went back to the era of the pre-1923 Grouping railway companies and were still applicable in my time on the footplate. The wider procedures for national negotiation embrace all railway grades below Officer level. The industry was sub-divided by function. All employees below Officer level were represented by a specific 'Sectional Council' (SC) of which there were five, numbered 1 to 5. Broadly summarised - 1 represented salaried grades - clerical, etc.; 2, the motive power department - footplate, etc.; 3, the operating department - guards, signalmen, porters, etc.; 4, the commercial department - goods handling, cartage, etc.; and 5, the engineering grades. Each was structured to allow the staff representatives serving on their particular Council to be elected or re-elected by the employees whom they represented. This was done on a rotating basis with a percentage being elected each year, to retain continuity. The voting procedure was confidential, with sealed ballot boxes, very similar in concept to voting for local councillors.

Footplate grades were represented in the 'Sectional Council No. 2' grouping. Each Region within the national system had its own SC structure for each of the five Councils. The No. 2 Sectional Councils had nationally, over the history of the industry, gradually developed the most definitively organised structure of all the Councils. The arrangements were based primarily on the entry date to the footplate grades of each employee. This determined their seniority date and became the basis for nearly all the administration of the PTR Arrangements within each Region. Normal routine movement of footplate staff between sheds was not allowed outside our own Region. Thus, we could only gain promotion, or transfer within our grade, within our own designated Sectional Council area, in my case the Eastern Region of BR.

It was a complicated procedural structure that took some understanding, but which worked well. It was accepted by the staff as being the fairest formula that could be devised to safeguard our potential security of employment. Special provisions were included to cover cases of personal need, usually for compassionate reasons. It was possible for an employee to ask for a transfer to a shed outside their own Region - but these were 'one off' options and would usually involve the Regional welfare officer. This person would make enquiries into the individual case. If the circumstances justified a favourable recommendation on behalf of the applicant, then support would be given to the transfer request. Such transfers occurred only rarely, but it showed how the system could be flexible in appropriate cases.

Please understand the above and following paragraphs are simplified summaries to enable the essential basics to be understood - the full agreements required a 25 page, 6 in. x 10 in. size closely printed document. Many managers with little or no experience of dealing with footplate staff on a regular basis would admit to being unable to interpret them correctly without knowledgeable assistance. To those unfamiliar with the finer details of footplate grade employment they could be a veritable minefield. Nevertheless, they served their purpose well to ensure parity over the entire rail network. I was to benefit considerably from understanding them.

When I applied for the Cambridge vacancy I was not the senior passed cleaner at Southend. There were hands with higher seniority to me still cleaning. This meant, if appointed, I jumped up the seniority list over them to secure my higher grade appointment. This was quite in order as I was moving away to gain promotion where my seniority date would be in the correct sequence at my new shed. Thus, this did not create any financial penalty at my existing shed to their earning prospects. It also gave me the opportunity, under the PTR Arrangements, to 'close' the shed at Southend. This was a procedure that prevented anybody else from another shed being appointed to a firing vacancy at Southend in advance of myself. I had the right to register my wish to return in due course in my correct seniority order under what was known as a 'preference move'. This had to be registered within 14 days after my arrival at Cambridge. By moving and taking advantage of the PTR Arrangements to exercise this right, all the hands more senior to me at Southend could achieve promotion, as the shed was no longer 'open' to applicants from other sheds, until after my return. After all hands senior to me had gained promotion to permanent fireman, the right to exercise my option to transfer back there to claim the next vacancy in my correct seniority position was then offered. Only after this was either surrendered, or exercised, could the shed again become 'open' and anybody from other sheds become again eligible to apply for a vacancy at Southend.

I had an uncle who lived in Cambridge and was able to secure me suitable lodgings. Hence why at our 'mini-council of war' my name became the one to apply for Cambridge in the first place. Thus, we solved our promotion prospects. Nobody had previously thought to 'close' the shed, and we were losing out. My seniority date met the requirements to qualify for a fireman's position at Cambridge.

The application of the PTR procedures were confined to operate as 'stand alone' arrangements within each Region, as already explained. This restricted staff movement to manageable proportions. Today, altered arrangements apply as the total number of footplate staff is drastically less than in the days of steam, and they are no longer all under the jurisdiction of one company since privatisation.

My application for the Cambridge vacancy was made in early November 1952. When all applications were in by the advised closing date, the most senior ones, equal to the number of vacancies, were informed they had been selected. This was subject to passing the required examinations. On 5th December my attendance at Stratford was required for written and oral exams on my knowledge of the rules and regulations, and of engine management. Then followed a practical test out on the road taken by our chief inspector, Mr Weavers, on class 'B1' No. 61008 *Kudu*, from Stratford to Shenfield. Everything was satisfactory and after a medical at Marylebone a few days later, my promotion was verbally confirmed. If any of the proficiency examinations had been failed, a possible two more chances were allowed. A third failure meant my employment in the line of promotion would have been terminated. In such a circumstance the option might be offered of staying on as an adult cleaner with no prospect of promotion and no more firing duties, or possibly alternative employment might be offered, perhaps as a general shedman. To be discharged from railway employment was almost unknown, for the simple reason most departments were short of staff. Transfer to a permanent way gang was a more likely option, if the motive power department had no suitable openings available.

If, at anytime during my subsequent career, a periodic medical examination was failed, especially the eyesight test, then a similar loss of job in the line of promotion could occur. Employment on restricted duties, e.g., confined to yard shunting or shed turning of engines, etc., might be offered if the medical condition permitted. This is an aspect not always appreciated. We could spend many years on the footplate and then, out of the blue, lose all we had achieved through a circumstance beyond our control. Generally, management were sympathetic in dealing with this kind of situation, but the ultimate was dismissal if they had no suitable alternative work available.

Reporting for duty on Monday 29th December found me allocated, from 5th January, to the pilot shunting link. My regular mate was to be a driver Sam Cooke, who was on the sick list. We never met. My new motive power superintendent was Colin Morris whom one did not expect to meet, unless in disciplinary trouble - to be avoided at all costs! No letters can be traced to advise who my new shedmaster may have been as all correspondence is signed on behalf of Mr Morris. Perhaps there was not one appointed.

The pilot link was the junior link for firemen at the shed and comprised 18 sets of men. We shunted all the yards and carriage sidings. The accompanying table details our work roster.

Table One - Cambridge Pilot Link Work Roster Winter 1952/53

Week	On Duty	Diagram
1	5.15 am	Carriage Sidings - north end of station
2	12.15 pm	Carriage Sidings - north end of station
3	8.00 pm	Carriage Sidings - north end of station
4	RD Relief	Various duties - different each day on day shift
5	RD Relief	Various duties - different each day on late shift
6	RD Relief	Various duties - different each day on night shift
7	5.30 am	Up Yard
8	1.30 pm	Up Yard
9	9.30 pm	Up Yard
10	5.15 am	Down Yard
11	1.00 pm	Down Yard
12	9.00 pm	Down Yard
13	5.35 am	Coal Field Yard
14	1.35 pm	Coal Field Yard
15	9.35 pm	Coal Field Yard
16	4.30 am	Carriage Sidings - south end of station
17	12.15 pm	Carriage Sidings - south end of station
18	8.15 pm	Carriage Sidings - south end of station

'J67/1' class 0-6-0 No. 68509 withdraws a rake of wagons from Cambridge goods shed on 12th May, 1953. Cambridge South signal box is on the left and the main through goods roads are in the centre. *R.E. Vincent*

'J69/1' class 0-6-0T No. 68600 is hard at work shunting in the goods yard north of Cambridge on 29th July, 1953. *A.R. Carpenter*

It was an excellent link to be in as we were readily available to the foreman for main line duties if required. It also enabled me to learn thoroughly the track and signalling layout of the station area. Rest Day Relief (RD Relief) turns of duty covered the various crew days off that were rostered at the frequency of 1 day per fortnight, throughout the link. All shunting pilots were continuously manned for the full 24 hour period except Sundays, thus extra time was required at the beginning and end of each 8 hour shift to book on duty, read the notices (15 minute allowance), and then to walk to and from the yard or sidings concerned. Access to each location had a specified walking allowance along a designated walking route. These were agreed between management and the union representatives to reflect best, i.e., safest, practice. Walking times were calculated at about 5 minutes per quarter mile, to allow for the need to carry bags, etc., and used public roads and foot pathways as far as possible, with a need to cross over or walk beside running lines reduced to the minimum.

Originally, less safe procedures had been followed with managers expecting staff to take the shortest walking route between two points with a much reduced regard for safety. In the former days of 'one crew to one engine' the need to walk to relieve another crew was considerably less prevalent. With the increasing abolition of this practice, particularly post-1919 when the 8 hour working day was introduced, engines became either common-user or were multiple-crewed. The need to relieve another crew away from the shed became more necessary. Managerial attitudes had to be reviewed under pressure from the unions who urged that safer walking routes should be designated (and the extra time be paid for). These often incurred higher cost to compensate for the longer distances that were agreed, and hence the former reluctance of some former pre-Grouping private railway company managements to concede the need for safer routes. After the 1923 Grouping most surviving problems were to disappear with increased safety awareness taking precedence over strict cash economy. Today, ever more stringent safeguards are being applied with a greater provision of properly made up pathways being provided on the authorised walking routes.

In 1953 the station was still lit by gas - a remarkable survival for such a principal station. Possibly, the last major station by this date within the Eastern Region still echoing each night to the unique sound of gas lighting throughout its platforms. There were many dark corners hidden in shadow that gave it a spooky feeling in places - very eerie. Platforms 3 (for Bletchley) and 6 (for Kettering and the 'Loop Line' trains to March via St Ives), offered several dark nooks and crannies, popular with courting couples as they bid each other farewell. The last service to Bletchley was at about 9.45 pm. We would shunt the empty cars in for this usually about 9.15 pm. Sometimes this would be done earlier if our shunter had noticed any couples waiting. We aimed to provide a bit of comfort, with the lights off, until the guard came to prepare the train! One wonders if such a personal service still survives - sadly the Bletchley trains have long since disappeared, but perhaps elsewhere? It is little touches such as this that help to make life a happier experience.

When Cambridge was granted the status of a city about the time of the Coronation, in June 1953, it was announced HM The Queen would be arriving

Class 'E4' 'Intermediate' 2-4-0 No. 62780, complete with stovepipe chimney, at Cambridge shed in the winter of 1953.   *Author*

Class 'E4' 'Intermediate' No. 62784 on Cambridge shed in 1953 equipped with the last surviving ex-GER round-topped 'water cart' tender originally built for an oil-fired engine.

Author

by train to do the official honours. Very miraculously the gas lighting couldn't be swept away quickly enough, but the resultant, better, but more clinical fluorescent variety somehow destroyed the former more intimate atmosphere.

With Sam Cooke being off sick a succession of young junior drivers became my mates whom I might not otherwise have met. The first of several was Bill Last who in more recent years has become better known through his talks to railway societies in the eastern counties area. He also helped Alan Bloom at his Bressingham Steam Museum with the operation of the fleet of preserved main line and other engines, either steamed or on static display there. My acquaintance with Bill was renewed one Sunday, some years ago now, at Bressingham on *Oliver Cromwell*, by arranging to be his fireman for the day. This was the last normal service engine to work in steam on BR in 1968, and is preserved as part of the national collection. We had a delightful time together going down memory lane in between providing footplate rides for the public - then still allowed. On the first of several turns together, on 5th January, 1953, we had an 'Intermediate' class 'E4' 2-4-0 tender engine No. 62781. The next day another popular young Cambridge driver, Len 'Dusty' Miller, was my mate on No. 62780. Again, as with Bill, we were to share the footplate in the future.

The little 'Intermediates' became a firm favourite. When first built in 1891 they were a middle-sized passenger engine class, hence 'Intermediate'. By the 1950s they were the smallest GE passenger tender engines remaining in service, but the nickname still stuck. They were a very strong engine for their size. For a short period after being allotted to a new regular mate, Alf Chandler, we had No. 62794 as a semi-regular engine. This engine, and then when it was transferred to No. 62784, another 'E4' we frequently worked on, had one of the last surviving inward curving top 'water cart' type tenders, originally built for engines with oil firing equipment. The more normal coal-carrying tenders had an outward curving profile to support the top valance side sheets. No. 62794 was unique in my experience, in running for a time with the cabside number E62794 which was a combination of the early and later styles of BR fleet numbering. Another engine type that became very familiar was the class 'C12' ex-GN type Atlantic (4-4-2) tanks, particularly Nos. 67360 and 67367. Members of class 'F6' 2-4-2 ex-GE tanks, were also allocated to the shed. Both types performed well on our carriage shunting duties but were totally different. The class 'F6s' were by far the more comfortable to work on. Several of them were also stored out of use round the back road of the shed, together with a few class 'E4s' for a time. They were serviceable, but surplus to requirements.

After three weeks, which gave a comfortable period to settle in, rostering for main line work began with a vengeance with the fourth week keeping me well occupied. Monday, it was off to Hitchin and return with Stan Houchin on class 'B17' No. 61636 *Harlaxton Manor*, and again on Tuesday, with class 'B1' No. 61300 (his regular engine, class 'B17' No. 61663 *Everton*, not being available) when we worked the 3.14 pm goods to Hitchin and back with the 9.35 pm passenger on each day. Wednesday took me to Temple Mills with Cecil Abbs on class 'WD' 2-8-0 No. 90302, up with the 2.10 pm goods, and on class 'K3' No. 61888, down with the 7.05 pm goods. Next, on Thursday, to Whitemoor Yards, March, via St Ives with George Stigwood on class 'WD' No. 90569, on the 4.55

No. 62785, the final class 'E4' to remain in traffic was also the final 2-4-0 engine to work on BR and is now preserved in the National Collection after restoration to her original 'as built' condition. Here we see her at Cambridge station departing for Newmarket in 1958. Note the full tender cab provision, very useful when working tender first.   *Author*

Class 'D16/3' No. 62585 approaches Cambridge with the 4.24 pm train from Bletchley on 12th May, 1953. The former London & North Western Railway Cambridge Goods Yard signal box can be seen in the distance.   *R.E. Vincent*

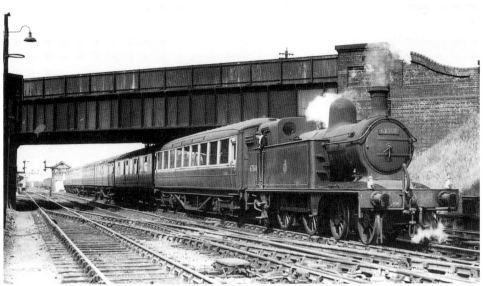

'C12' class 4-4-2T No. 67360 shunts the stock for the 6.10 pm buffet car train for King's Cross on 12th May, 1953.   *R.E. Vincent*

Sister engine No. 67367 at Cambridge shed in 1953. These two engines were regularly used as carriage shunting pilots throughout my time at Cambridge.   *Author*

Class 'B17/1' 4-6-0 No. 61600 *Sandringham* near Bishops Stortford on a down Cambridge express in April 1952.   *Brian Morrison*

Class 'B17/6' No. 61627 *Aske Hall* being prepared for its next turn of duty at Cambridge shed in 1953.   *Author*

pm goods and home passenger. Not 'on the cushions' in a passenger train, but in a very rough riding 'Queen Mary' type ex-LNER platform design 20 ton brake van (so called because they first entered traffic about the time of the late Queen's Silver Jubilee Coronation with her husband, HM King George V in 1935). These were a then new concept in brake van design, constructed with a longer than usual wheelbase to withstand a tough life. It was said they were just like the late Queen (who was affectionately considered to be a 'good, strong, tough old lady'). This might be an apocryphal story, but these vans were definitely known as 'Queen Mary's', so there has to be a connection somewhere. (They continued to be built as the BR standard brake van design, having proved so successful in withstanding the rough and tumble of goods train operation. The BR-built ones were mostly fitted with the 'Oleo' type hydraulic buffers and roller bearing axleboxes.) This was followed on Friday by firing to an Ely driver, Bill Lockwood (*see also below*), to Whitemoor and back via Ely North Junction on class 'J17' 0-6-0 No. 65512, outwards with the 7.05 pm goods and back with the 10.00 pm goods to Ely. Then on Saturday came a little gallop to Ely and back with Cecil Abbs again, on class 'K1' 2-6-0 No. 62054, on the 6.04 pm passenger, returning with the 7.30 pm goods. Finally, to round off this week of hectic route-learning over strange lines, with over half of it in darkness, a gentle Sunday turn with driver A. Drayton (I never learned his first name) on class 'J15' 0-6-0 No. 65461 carriage shunting. Not bad for one week and my first one as well out on main line duties since moving from Southend.

It certainly whetted the appetite for more. It was whispered afterwards that my abilities were soon enquired about by the foreman , 'What's he like, and can we roster him for main line duties regularly?' It was also whispered that the reports were satisfactory! My past experience at Southend was proving to be useful. This baptism of fire, so to speak, meant working on four classes of unfamiliar engines, 'J15', 'J17', 'K1' and 'WD'. Not bad for one week! The 'J15s' were known by us as the 'Small Black Goods' (the class 'J17' were 'Big Black Goods'); the 'K1s' as 'Baby Bongos', being a smaller version of the larger 'B1s'; and the 'WD' stood for War Department, known to us as 'Austerities', having been built cheaply for war service, mainly overseas. Some called the 'J17s', 'Short Box Knockos', but I always understood this term applied to the larger 'J19s' (and 'J18s' from which they were rebuilt) which were smaller than the 'Long Box Knockos', class 'J20', referred to in the previous chapter. The 'J19s' knocked in the axleboxes like the 'J20s', whereas the 'J17s' did not have this knock.

Just to ensure there was no swollen head developing, the following week it was back on yard shunting and shed duties. This included a turn on my first 'Claud' 4-4-0 with driver Bill Nordon on class 'D16' No. 62607, when we shared the day together carriage shunting. Some of these engines still retained the GE-style air-operated reversing gear and were very popular on shunting duties - no energetic winding to and fro of the more normal hand-operated wheel! 'Clauds' were so called after the name carried by the first member of the class *Claud Hamilton*, named after the then Chairman of the Great Eastern Railway, Lord Claud Hamilton. It had been specially prepared for exhibition in Paris just after it was built in 1900 - and earned a gold medal for excellence. She was one of only two GER engines to carry a name. She was also numbered 1900 in the

'K1' class 2-6-0 No. 62040 on a March-Ely-Cambridge freight train in June 1952.

P. Ransome-Wallis

Shunting in progress in Whitemoor down hump yard on 21st May, 1957.

engine list to reflect the date. As this number was well in advance of the previous highest number in use, the remaining 120 engines of the class that came to be built were numbered backwards in successive blocks of 10 - a most unusual practice. (The other named engine was *Petrolea*, a larger version of the 'Intermediate' design, that was equipped to burn a waste by-product from the GER gas works that produced the gas for carriage lighting.) Life was very definitely developing in an interesting manner.

The trip with the Ely driver, Bill Lockwood, became the most miserable and memorable of my time at Cambridge, in no way the fault of Bill, who was a good mate to fire to. No. 65512 had a small low-sided tender full of dust as the staple diet for the fire. Most, by this date, had a larger higher sided tender which would have been very welcome had we had one. Normally, a low-sided one would not have been a problem, but on this particular wild and windy night on the outward journey the wind was rising ominously. By the time of the return trip, it had risen to full gale force coming at us side on, straight off the level fenlands with nothing to break it up. We had a full load of loose-coupled loaded coal trucks, forming a long and heavy train, probably about 500 tons trailing load. The dust was very difficult to get into the firebox without losing most off the shovel blade. By turning the blade well towards the vertical facing the wind (with my backside likewise pointing at the wind - very cold and uncomfortable!) it became possible after a fashion to fire in a partially successful attempt to retain as much as possible on it. This required a deft flick of the wrist at the last moment to feed what was left on the blade into the firehole. It was back and arm breaking work. The low tender meant we had a much more exposed footplate open to the elements, that were absolutely merciless. How much of the dust was simply blown away by the winds from off that tender, and my shovel, is anyone's guess - it was quite considerable (as was the amount of it swirling around inside the open back of the cab because of the low-sided tender). By the time we got back to Ely, the arms and back ached so much they felt as if they were badly bruised. The gale was so strong we were barely managing 25 mph with the engine being driven very hard indeed to achieve this. We both looked and felt like chimney sweeps. It was a real struggle to maintain adequate steam, as we doggedly fought our way through the darkness over this level fenland road, but we survived and got through with some delay. Owing to the gale, Bill had to work the old lady very much harder than usual, which meant more coal and use of the boiler injector, all of which took its toll on the boiler pressure. It took a couple of days for my body, and sore eyes from the swirling dust, to stop aching. Fortunately, No. 65512 was a good steamer, otherwise our efforts may not have been enough. Throughout all of my footplate service no other trip came anywhere near to being a comparable experience. Fortunately it was not raining. Fen country could be a hard taskmaster when the weather really stirred itself.

Then came a surprise. For the next three weeks the roster showed shunting in the up hump yard. Steam had recently been replaced by the then brand new 350 hp diesel-electric shunters (known as the class '08' type in later BR days). The fireman was not needed, and therefore booked 'spare as required' - but not for long! Another new route to learn came when working with Sid Gallard to

Ivatt-designed class '2MT' No. 46403 on Cambridge shed in 1958. Examples of the slightly modified later BR version were on the Cambridge roster throughout most of the 1950s, being mainly used on the Colne Valley route services, and very popular and successful engines they were too, displaying prodigious haulage capacity relative to their moderate size.   *Author*

King's Lynn shed on 4th October, 1953 with 'D16' class 4-4-0 No. 62579 nearest the camera.
                                                                              B.K.B. Green

Colchester and back via Long Melford both ways, on class 'D16' No. 62562, on the 8.35 am outwards and returning with the 2.01 pm, both passenger workings. We did not go onto Colchester shed to turn, instead being sent down the Clacton branch to turn on the St Botolph's triangle, taking water in the station there, the only time my work took me over part of this branch.

Another 'first' was to work on an ex-LMS-built class '4' Ivatt type, 2-6-0 No. 43003 fitted with the less successful double chimney draughting arrangement. In this original form they became christened 'Flying Pigs'. Enginemen are notorious for their often sardonic capacity for humour. These engines were frequently incapable of moving swiftly, i.e., they didn't 'fly', being often shy for steam. Their soft exhaust created insufficient draw on the firebed. They could be real 'pigs' if you didn't manage your fire very carefully. A visit to Derby works discovered No. 43027 just ex-works modified with an ugly experimental single stovepipe chimney, rather like a stumpy version of the more elegant GE style stovepipe chimney. This trial must have been satisfactory. The BR-built series were delivered with single chimneys and for reasons unknown were given the nickname 'Doodlebugs' after the World War II 'V1' flying bombs. They became a very successful and respected prime mover, as the Midland & Great Northern (M&GN) section quickly discovered. The preserved example, No. 43106, is sometimes referred to as a 'Flying Pig'. This is not strictly correct as the term was only true for the original double chimney examples, for the reasons just explained. We also had three of the smaller Ivatt LMS-designed and BR-built class '2' type 2-6-0s on our allocation, in the No. 4646X number series. These were known by us as 'Mickey Mouses' because of their diminutive size which belied their prodigious capacity for work. These were normally used over both the Colne Valley and Long Melford roads to Colchester and, unlike their larger siblings just mentioned, were excellent little engines, very popular with the crews. They also came complete with tender cabs, like the larger machines had. They were very suitable for these routes.

More mature readers may recall the serious floods that covered many areas of East Anglia in early 1953, when just over 300 people perished. This short-lived but very disastrous period inevitably played havoc with rail services throughout the affected areas - which were many. Monday 9th February found me booked with John Mott on class 'D16' No. 62526 to work the 1.58 pm Ely to King's Lynn, 4.18 pm Lynn to March, and the 5.40 pm March to Cambridge, all passenger workings. (To railwaymen King's Lynn was always known as 'Lynn'.) Alas, it was not to be. We got as far as Downham Market from Ely to be allowed eventually to enter the station at dead slow speed. The flooding was everywhere, including some of our tracks under water. It was a very peculiar experience with extreme caution excercised. How our passengers continued their journeys after leaving our train we never did discover. We returned to Ely working tender first, to leave our 'Claud' and cars there. We were instructed by Control to take over class 'WD' No. 90275, towing class 'J67' No. 68502 and class 'D16' No. 62579, back to Cambridge. All had become trapped at Ely with the flood disruption. Many diagram workings were abandoned to be replaced with emergency 'ad hoc' arrangements. These were initially on an hour by hour basis, but very soon by emergency flood workings. These had a degree of

An up class 'F' freight train headed by 'WD' 2-8-0 No. 90075 approaches Mill Road bridge, Cambridge on 12th May, 1953. Coldham Lane signal box can be seen in the distance.

R.E. Vincent

Driver Alf Chandler in the cab of class 'J67' 0-60T No. 68516 keeping a sharp lookout. Alf was my regular driver for most of my time in the shunting pilot link at Cambridge - a true gentleman. The close proximity of the houses in Mill Road to the down yard headshunt can be seen.   *Author*

organisation within the constantly changing situation. It was a challenging time with many special demands made upon train crews and railway staff generally. Fortunately, not repeated since, and let us hope, never again. These were the floods that submerged nearly all of Canvey Island in the Thames Estuary where the population suffered very serious deprivation for weeks afterwards, even though the waters had by then receded.

One of those little oddments that are a kind of 'gem' among diagram rosters came my way at this time working with Charlie Stubbings on class 'J17' No. 65548. We travelled 'on the cushions' to Histon (on the St Ives Loop Line) to relieve the morning crew on the Histon goods pilot. The Chivers Jam factory, located here, kept the station yard busy. We worked the 1.55 pm goods to St Ives, shunted the yard as required, then 3.00 pm goods to Swavesey, again a quick shunt of the yard as required, 4.00 pm goods back to St Ives for another quick shunt of the yard, and then 5.20 pm goods to Cambridge. It made a very pleasant day out where time seemed to stand still and yet disappear because you were on the go without being really conscious of it.

Mention of St Ives recalls the bank that existed at Somersham on this Loop Line to March. (So called because it looped round the other main route from Cambridge to March, via Ely.) Not an over serious obstacle in itself, but one that could cause dismay if we had an engine with a dirty fire that had worked throughout from the Temple Mills yard, in East London. We would relieve the in-coming crew on the down goods line at Cambridge. If we were struggling to keep the show on the road in a going order, this little bank could upset matters if the fire was not carefully managed. One useful dodge was to get the boiler as full as possible while the driver slowed for the sharp curve through St Ives station. The fire would be nursed as he re-applied power to pull away towards Somersham and hopefully get them swinging enough to rush the bank. This was alright so long as we weren't struggling with a class 'WD' engine. These were officially limited to 35 mph, although some sources claim 40 mph. My recollection is the lower speed, which would be 'stretched' if the end justified the means! Such tricks and knowledge were being learned all the time, and in this example, trips to Whitemoor soon came regularly.

My new rostered regular mate, Alf Chandler, had opted to spend his remaining days in the pilot link owing to health problems. He was a very good mate, who took an interest in my progress. He was another one of nature's gentlefolk. My remaining time at the shed was with him until returning to Southend, in between frequent absences on main line duties. It was always a pleasure to come to work with Alf. We lived nearby to each other and would usually walk home together. His wife was a very softly spoken gentle lady. Once he had come to know me, we regularly shared the driving. He found the long reversing levers, in particular, difficult to manage with the frequent changes of direction in shunting operations. I would do the firing in between shunts while the shunter was coupling up and checking round the train. If my driving was not up to standard, Alf would gently say, 'Not like that, my boy!' It was more than sufficient. One soon learned, and very useful experience it proved to be. He taught me how to do rough shunting in a gentle manner. Rough shunting is when you 'hit up' the wagons in flat shunting yards and then stop quickly. Some drivers would just slam the engine brake full on immediately. This could badly shake the trucks and their contents. Alf demonstrated how to make a partial brake check to get the couplings stretched out first before applying the secondary full brake force. It was so simple, yet some drivers just could not, or would not, do it.

In the pilot link we learned to appreciate the semi-regular shift pattern, whereby we were rostered on duty on or about 6.00 am, 2.00 pm and 10.00 pm in a three weekly cycle. There were some exceptions, but not too many. Except, that is, until the call of main line work beckoned! Then we could be booked on literally at any single minute round the clock and be rostered in very haphazard fashion one week to the next. When the prospect of such work was offered to a mere 17-year-old stripling, could he refuse, did he want to? There was no contest, the main line won every time! These duties, as already observed, were exceptional with the minimum age allowed on the running lines officially set at age 18. With the special dispensation granted for the duration, we did it, nights and running line work, enjoyed doing so, and gained valuable experience. The soft, cuddly, rules at work culture designed to 'look after' you, that apply nowadays prohibiting both practices are a questionable restriction. Are they necessarily for the best? They never did me any harm.

In my youth random vandalism and violence were hardly known, and respect for society and the laws of the land were taken for granted. As youngsters, if we stepped out of line, a cuff round the ear from the local policeman with his rain cape soon straightened you out before you grew up to became a potential menace. Instant justice, no courts, and you learned respect for your elders. We would walk, or cycle, to work at any time during the night along darkened streets and think nothing of it, with hardly a moment's worry. If only one could enjoy such unrestricted freedom everywhere today! Sadly, such unofficial instant retribution against today's youth who transgress acceptable behaviour is banned and everything is handled with dubiously effective formality creating criminal record histories and the like. By age 16, we were treated as an adult member of society, and expected to respond and conduct ourselves accordingly. Of course, we got up to mischief, but not of the violent kind increasingly plaguing society today. My old grandad (who fought in the Boer War and was a company sergeant-major in World War I) often used to quote the old saying, 'If you don't bend 'em when them twigs, you'll never bend 'em when them boughs' and never have truer words been spoken. Our lives on steam engines could be tough at times, but our more old fashioned upbringing did help us mentally to accept it. It was no good expecting sympathy when you suffered the inevitable cuts and burns out on the road; you dealt with them as best you could and just carried on. Unless it was sufficiently serious to justify stopping the train (very rare), you had no alternative, it was the life you had opted for in the first place and went with the job.

One interesting engine we had was one of the last survivors of the ancient class 'J66' 0-6-0 shunting tanks No. 68383 built in 1888. She had an unusual curved top profile to the side tank inside the cab on the fireman's side. Very useful for cat napping on when a suitable chance offered itself in between periods of shunting! She was a regular for shunting the down yard, which was always busy. This was a level yard with the headshunt going northwards under the large girders of the Mill Road bridge that spanned the north end of the station tracks. A busy area with the shed outlet, up and down main lines, up and down goods lines, the yard headshunt, and the up yard arrival line, all alongside each other. It was a place to exercise the greatest care when walking about the tracks, especially to and from the enginemen's cabin by the down goods line. There would be a steady procession of loaded goods, mainly coal, trains up to London, and goods and coal empties down from there. These operated between Whitemoor and Temple Mills yards more or less continuously from early Monday to early Sunday mornings. Today's residents of the properties adjacent to this area enjoy a very peaceful life by comparison to their forebears of 50 years ago. The constant clanging of buffers with the shunting and general noise of train movements starting and stopping was non-stop round the clock, except for Sundays when it did ease off to a comparative quiet. Believe it or not, they possibly were not aware of the noise! At home we lived alongside Southend Airport. Aircraft would fly overhead, the windows would rattle and, yet, we didn't consciously hear them. Visitors would remark on the dreadful noise, and how did we put up with it? On many occasions, one of us would say, 'What noise?' Daft, really, isn't it, but the truth!

The 2nd March found me being taken off the down yard pilot and heading for Norwich with Bill Eley on class 'B17' No. 61622 *Alnwick Castle* working the 2.33 pm passenger Cambridge to Norwich. On this day there was a blanket fog for most of the way. It was my first trip over this road, and not very enjoyable for either of us. Bill had to keep half an eye on me to say when and when not to put coal on the fire. It is in such conditions that a considerable extra strain is placed upon the driver. I was unfamiliar with the road, it was thick fog, and he had a passenger train to run as near as possible to the booked schedule. He couldn't rely on me for signal observation in such adverse conditions. We had never worked together before, but fortunately it was daylight on the outward trip. Obviously I was fully competent with the engine management in the sense that Bill could rely on me to fire correctly when told to do so. I kept a keen eye on the boiler water levels, but had to rely very much on his guidance, and he upon his own knowledge and skill. The last thing he needed was for me to be firing up just before a signal sighting was due, or he was soon to close the regulator. In each case the drifting smoke would become a problem, hence the need for his instructions. We managed, but it illustrates the kind of hazardous situation that could occur. We had left Cambridge in decent weather, but by Ely it had turned nasty and remained so throughout to Norwich. Fate was to decide that this was to be my only run throughout over this road, which is why it remains so imprinted on the memory, with visibility for most of the journey barely 50 yards, often less. Bill was very thankful when the day was over. My day had by far the less onerous responsibility, but it was no pleasure for me either. Running trains in thick fog in the days before modern aids were available to assist signal reading, was not for the faint-hearted. Our return working was the 5.29 pm class 'D' fitted goods back to Brandon. We attached wagons at Wymondham and Attleborough *en route*. After stabling our train at Brandon, we returned LE back to Cambridge.

A King's Cross Pacific No. 60017 *Silver Fox* at Cambridge shed in 1953.   *Author*

Road repair work outside the entrance to Cambridge shed. W. & J. Glossop's Sentinel steam lorry MT 3600 was still in daily use in 1953.   *Author*

The next new road to be learned was to Sandy on the Saturday night of 14th March on the 'Nor-West' line to Oxford (a former London & North Western Railway branch); on this occasion with Bill Barham on 'Short Box Knocko' class 'J19' No. 64669. We booked on at 9.00 pm, to work LE to Sandy. Here we picked up the return goods from Yarnton (beyond Oxford) stabled in the sidings there. We were back into Cambridge down yard and off duty by 5.00 am Sunday morning. This line had the odd gradient or two, including Gamlingay bank, and I can remember as we went outwards LE running tender first, noticing most of the stations were still lit by oil lamps enclosed in quite magnificent glass-faced lanterns. These were decidedly larger than was normally provided in such cases, with the station names inscribed on the glass across the wider top portion of the lantern. Towards the top of one bank there was an orchard belonging to a crossing keeper. In the season he was known occasionally to hand up a bag of apples if you were working slowly enough as you lumbered past with a goods train. Passenger trains didn't qualify as they were going too fast. The driver was expected to continue at a slow speed until the guard had collected his bag also! I never benefited from this kindness, not being at the shed long enough to see the autumn in fully.

Five days later, my road knowledge was to be again extended, this time with a trip through to Bletchley 'on the cushions' with Ken Aubrey to report to the shed. We were told to prepare and bring back a 'Claud', No. 62525, towing a 'Long Box Knocko', No. 64683. Trips like this are very useful for learning a road, as you are not rushing. The driver has less to concentrate on with no train to control, and can spend more time describing the various features, which Ken was kindly doing. The single line sections between Bedford St John's and Sandy were memorable for the enormous metal single line train staffs used. Presumably a relic from the ex-LNWR era, prior to 1923. They had numerous thick metal rings around the very (in excess of 2 ft) long tubular shaft. They were awkward and heavy objects to stow away in the cab. The platforms on this stretch had the wooden fence palings common to LMS stations. Unfortunately some got broken at one station when the signalman missed the staff and the only option was to throw it on the platform for him. Although we were not going very fast, the weight was enough to cause this damage. I could hardly believe my eyes as it happened!

On 1st April with Ben Revill we went 'on the cushions' to Brandon to relieve the crew on a ballast working, on a 'Standard' class 'J39' No. 64968, to work back to Cambridge. The weather was a considerable improvement on the last visit to this peaceful Norfolk township, with no fog this time. It was the only occasion for me on one of these engines at Cambridge. Later in the same month, we were in harness together again working over yet another new stretch of road, when we were called in to work by special messenger. Booking on at 10.20 am, we prepared our mount and then worked the 11.40 am special empty vanfit train to King's Cross goods yard. We had a good load, 60 on, weighing somewhere about 475 tons with the brake van. This was over the load, but Ben said we would take them as King's Cross were desperate for them. Fortunately, we had a good strong engine, 'Footballer' class 'B17' No. 61656 *Leeds United*, and returned LE. My wages were earned going up road that day, but the return trip

Class 'D16/3' 4-4-0 No. 62588 at Cambridge shed in early 1953 during the severe winter that seriously affected East Anglian train services. This class comprised many variants, this engine having the later LNER-style wheel valancing and rebuilt with eight inch diameter piston valves.
Author

Class 'D16/3' No. 62518 at Cambridge shed in 1953. Notice the GER-style smokebox door with circular ring. *Author*

was easier! This was my first trip up the Great Northern (GN) route, equipped with some of the unusual ex-GN pattern somersault type signals still in use on the main line. We had a good run up. This was to be the forerunner of a close association with the King's Cross goods yard. With the peculiar benefit of hindsight, it was quite uncanny how my footplate career was to prove so very helpful in my subsequent management career. A good ground level knowledge was gained of several places to be under my control at a later date.

The constant challenge of trying to learn all the roads over which Cambridge men worked and the wide ranging knowledge being gained in such a quick succession, certainly ensured adequate variety. On occasions, it became more than this, it was positively hard work. Learning the various gradients, when it was necessary to have a good fire on, when it was possible to relax and let gravity do the work, all took time. Sometimes an engine would be shy for steam and without this detailed knowledge, the work could become very difficult. The average riding qualities of most engines, particularly the 'WDs', and the 'Jazzer' 'K3s', often caused us considerable discomfort. Bruised ribs and elbows were suffered on several occasions. Never once during my nine months at Cambridge was insufficient steam produced, although there were one or two near misses, but never an actual stop for shortage of steam, or 'blow up' as we called it.

On one occasion on a very poor and rough class 'WD' engine - which were generally reliable steaming engines - we had one very reluctant performer. My anxiety mounted at the declining loss of both pressure and water level in the boiler as we struggled southwards up Elsenham Bank towards the summit heading for Temple Mills. My mate, who was not in the least perturbed - or at least this was the impression he gave - leant across the cab to suggest if I was that worried, then turn the empty tool bucket upside down and stand on it to make sure the water was still visible in the gauge glass! This did relax me a bit while continuing to fire little and often to keep the brightest possible fire and let fate take its course. We were each doing our best to keep the show on the move. We went over the top of the bank with both boiler injectors turned full on at the last moment, with just 105 lb. of steam pressure out of a possible 225 lb. - not a satisfactory situation. By the time we had rolled down the other side of the hill through Stansted the injectors could be shut off with the water level back to a safe margin. Gradually, the pressure recovered - vital in case Bishops Stortford's distant signal was against us and we needed the engine steam brake. We had relied on the tender handbrake to control our steady downward descent until then. It was an object lesson in proving that worrying does not solve a problem, only diligent thought and skill may do so. It was another useful lesson learned! Experience gradually gave you the confidence to know when, and when not, to take certain actions within the required margins of safety. We had relieved March men on the up goods line at Cambridge and inherited a dirty fire (caused by very dusty coal) that the March fireman had used the pricker on far too much, and clinkered the firebed up. It was a hard night's work, but this happened. A rough trip taught fresh skills - very useful for future occasions!

Another speciality around this period of spring 1953, was the supply of fist-sized coal eggs of compressed dust mixed with a lean cement mix for fuel. 'Austerities' were notorious for their rhythmic fore and aft movement on the tender drawbar as they proceeded with a regular semi-circular motion imparted to the cab. It was akin to a form of 'rock and roll' style action with the ever-present clankety-clonk, clankety-clonk, from the valve gear and axle-boxes, which could be very uncomfortable. The coal eggs were like marbles. To control them was just impossible. The cab floor would be ankle deep in them. Nor could we prevent them from rolling off the footplate out onto the ballast, try as hard as we may. Very easy to shovel but very difficult to maintain our balance. Stepping back and forward with the right foot as we swung each shovelful whilst pivoting on the left foot was not very funny at all.

A particularly unpopular fitment in the fireman's top corner of the 'WD' cab was the large 'Detroit'-type sight feed oil lubricator. This always caused a slimey, oiley gunge to build up on the cab floor underneath it - exactly where we wanted to stretch our feet when attempting to snatch a breather perched on the hard wooden tip-up seat. Being located high up into the cab roof, these lubricators were difficult to fill with the thick cylinder oil, resulting in frequent spillage. Efforts to clean off the gunge with the slacker hosepipe were rarely successful. We had little choice but to put up with it as best we could.

'Austerities' were a fairly reliable engine, and if handled right, would keep plodding away all day and be masters of the work. We accepted the rough riding qualities - we had little choice - and took care not to let our ribcage become too bruised against the cabside window opening. Only once did I ever have the luxury of a decent riding engine. No. 90029 was ex-works in sparkling clean black. She rode like a carriage with no knocks or rattles and steamed to perfection. My mate said, 'Enjoy it son - you'll never get another trip like this on a 'WD'!' He was right.

It shames me to admit it, but the only occasion to cause me acute embarrassment throughout my footplate years was on one of these lumbering workhorses. It was a really scorching hot Saturday afternoon with no breeze to speak of. It was the end of a particularly gruelling week of awkward turns and long hours. We were steadily 'clankety-clonking' our way along the Lea Valley on the gently falling gradients towards Ponder's End. With a completely clear run up in fine style, yours truly was doing all the right things. Approaching Sawbridgeworth heading south with a decent fire on after giving the customary help to my mate with the signals through Bishops Stortford and Spelbrook, the cab floor was washed down and swept clean ready for a decent breather. It was good to earn a break and cup of tea out of the can knowing the fire would almost certainly take us into Temple Mills without further attention being needed. Then it happened! My mind was a total blank until we swung onto the goods line at Ponder's End amidst much amusement from my mate. He claimed it was impossible to doze off on a rough riding engine, especially on a 'WD'. He was amazed - if he hadn't seen it with his own eyes, he said he would never have believed it! He purposefully left me alone just to see how long it was possible for anyone to survive sound asleep. To manage 17 miles must have been a record! The injector had been working and on 'WDs' these made a very loud singing noise. When he turned it off, this should have woken me - it didn't! Needless to say the tale went the rounds, starting with our arrival in the cabin at Temple Mills. As my mate said, the fire was good, and the boiler water level was good. He left me alone so he could hang me afterwards with the tale. It never occurred again - it was simply not done.

Further route knowledge was acquired when relieved from firing to my own mate Alf Chandler, at short notice on 30th May. A young passed cleaner climbed onto the engine, clearly short of breath, to explain he had been sent to take over. 'Look sharp and travel "on the cushions" to Ely, there to relieve a fireman whose hours were up and join Chris Easy on class 'D16' No. 62571', came the hurried instruction.

A quick dash just caught a train about to depart. On arrival at Ely, an equally quick explanation to Chris about my lack of road knowledge, and we were soon on our way. We worked the 4.50 pm to March, then 5.35 pm to Peterborough East, returning with the 6.35 pm to March, then forward with the 7.46 pm to Cambridge via Ely and Newmarket, all passenger workings. Having done this, instructions were given to finish my shift with Alf on the pilot - it was expected that you earned a full day's work! The 6.35 pm was a heavy 10-coach restaurant car express from Birmingham to Yarmouth and Norwich, formed with ex-LMS coaches. It was a good loading for a four-coupled 'Claud' to March. My first express working on one of these graceful looking engines, successfully completed - one felt very pleased! Having explained my lack of road knowledge, my courage failed to explain this was also my first main line trip on a 'Claud' in case Chris refused to have me, which he would have been entitled to do. Fortunately, my fears were soon behind me as we got going after leaving Ely on the 4.50 pm, Chris proved to be a very considerate mate to fire to. These engines had 7 ft diameter coupled wheels, the largest of any engine then still working in Britain. They gave the illusion of moving in a very regal-like manner with an easily recognisable ringing sound made by the side coupling rods. A very distinctive class of engines that had a long and useful life. Some still retained their original GER ornamental valancing covering the coupled wheels. With their slower rotating wheels, this gave them the appearance of a graceful skirted lady as they seemed almost to glide sedately by.

The next day it was off to King's Cross again, this time with Bill Dewhurst on a class 'B1' No. 61287, working the 1.50 pm passenger up road, returning with the 6.21 pm semi-fast passenger down road. (You always went up to London, and down from it. All running lines were designated accordingly.) This was another section of new road, into King's Cross passenger station, to file away into the ever busy brain. The next day again had me going to Peterborough, but to the North station this time, and another new section of road. This time with Bill Creek on another class 'B1', No. 61302, which included working the night postal train for a short section (just to confirm that shifts could be erratic!). Alf pulled my leg about this saying it confirmed my ever expanding abilities. My view said it was because there was nobody else available, which I'm sure was nearer to the truth!

On 6th June, the road via Newmarket to Bury St Edmunds was added to the ever growing list when firing to Fred Nunn on class 'J15' No. 65405. We worked the 4.10 pm passenger to Bury, the 7.20 pm passenger to Cambridge, then the 10.17 pm passenger to Newmarket, returning with the 11.00 pm empty cars to Cambridge. We stood at Bury alongside the final passenger working preparing for its sad trip over the Bury to Thetford line, which closed to passengers on that date. The engine

Class 'F6' 'Gobbler' 2-4-2T No. 67236 leaves Bury St Edmunds with the 1.44 pm for Thetford on 25th April, 1953.   *G.R. Mortimer*

Class 'J15' No. 65391 is seen on Bury St Edmunds shed bearing the headboard 'Thetford Flyer' on the last day of passenger services to Thetford, 6th June, 1953.   *Author*

'D16' class 4-4-0 No. 62576 after arrival at Cambridge from Bury St Edmunds on 13th May, 1955. The train is standing in Platform 6. The engine release crossover for Platform 5 is in the right foreground.   *Eric A. Brookes*

was suitably inscribed on the smokebox, ready for the final departure. The official closure date was on the 8th, but with no Sunday service, the 6th became the actual date. In the later Beeching and post-Beeching eras, we can all too easily forget that branch line closures on a quite extensive scale had also been implemented during the preceding decade before his time; likewise, many lesser branch lines had succumbed during the post-1929 depression era when competition increased from developing motor bus services. In the 1950s the private car became a major culprit in causing rail retrenchment. Beeching simply hurried up the inevitable reductions that had to be faced up to by the railway industry.

As if all this was not enough, on 9th June, my 18th birthday was celebrated on another class 'J15' No. 65442. More new territory was covered with Chris Norden, by firing on two round passenger trips to Mildenhall, out with the 6.25 am and 10.23 am, and back with the 7.35 am and 11.50 am. These were my only trips over this quite delightful rural backwater, which, like so many other country branches, has long since been surrendered to the motor car, although it survived long enough to be dieselised before doing so. My special date is shared with none other than the world famous 'Father of Railways', George Stephenson - reflected glory, indeed! Reaching age 18 also made me a fully legalised main line fireman - not that it made one iota of difference! It also meant enlisting for National Service call-up into the armed forces. BR were keen to see us ask for deferment, as footplate grades qualified for this due to the on-going staff shortages. Being keen to get it over and done with, I went to enlist and did not ask to be deferred. Events proved this to be a wise decision.

The 11th July gave me my first and, as it turned out, only trip while at Cambridge on a 'B12' '1500' since leaving Southend. With No. 61557 and Arthur Pratt, we worked the 1.23 pm special passenger to Liverpool St and the 4.25 pm special passenger back. It was very rare in the earlier 1950s era for one of these engines to work up to London from Cambridge, or for one to be crewed by Cambridge men anywhere other than occasionally to Ipswich. In the later 1950s it did occur more often, when some '1500s' were allocated to the shed. But in 1953, while Ipswich men worked into Cambridge most days with them, our men usually had 'Clauds' for the Ipswich turns as we had no 'B12s' on the roster. This day was memorable - apart from the extra road knowledge! We inherited a dirty fire, but managed to keep time alright until after the easy steaming along the Lea Valley. Running down the fire ready for arrival in London, in my ignorance of the road, the steep curving climb up from Copper Mill Junction (north of Temple Mills) round to Clapton Junction (on the Chingford road) pulled the fire so much, we nearly came to grief. From having a comfortable trip, it all went pear shaped and by Clapton station the rot had well and truly taken hold. Arthur could do little about our predicament with his handling of the engine. He did manage, but only just. It was a close run thing to maintain sufficient steam pressure to stop the brakes dragging. Fortunately the water was well up in the glass passing Copper Mill Jn which just saved the day. As we tipped over the top of Bethnal Green Bank to drop down into the terminus, there was barely enough water to be safe. Unfamiliarity with the road had caused my engine management to let the side down. Yet another lesson learned for another time! Arthur was a bit put out by my error, but understood why it had occurred. The fire was thoroughly cleaned before the return working and an entirely uneventful trip home.

Every so often we were booked on shed as required, which usually meant engine preparation and disposal duties. Sometimes we drew the short straw. If it was all the latter, then by the end of the shift you were absolutely filthy, covered in ash, and ached all over. Shovelling clinker, with the short or long slice (on some other regions known as a 'paddle') out of the firehole, raking out ashpans and emptying smokeboxes with the wind swirling around could be pure misery. Even worse if it was raining. These were the less desirable aspects of the footplate calling, but had to be done, irrespective of the weather. Trains do not stop because it rains. On the GE section we always disposed of our own engines, unlike the GN section, for example, where at King's Cross we did not do so. Most days included the task of fire cleaning, and ash disposal. Once a shift was bearable, but a full shift of it was different! Nobody enjoyed these duties, but they were an inbuilt part of the job. Engine preparation was better, but could be hard work if you had to go hunting for fire-irons to make up the required equipment. These were heavy and awkward things to carry around the shed. They required extreme care not to hit anybody in the often dimly lit and murky atmosphere that occurred inside a shed building. These are the sort of occasions when those who consider footplate work to be 'romantic' should have been around to try it!

Likewise, when working hard trying to get enough steam from a reluctant kettle. Usually you were sweating profusely, more than likely having a most uncomfortable ride and, for whatever reason, the engine did not want to boil. And this, no matter how many tricks of the trade you tried! Or, the engine was not bad, the ride was not bad, but the weather was just awful. Freezing cold down one side and hot from the fire down the other. Maybe soaked to the skin if you had an exposed cab, such as on a 'J15', or working tender first. All included in the daily grind that we took for granted and part of the unwritten job specification. Glamourous? Few of my many former colleagues would think so, as much as most of us normally enjoyed the work. This was the reality of what it could be like - not always, but quite often. It is helpful to record such realities before the thousands of us who did it to earn our daily crust, have departed to another place.

Tuesday 28th July took me to Hunstanton with Fred Gotobed on 'Claud' class 'D16' No. 62531. We went 'on the cushions' to Hun'ston (as it was known), to work the 5.00 pm passenger to King's Lynn, and 7.45 pm express non-stop, Lynn to Cambridge. This was my first real challenge on a 'Claud', being a bit over 41 miles, in 55 mins, with little chance for a respite. We arrived right time with seven Gresley buckeye wooden, bow-ended corridors - not excessive, but enough to cause trouble over this mainly flat fenland road, had I done it wrong! It was my only occasion to work a passenger train through Ely station without stopping. We repeated the exercise on Saturday with the same engine, departing Lynn at 6.28 pm with a normal passenger service with stops *en route*. In between these two trips was a day on the Coalyard pilot with Alf on class 'J67' No. 68530, and a goods working to Brandon with Bill Haylett. We returned from Brandon to work via Ely North Jn curve to March, on our class 'WD' No. 90510. This was my only trip over this curve. The week was completed by a trip with 'Dusty' Miller with class 'B1' No. 61300, on a fruit special, Swavesey to Whitemoor, then LE back for a cattle special, St Ives to Cambridge.

To travel over the - in those days - very rural and scenically pretty Colne Valley road was a pleasure that only once came my way. This peaceful byway ran from Haverhill via Halstead to the delightfully named Chappel & Wakes Colne station. The route followed the verdant valley of the River Colne. It was some six miles shorter than the alternative route between the same places that took to the higher ground to run via Long Melford. Halstead was a real country market town where time seemed to have stood still. The station had a useful-sized goods yard and in its time had been a hub of activity. Alas, by the early 1950s, the ominous signs of decline were beginning to appear, although it would be another decade before the inevitable came to pass. In 1953 the line was still serving a useful purpose. On 17th August, with Charlie Pumfrey on our little 'Black goods' class 'J15' No. 65458, we worked the 6.25 am through passenger service via Halstead to Marks Tey, the junction for the Ipswich main line, before returning over the same road with the 8.41 am service to Haverhill arriving at 9.42 am. The day's work was completed by travelling to Long Melford 'on the cushions' to work the 12.27 pm service back to Cambridge with class 'B2' No. 61639 *Norwich City* - a total contrast in motive power (and, a good old rattler she was too, giving us a very lively ride, which probably explained her use on such a secondary service, to complete the required mileage for her next overhaul). The direct route via Halstead had been constructed by the small Colne Valley Light Railway Company and was not strong enough to allow main line engines to traverse it.

Oops! This sequence of photographs show that once in a while things can go wrong. On this occasion, in 1953, a little unplanned gardening by class 'D16/3' No. 62575 which came to rest just short of the cottage immediately alongside the main line at Coldham Lane, Cambridge, having ploughed up the rear garden, in a mishap that required the Cambridge breakdown crane with a special closure of the line on a Sunday while engine and tender were recovered. A roof section has been removed to give clearance to allow lifting gear to be attached to the rear drawbar framing. The section would be replaced later when the engine had been re-railed. The engine suffered only minor damage and after a good clean up was soon back at work.   *(All) Author*

'J15' class 0-6-0 No. 65390 on a Cambridge-Kettering passenger train at Godmanchester on 5th July, 1954.   *E.H. Sawford*

'J15' class No. 65405 on a local freight at Godmanchester in 1953.   *E.H. Sawford*

Sadly, my time was running out as advice had been received that my preference move back to Southend was coming up, sooner than expected. Before it did, a final bit of yet more road learning filled in another piece of the Cambridge jigsaw. On 29th August a derailment at Whittlesford occurred after Sid Hall and I had worked up to Temple Mills with class 'WD' No. 90087, on the 11.00 pm goods from Cambridge. On our return working with 'Baby Bongo' class 'K1' No. 62036, while working the 4.05 am Broxbourne to Cambridge goods, we were diverted at Audley End to run via Bartlow (on the Colne Valley road) to Shelford to regain the main line - a kind of swan song!

The 14th September found me briefly back at Southend to fire to my new regular mate, Harry Loker on our regular class 'B12' No. 61578, before entering the RAF on 2nd October to learn all about aircraft cockpit instrumentation. This has no place in these memories, except to say it was an excellent two years that took me to many countries that would not otherwise have been seen, in pursuit of experimental development work on new jet fighter aircraft.

My all too short spell at Cambridge shed had been exceptionally enjoyable. The decision to go there was a good move. Frequent mention has been made about the regular learning of new road knowledge. In the final round up, the full list of all the roads run by Cambridge men was not quite completed. To be fortunate enough to work over so many of the routes worked, within so short a period, confirmed just how beneficial had been my time in the pilot link. The route knowledge gained was to prove of inestimable value.

In 1953 one of the regular Cambridge engines working to Kettering was for many months the class 'J15' No. 65391. She took the standard rake of three ex-LMS main line corridors to and fro for most of my time at the shed. It made a fascinating sight to see this long-funnelled antiquity at the head of a main line formation. My abiding memory as a passenger is the rattle of cinders on the metal coach roofs of the LMS stock as she blasted her way forward via Thrapston onwards to Kettering and then brought me back again, later in the day. A memory of not only a particular line, but also of an older lifestyle it was my good fortune to experience before it disappeared for good.

The loss of so many country branches has influenced the social structure of the areas they formerly served. Today, the rural lines that do survive have mainly unstaffed stations with very minimal facilities, which is considerably better than no line or no facilities at all. Cambridge shed, once a principal shed supporting several sheds within the former Cambridge operating district, is now just a signing-on point. The large shed complex has disappeared. The comparatively small number of train crews now allocated there work over less than half of the route mileage that was covered in my time. They can no longer work to Oxford or Swindon via Bletchley; to March or King's Lynn via the St Ives Loop Line; northwards from Whitemoor via the GN/GE Joint line via Spalding; to Kettering via Thrapston; to Hunstanton from King's Lynn; to Ely via Newmarket; between Long Melford and Thetford; to Mark's Tey (for Colchester) either via Long Melford or via Halstead; to Audley End via Bartlow, or over the Mildenhall branch, all these routes having long since been closed. The branch from Elsenham to Thaxted had already closed shortly before I went to the shed. I very nearly came to work the last train of all to enter Thaxted station, in June 1953, to commence track lifting. On the credit side, there is now an absolutely excellent electric service between King's Lynn and London, both into King's Cross and Liverpool St stations, so it is not all doom and gloom.

Some of these lines would not have survived anyway, given the growth of alternative transport modes. The line to Bletchley has already been partially re-opened to passenger services and plans to re-instate further stretches of it are under review. Whether this will ever include re-opening at the Cambridge end is not certain. If proposed plans to develop the former joint line route that ran northwards from March achieve reality (which has to very doubtful south of Spalding), then the loss of the Loop Line via St Ives may yet be regretted, but such a development is just speculation. With the ever expanding growth of the home counties population, the loss of one, or even both, of the routes to Mark's Tey (still open from there back to Sudbury), might become subject to review, although to what extent the track bed has survived, particularly in the Haverhill area where much development is taking place, may preclude such ideas. If only the line of these lost routes had been safeguarded in county structure plans, the story today could well have been very much different.

Expressing such thoughts may be good for the soul, but in reality does little good, and can make you feel sad. Let us continue our journey and leave such melancholy observations behind us.

'E4' class 2-4-0 No. 62785 hauls the 10.23 am Cambridge-Mildenhall train away from Cambridge on 29th July, 1953, passing Coldham Lane Junction. The branch tracks to Newmarket are clearly visible in the foreground.   *A.R. Carpenter*

Chapter Five

The Footplate Years - Return to Southend

Coal and how it affected our firing - what a fascinating subject! Before resuming the story at Southend, following my return to the shed from Cambridge, the effect of this most essential commodity, the 'black diamonds', upon engine performance will be of interest.

Shortly after starting at Stratford a prank by a senior driver led me to believe, having been fed a long build-up story with a dead pan serious face, how difficult it was to fire engines on the main line with hard Yorkshire coal. He was adamant you could only get the best results by firing it 'shiny side upwards', as to do otherwise led to all sorts of trouble. Silly as it seems, the fact is he was sufficiently convincing to create concerns about what to do, in case my efforts were wrong!

Needless to say, the first time you actually picked up a shovel you immediately realised the joke was on you! This was a vital ingredient of the life - an excellent camaraderie became yours if you got stuck in to learn what being an engineman really meant. You earned your acceptance from your fellow workmates, shared the rough with the smooth, and above all else kept a decent sense of perspective, which included many little bits of humour. To do, or to be, otherwise, could create untold personal drudgery, if you took the life too seriously, with no ability to smile at yourself. A sense of humour was essential to balance the less welcome aspects of the footplate calling.

The truth is we did sometimes get it wrong, but not usually because of shiny coal. More often than not, it was because of the total absence of any shine. A vital skill we had to learn was how to create steam with just dust, when the absence of even a limited quantity of small lumps could severely test our abilities. The most careful attention was needed to create a decent thickness of firebed without blacking it out, during the engine preparation. With normal coal during our preparation duties to get the engine ready for the day's work we spread the body of fire, left for us by the shed firelighter under the firehole door, over the grate and fed a decent charge of lumps in. This, we left to 'cook' for the 20-30 minutes required to do our other duties, before building up the firebed ready for the trip.

With dust this was not possible. If we had been left a good body of fire sufficient to cover the entire grate it was spread forward very carefully so as not to lose too much through the firebars, remembering it had also been built up during the night using the self same dust in the tender or bunker coal space. If there was insufficient fire initially to do this, we spread it as far as possible. To this was added a layer, and later, spread it further towards the front of the box, before adding the next layer and so on. As we carried out our other preparation procedures, we regularly had to pause to sprinkle a thin layer over the fire. It was essential to make sure each sprinkling had fully caught alight before applying the next one. If we rushed it, which was the greatest temptation, then disaster followed! If we did it correctly then we at least commenced the journey with a sporting chance of a reasonable trip. It was a particular art, like so much else to do with steam engines, that was acquired by experience and teaching handed down by others.

Southend was fortunate to have a standard concrete bunker type mechanical coaling tower which took away the manual effort of hand coaling from a raised stage. Unfortunately, it also meant we could receive anything in a loco-coal truck that looked black and was euphemistically called 'coal'. The manual coal stage sheds usually had lumps supplied, even if of a small size, because of the handling problems with dust. I expect it was supplied sometimes, although I never heard of this and never experienced it at a manual coaling shed.

We suffered the infamous National Coal Board (NCB) brainwave to solve their problem of huge stockpiles of slack dust. These had accumulated in the days before modern coal-fired power stations and cement works needing a diet of such material. The NCB backroom experts developed a product marketed as 'Nutty Slack'. This was a blend of small cobbles and dust, offered to the domestic market. Housewives soon discovered how dirty their houses became and refused to buy it. The next NCB *magnum opus* in brain cell technology sieved out most of the nuts and offered the residue to BR at a cheap price. With both organisations being government owned it was a foregone conclusion that BR would be expected to ease the NCB's problems. Wagons of 'nutty slack minus most of the nuts' began arriving to become the staple diet for a time of the coaling plant storage hoppers. We had some interesting trips during this time! We all had to struggle, with help from our drivers, to keep the kettle on the boil. The gradients of the Southend road required considerable skills in engine management to ensure time was not lost. It was filthy stuff to work with, being well-nigh impossible to damp down as water will run off the surface of compacted dust. It would swirl round us, get into our neck collar and eyes, and make life a sheer misery. The required firing skills were quickly learned - it was a case of sink or swim!

Fortunately, Southend shed in the earlier 1950s had a designated strategic coal dump. We could supplement our basic pay after completing the normal day's work by unloading this coal, always lumps, never small sized material, manually into the stockpiles to earn 10s. per 16 ton truck, which usually took one person about four hours to do. We were not paid for the hours it took - just the 10s. bonus on a 'job and finish' basis. This represented a small fortune to us youngsters and everybody scrambled to get this perk. Twenty-one ton trucks took about five hours to empty and paid 12s. 6d. As a cleaner on 1s. per hour pay rate, to earn 2s. 6d. per hour was a real bonus.

The real perk came later! It provided a ready, but strictly unofficial source of lump coal to supplement the dusty material in the tenders - need one say more? During engine preparation, so long as we were nearby, enough lumps would be scrounged to build up a reasonable firebed. We could then add the dust and if one was careful it made the trip that much easier in consequence. How the powers that be explained the massive shortage between tons stacked and tons reclaimed when they came to clear the stockpile, nobody ever explained! The shortfall discrepancy must have been enormous, as we were always nibbling away at it to build up our firebeds! There were strict instructions telling us not to, threatening the most dire consequences if we did. The proverbial blind eye was the order of the day, as management knew it was to avoid delays.

It did not solve the problem at Liverpool St when getting the fire ready for the homeward trip - no lumps available! Or at Southend, if you were not alongside the dump and likewise unable to scrounge the lumps! The *modus operandi* at Liverpool St was to arrive with a good, well-burnt-through depth of fire and with the water low in the gauge glass to minimise the risk of blowing off under the overall roof. The skill came in gauging the minimum safest level of water required to go down the steep gradient of Bethnal Green Bank and into the terminus. Blowing off under the station roof was the ultimate crime that could quickly bring the smoke inspector scurrying over to make a report out. The noise would drown the station announcements, and even maybe dislodge old soot from the high glass canopy that might fall upon passengers. We would go to any amount of trouble to thwart the unwanted problems of a disciplinary Form 1 'Please Explain' which it was essential to avoid at all costs. Having the water low in the boiler gave you the margin required to put on the injectors to prevent blowing off. By carefully sprinkling the firebed with dust at intervals we could maintain the depth of fire ready for the return trip. By such tricks we hopefully were prepared for the stiff climb up the Bethnal Green Bank out of the terminus from a 'cold' start. It certainly made a change from normal routines, when dust was on the menu. Fortunately the NCB fiasco lasted only a few weeks. Our managers soon got fed up with the service disruptions caused by engines short of steam and better quality coal was restored.

Other variations to use up the large stocks of dust the NCB had accumulated, were the supply of coal eggs, already mentioned. Another alternative were the large sized briquettes which had to be broken with the coal hammer before firing, unless we had a thick fire on. Firing a thin fire with unbroken briquettes could cause loss of steam pressure with too much cold air entering through the firebars and bypassing the briquettes, lowering the temperature in the firebox as a result. This cooler air would cause the loud vibrating noise that signified holes in the fire. Both the eggs and the briquettes were preferable to the 'nutty slack without the nuts'. We could at least damp down residual dust with the slacker pipe. To maintain a semblance of a tidy and clean footplate was possible with the briquettes but almost impossible with the eggs, except when stationary.

To fire an engine properly is a very skilled art to learn. Anybody can heave coal into a firebox. The skill was knowing when and how to do so, according to the coal quality and work demand. Every engine could be different and, often as not, nobody could explain why. Apparently identical engines could require different ways to fire them to obtain the best results. Two of our regular-manned class 'B1s' Nos. 61335/36 illustrated this very clearly. No. 61335 became my regular engine. She steamed best with a thinner fire at the back and a thicker fire at the front of the firebox. No. 61336 in common with most of her class, was exactly the opposite way round - thicker at the back and thinner at the front! If you fired the former like the latter, you were quickly struggling for steam. Nobody knew why; many thought they did, but no satisfactory explanation ever emerged. We kept our secret to ourselves as best we could which helped to ensure other crews did not try to 'steal' her before we booked on duty. She had a poor reputation, and we encouraged others to think this was so! The reason being, if another crew were booked on a known 'dud', they might try to fail it in the hope of getting a better replacement. Any regular-manned engine was usually a better option, if the running foreman could be persuaded. Anything was fair game if you could be convincing enough!

We had to treat each engine as an individual machine and use whichever firing technique produced the required result related to the driving style of our mate. Some drivers were heavier, or harder drivers, than others. Some would drive with shorter cut-offs, with the reverser notched back nearer to mid-gear, and wider-open regulators. This achieved better use of the expansive properties of the superheated steam as it went through the cylinders. Other drivers would drive with a longer cut-off and a less open regulator. This method at any given steam pressure, used a little more steam for identical work. The former style gave a softer exhaust and lighter draw on the fire, the latter gave a stronger exhaust and a heavier draw. The former required a more careful firing to avoid creating too thick a firebed, which could reduce the heat values and inhibit steam generation. The latter gave a stronger exhaust and made it easier for the fireman to be less careful with the firebed thickness and often easier to maintain full steam generation, but at the expense of a slightly heavier coal usage.

If we had indifferent coal, maybe of lower calorific value, the stronger exhaust would assist the fireman as it helped to achieve the required heat in the firebox more easily. The driver who worked the engine in the softer, more economical style, could cause difficulties for his fireman, if the fireman was too heavy handed with the firing. If the pressure dropped due to the inadequate draw on the fire not keeping the coal up to full heat, the driver would have to work the engine that little bit harder to compensate. This in turn could liven up the fire to achieve the required pressure. Some engines would steam better with a thin fire, irrespective of how the driver handled the engine, while others needed a thicker fire - to the unskilled fireman, a totally baffling situation. Most engines would steam better with a thicker fire to the back end of the firebox and a thinner fire to the front. Others, including most class 'B12s' which had a very shallow firegrate, were the reverse, steaming easier with a good thickish fire to the front and a less thick fire towards the back of the box. The design of the ashpan could have a marked influence on the steaming ability of a boiler. Each class of engine had a different ashpan layout governed by the axle spacings and height of the firebox foundation ring above the axles which influenced the ashpan depth and therefore its ash capacity. On longer runs this could get critical with some engines when the ability of the air to reach the firebed in sufficient volume became restricted as the pan became filled with ash. Less air meant less oxygen, which meant less heat - simple really, but often not properly understood by some firemen who could not be bothered to use the air damper controls to assist, or retard, coal consumption to adjust their firebed temperature to the demands being made of it by the driver, relative to the work being done.

Good engines, with cylinder valve events set correctly with the motion pins not worn, could be fired with a thinnish fire all over the box kept at white hot heat with a little and often firing style, dependent upon the calorific value of the coal. When an engine with higher mileage was approaching its time for overhaul, the valve settings could become uneven due to motion pin and axlebox wear. This caused the exhaust beats to get out of true creating an uneven draw on the firebed. The fireman would then have to fire more coal to some parts of the firegrate than to elsewhere. If the engine had developed a rough riding quality, the vibration might cause the firebed to shake down the sloping grate towards the front part of the firebox creating too thick a firebed, when not wanted. Thus, loss of temperature because the air could not fully penetrate it to achieve proper combustion, could cause loss of steam pressure. If a fire was dirty with heavy clinker building up on the bars, this would inhibit the airflow to the firebed, and again caused loss of steam pressure due to lower firebox temperatures. With fine dust it was less easy for the air to penetrate easily up through the firebars and through the firebed to achieve good combustion, which explains why dust was such a problem. Too thin a firebed and you ran the risk of holes developing allowing cold air into the firebox; too thick a bed would choke the air through it and give reduced combustion. Both created lower firebox temperatures. If, additionally, you had not got good steam coal (i.e., with the higher calorific values) - more problems! And this is before you discover the particular firing technique best suited to the particular engine, or your driver if he is not your regular mate. Obviously, we understood how most engines would perform, gained through regular experience of them, but once in a while we could get well and truly caught out by any number of reasons, such as dirty boiler water overdue for a washout. A serious build-up of sludge on the foundation ring between the inner and outer firebox wrappers would impair the ability to boil the water. It would even be possible in extreme cases to rest a hand on the outside of the firebox foundation ring because it was so cool due to poor heat transmission from this cause. Dirty water with many sludge-like particles in it inhibited heat transfer to the water, and could also become frothy as a result. In extreme instances this froth would carry over with the steam into the cylinders, causing priming. Water, being a liquid, does not compress, therefore the risk of smashing off the cylinder head had to be avoided by opening the cylinder drain cocks in this situation. Severe priming could often be contained by running with a lower boiler water level, but this could be risky with frothy water giving a falsely high water level in the gauge glass, if a careful watch was not kept. In severe instances of this occurring - an extreme circumstance will be related later in this chapter - loss of time could develop, irrespective of the coal quality.

We haven't yet considered external factors such as the weather. If it was foggy, or the cylinder gland packings were blowing badly creating a similar effect, the driver would be relying more than usual on his mate to assist with reading the signals. The last thing he wanted in such circumstances was his fireman being more occupied with poor coal. Interesting, is it not? This was frequently the reality of life on the steam footplate, especially in my earlier years, before maintenance standards improved. The really thick green 'peasouper' fogs (known as 'smogs') prevalent in larger built-up areas, and especially in London, that disappeared in the later 1950s as the Clean Air Acts reduced the problem, were a real hazard to us until the new legislation, by and large, eliminated them.

It all took time to learn and hence why young firemen started on the shunting engines where mistakes in firing could be more readily overcome. Later, we gradually gained promotion up through the links, before being allowed on the more demanding workings where a mistake in technique could cause delay to the service. At Southend it was the practice for youngsters to be sent out on daylight goods workings, riding with experienced firemen who would let us have a go. They taught you how to do it. Riding like this was very useful, as we were learning the road as well. These trips were strictly unofficial, but were our foremen's way to help us become of more use to them as potential firemen. We were never allowed to record these trips on our time tickets, which had to show 'cleaning' to avoid higher authority challenging the practice. A complete nonsense really, because it was for the overall benefit of the shed. It was easier for a country shed to permit such practices. At Stratford, the shortage of passed cleaners prevented the practice anyway, but they had a considerably wider variety of shunting work for novices to gain experience on. Many smaller sheds could not offer such opportunities with nearly all running line work only and hence the chances to ride out.

When steam generation became a problem, the need for a driver and fireman to work together became more important. A good driver would know the subtle changes of gradient that could permit him to help his fireman by easing the engine a little on favourable grades, even for a short distance. Likewise, a good fireman would know when to help his driver on adverse grades by offering as much steam as possible by mortgaging the boiler water level, if circumstances allowed. With help from his driver he would hope to recover a higher level over the next favourable gradient. By providing the highest steam pressure he could manage, this limited the need for the driver to work the engine harder and thus use up more of the precious steam. It often became a chicken and egg situation! More steam used equalled more water used. This equalled more coal needed to replace the usage, when at the same time, for whatever reason, the lower production of steam was causing the driver to use more of it. He had to do this because of the lower pressure, in order to maintain the scheduled train timings. Life was rarely dull!

Many a struggle has been enacted on the footplate, frequently due to poor coal, unknown to the outside world. You had to keep the show on the road, if humanly possible. Lost time booked against the engine was a serious 'black mark'. Herein lay the art of teamwork. Driving and firing engines in tip-top order, with good coal, was to us relatively easy. Not dissimilar to preserved steam on the main line today, although, with one important difference for today's crews. They have not the opportunity to get everyday experience with regular mates, like we had. They might therefore struggle as a result, but rarely because of the mechanical condition of the engine, although still possible due to the coal quality. Life on the footplate was often a challenge that went unsung and unrecorded. If you lost time, then explanations would be required and your sins exposed. Hence the art of chatting up the guard to square his journal when only the odd minutes were involved!

Most guards would 'lose' these odd minutes if they could, but some would not and insisted on 'time is time' and compiled their journal accordingly. It is perhaps not realised that drivers were not in charge of their trains - the guard was. The guard had a company watch, drivers never did, remarkable as this might seem, when it was the driver who was responsible for running to schedule. The guard would allocate the causes of delay by using his own observation and judgement. The driver was responsible for the safe working of the train out on the road, but it was the guard who controlled when it would depart after each station stop. This worthy kept the record, i.e., the journal, for submission to his manager at the end of each shift for scrutiny of any delays. These were primarily allocated under five headings - (i) engineering; (ii) operating, i.e., signalling; (iii) station work; (iv) motive power, i.e., the engine; and (v) other causes, e.g., weather, etc. Engine performance in running to the schedule timings *en route* was always closely monitored, and hence my earlier comments about the differing standards in respect of this activity today. Needless to say, there were frequent disputes between the various traffic departments - signalmen, guards, drivers, or station staff, as to who was responsible for causing a delay. If it was collectively possible, they would blame, in this context, the 'outsiders', i.e., the non-traffic agency - the engineers. The operating, motive power, and engineering managements (and remember engineers came in three categories - track; technical signalling [as opposed to operating signalling]; and structures) would regularly get involved in inter-departmental disputes. Each tried to pass the buck if they could, when a heavy delay had to be accounted for - it was all part of the survival process to safeguard your own department. No manager was prepared to accept a delay he felt his department was not responsible for. In the final round-up in the annual summaries of who caused which delays, the honours were usually about equal, despite all the internecine wrangling! But, if they didn't each strongly contest their corner, then the weakest became liable for the most delays, with consequent adverse judgement of their performance by the Regional Board. In the final analysis it had only limited value, because the real sufferer was almost always the customer.

We have strayed a little away from the direct subject of coal, but I hope these explanations remove some of the mystery of the factors that could influence train workings.

The final time that coal was to really hit the headlines came with the pending introduction of the Clean Air Acts. The need to curtail smoke emissions, not only in Liverpool St, but also everywhere else in built-up areas, made an impact when Welsh coal was introduced to normal hard coal areas. Until we learned how to use it, there was serious fun and games with engines short of steam, either because the coal hadn't burnt through properly, or because it had, but had swelled up and brought the firebox brick arch down! Welsh coal is a near-smokeless fuel. It is a superb but soft and fragile fuel which takes much longer to get hot and swells when it does. It requires a totally different firing technique to the smoky, quicker-burning, but non-swelling, hard fuels we were familiar with. Welsh coal was introduced in 1957, by which time I had departed from Southend to pastures new on the GN suburban services out of King's Cross. We

A general view of Southend shed taken from the upside of the station track layout in 1955. This records the scene as it was just before the advancing overhead electrification works spoiled it forever. To the left is the white-coloured concrete oil hut used for storing inflammable products; centre left is the water tower with the circular water softening tower immediately behind it; and to the right is the shed building. The nearest windows underneath the water tank were for our messroom, the next window along the front above the engine smokebox, was a non-inflammable and equipment store; and the bay-fronted window was the shedmaster's office. The ground floor level housed the water valves and pumping equipment for the main tank and the softening plant. The low white-coloured concrete bunker to the right of the shed building entrance was the sand bin.   *Author*

Engines on view at Southend on 8th May, 1955. *From left to right:* Class 'B17/2' No. 61611 *Raynham Hall* on the oil stores road; class 'B1' No. 61370 on the run-round road; class 'B12/3' No. 61576 on the No. 2 shed road, another 'B1' class locomotive on the No. 1 shed road and finally class 'J69/1' No. 68632 on the sandbox road.   *Author*

had a dreadful two or three days mastering the skills needed to use it, and the service suffered catastrophically until we did. Some classes of engine suffered less than others due to their different draughting arrangements, but all had their teething problems. With the larger engines with bigger fireboxes, the problems were not so acute, but the techniques had still to be mastered. One problem was to understand when to start letting the fire get lower towards the end of the shift. Many were the firemen who arrived back on shed, in the initial days, still with a boxful of hot fire because the slower burning Welsh product had not finishing doing so. Within a week, all was nearly back to normal and we became masters of it as if it had been our coal for years. Experience soon came to our rescue!

The most telling comment one can make was the almost total absence of any guidance being offered to us. Welsh coal appeared overnight in our bunkers and we just had to get on with it. I recall a simple instruction in the daily notice case to advise that henceforth all suburban engines would be supplied with Welsh smokeless fuel. There was no guidance as to the full significance of what this meant. Today, training courses would probably be organised, and no doubt examinations required to certificate the required competence! I am sure that, on balance, the older more rough and ready management style of assuming you were capable, even if a slight hiccup occurred, was the better approach. However, it would have been sensible to warn us of potential pitfalls when these can be foreseen - we were not warned, and many of our drivers had no previous experience of Welsh coal to help us. A note of explanation in the notice case would have prevented much of the hassle that occurred.

A hero's welcome upon returning from Cambridge was not expected, but some of the cleaners who were now regular firemen through the 'closing' of the shed to outsiders, did take the time to come and say 'thanks'. It was a welcome gesture. Southend was always a happy shed, where we would help each other.

It has been mentioned that class 'B12' No. 61578 became my regular engine upon returning to the shed. A cruel twist of fate affected my final turn of duty with my new regular mate, Harry Loker, before leaving to join the RAF for two years. Circumstances, beyond our foreman's control, forced him to provide an engine with the worst reputation possible because '78' was unavailable, much to my disappointment on such a special day. Operating problems earlier in the day had disrupted the planned workings which meant the shed could only offer the rough riding 'Bucking Bronco', the infamous class 'B17' No. 61613, *Woodbastwick Hall* - briefly mentioned already in Chapter Three. We were booked to work the 4.54 pm up passenger to Liverpool St and return with the 7.50 pm down passenger. It was generally accepted this engine did not go to London, with the higher running speeds required between Shenfield and London. But, it was this hated machine, or nothing. No engineman liked to see trains cancelled. We looked at each other and Harry agreed to take her. It was of course primarily his decision as the driver, not mine as the fireman. (Only once in my footplate career, did I as a fireman refuse to work an engine, to be referred to in Chapter Seven.)

No. 61613 was a real terror that shook you up in the most alarming manner and the subject of many complaints to the management. Eventually they had to

Class 'B12/3' No. 61523 on the 100 Foot Pit road at Southend. *Author*

A Sunday scene at Southend shed with class 'B12/3' No. 61575. Note the smokebox details highlighted by the locomotive's regular crew. *Author*

concede that major attention was required, even though she had not completed the required mileage to qualify for a main works overhaul. We were unofficially told not to be too particular about timekeeping, but no one wished to cause avoidable delays to passengers. Our own pride in the job was at stake, which was important in those now long ago times. If any encouragement had been needed to leave the footplate, then this last trip for the duration would have provided a good enough reason. It is difficult to describe the misery this particular engine gave us, as an extreme case. I will try, although I fear inadequately, to do so.

Imagine, if you can, a smallish boat taking a diagonal course through the waves - up, over, and down; up, over, and down - with a corkscrew-like rolling motion as it progresses forward. Then try to imagine each regular motion is continually buffeted with a judder in mid-movement as you are pitched sideways in the opposite direction to the previous roll by rogue waves crashing against the boat. This is a simple description but hopefully creates an image in your mind's eye. Now assume you are standing up and imagine trying to remain standing while this is happening and further imagine the boat is juddering from continually grounding on a stony beach, with a hard jarring sensation coming up through your feet and legs. How are you doing? Perhaps you may already feel just a little less than comfortable, although probably sitting down as you read these words.

Now in place of the boat imagine yourself on No. 61613, travelling at up to 60 mph on the curving Southend branch, and then at up to 70 mph on the main line. Now visualise the engine shaking and bouncing along with an irregular motion, broadly as described for the imaginary boat. Try to visualise how you might swing a shovel into the lower half of an oval-shaped firehole, with the cab jumping quite violently from side to side. The lower half of the hole is about 7 in. deep in the middle by about 15 in. wide at the maximum width. Across the top straight edge of this half-oval is a notched swing flap pivoted at the widest part of the opening, protruding outwards in to the cab, used to manage combustion by control of air admission. Through the lower space you have to achieve with your shovel, sufficient momentum to shoot the coal up to eight or nine feet into the firebox. Fortunately not too often, as the juddering vibration is helping coal forward to the extreme front of the box. Most has to be fired up to five or six feet into the box. The engine is savagely shaking you about from the constant lurching motion. This is accompanied by the continual thumping and banging from the badly worn coupled-wheel axleboxes immediately below your feet. Your ankles and leg muscles are receiving a constant involuntary massage from the shuddering vibration imparted through the cab floor boards. I needed to swing the shovel during the journey with short breaks to assist Harry with signal observations and to work the boiler water injectors as required. Relief from shovelling, but not from the vibration, came on favourable downhill gradients. Brief respite from the numbing vibration came while standing in stations. Firing was - unusually - done in the stations purely because it was easier to do so. Harry would open the regulator and off we went to experience it all over again . . . and again . . . and . . . Hopefully, this inadequate description does manage to convey a little of what it was like.

Driver Bill Frost, my regular mate for 15 months in the 'Bongo' Link, looking out of the cab of our regular engine. Bill had worked at Stratford shed for many years, firing on main line expresses, before eventually transferring to Southend shed. He never wore a BR issue hat, always preferring his cloth cap. We had many happy hours and journeys together, often made amusing by his never failing eye for a pretty lady passing by on the platform - it was all nice clean, harmless fun. We had many a smile watching people who had no idea they were being observed while we sat quietly out of view in the cab!   *Author*

We did it, because the alternative in this instance was to refuse to work the engine and two trains would have been cancelled. How do you define what is a rough ride and what is not? It is a subjective judgmental opinion, rather like when do you decide the sun is too hot to work in the garden? We claimed to management she was rough, indeed very rough. Management disagreed, until they could no longer do so. Until they did, we suffered the engine. We had our job to do, but then so did they. Our managers were struggling to overhaul arrears of maintenance within financial constraints imposed on them. Remember I am describing an event in 1953, well before the purse strings began to be eased with the 1955 modernisation plan. Other engines were rough, but less so than this detested machine, although they could still be very lively machines upon which to work a full shift. The name 'Woodbastwick' was extremely unfortunate, but very apt, as she quickly became known by a corruption of it that is best left to the imagination!

After saying 'cheerio' to Harry, my aching body was taken home to rest the pummelled legs and arms, and to allow the sore ribs that were black and blue with bruising to recover in a nice hot bath. Such a trip was exceptional, but these events happened.

The passage of time is a therapeutic healer, and two years working with the latest military aircraft technology did wonders for me as an individual. My time was spent working on aircraft instrumentation on all kinds of different fighter and bomber aircraft, from the piston engine Spitfire and Lancaster to the then most modern jets such as the Hawker 'Hunter' - then at the leading edge of military aircraft development when first introduced and we were the very first squadron to have them. It also returned me to civilian life keen to resume my interrupted career on the footplate. Weekend leaves had offered the occasional chance to keep my hand in, riding on the engines and having a go with the shovel, when travelling home to visit my family. All very unofficial of course!

Returning to Southend shed in October 1955, it became quite an experience to discover a railway being transformed in preparation for the new 75 mph dc electric train services. Also, to a Stratford works faced with its workload being reduced as modernisation plans were developed and introduced. The former arrears of maintenance had, by and large, been eliminated and engines generally were in a little bit better condition, although not perfect. As each new modernisation scheme came in, so fewer steam engines were required. It took time to achieve, but eventually the once considerable works itself was to succumb. Such an event we would not have believed possible, during the final heyday of steam on the GE section, when the new BR standard engines began appearing from 1951 onwards. In due course the GE became the first major area anywhere on BR entirely to abolish steam power - but this is racing ahead of the story!

My seniority now placed me into the top passenger link at the shed. Called the 'B1', or 'Bongo' link, we worked all the heavy 10-car business trains each morning and evening. My new regular mate became Bill Frost. His son, Peter, was also a fireman at the shed. Our regular engine was No. 61335. Our opposite mates were the senior driver at the shed, Fred Tomlinson, and his mate Keith Ian. Keith was to become a train crew supervisor at the Southend Victoria

Class 'B1' No. 61335 near Billericay on a down Southend train, waiting to proceed forward under 'Single Line Working' arrangements during an engineer's possession of the opposite running line during electrification works.   *Author*

Class 'B1' No. 61370 at Southend shed on the run round road in 1955.   *Author*

booking-on point for traincrew staff in the final years of his career before retirement in the mid-1990s. We had 12 weekly diagrams rostered to the link. For details, see the Table below. Six pairs of crews manned six regular engines, as explained in Chapter Two. It was an interesting link to be in, although the work was fairly routine and repetitive. Summary details were:

Table Two - Southend 'B1' Link Work Roster, Winter 1955/56

Week	On duty	Diagram No. and Working
1	4.55 am	2 - 6.18 to LS arr 7.37; 8.11 ecs to TF; LE to SX; home passr.
2	2.30 pm	4 - 3.54 to LS arr 5.24; 6.45 to SD arr 8.07
3	5.35 am	4 - 7.10 to LS arr 8.18; 9.50 to SD arr 11.16
4	12.40 pm	5 - EP; 1.13 to LS arr 2.30; 5.33 to SD arr 6.44
5	5.45 am	5 - 7.25 to LS arr 8.36; 10.18 to SD arr 11.38
6	12.35 pm	1 - passr to LS on 12.54 arr 2.10; 4.45 to SD arr 5.53
7	4.15 am	1 - 5.51 to LS arr 7.12; home passr or work as required
8	1.35 pm	6 - passr 1.54 to SX arr 3.16; 5.38 ecs to LS; 7.00 to SD arr 8.25
9	7.25 am	6 - 8.35 to LS arr 9.57; 11.17 LE to SX; passr to LS; relieve SX 72 men; 1.50 to SD arr 3.19
10	1.30 pm	3 - 2.54 to LS arr 4.18; 6.12 to SD arr 7.38
11	5.00am	3 - 6.38 to LS arr 7.56; 9.08 to SD arr 10.29
12	5.10 pm	SX 72 - 6.32 pcls to LS; change engines with SX men; 11.26 to SD arr 12.55
		(The 11.26 was the 2nd shift of Diagram 2, although not formally listed as such.)

EP = Engine prepared; LE = Light Engine; LS = Liverpool St; SD = Southend; SX = Stratford; TF = Thornton Fields Carriage Sdgs; ecs = empty coaching stock (or cars); pcls = parcels train; passr = booked to travel 'on the cushions'.

These workings record the basic roster for Monday to Friday services. They would be frequently altered to accommodate changed traffic requirements, particularly when booked to travel passenger, when an extra train working was often diagrammed, such as to work an excursion from Chingford to Southend. The on duty times for up morning workings included an allowance of 15 minutes for steam heating the train before departure, during the winter months. Booking on times were 15 minutes later during the summer period when no steam heating was required (except for sleeping car services - not applicable to Southend trains).

Our day might be livened up by some of the characters we had at the shed. Our senior shed fitter, Ben Goodman, was a real gem who loved to leg-pull and crack a joke at someone else's expense. His wicked sense of humour would delight in gently 'winding up' anybody who showed signs of being, or about to become, irate. His speciality was crisp one liner's, usually questioning the victim's parentage, while he set about effecting a quick 'fix-it' repair to keep an engine in traffic. Ben was a master with a spanner and lump hammer to coax reluctant boiler injectors to inject, or vacuum ejectors to eject to the correct inches of mercury, when they obstinately were refusing to perform. When it came to 'donkey pump' repairs (the steam-operated Westinghouse air brake pump) there were few better exponents of the secret and mysterious arts of making them last out. Thus, he kept engines in traffic until a replacement unit could be fitted, or the original one properly repaired. This would be either at night or during the next shed day for the engine. His activities would be accompanied by varying degrees of the artisan's own peculiar variety of colourful blasphemy. This encouraged matters along which would include any opportunity to have a leg-pull elsewhere. With his ever willing fitter's mate (who acted as a sort of supporting cast to the many verbal pantomimes) he - and the other fitting staff, likewise - would work in all weathers to keep engines available for their next turn of duty.

A running shed fitter had a rough, tough, and very dirty life. It required a particular kind of personality to stick at it, usually in adverse conditions of hot pipework or dripping hot water and oil, and yet remain cheerful. The changing of a broken engine spring (tender springs were less difficult) was always a loathsome job at the best of times. They usually brought forth a masterful performance of the art of colourful language. One of the printable phrases of Ben's that I can recall went, 'Come on you wobbly-eyed, cackhanded, twisted corkscrew cowson of a [lady of the night]' when trying to persuade a crookedly lined up nut to straighten itself onto the thread! It was no wonder that tempers would occasionally become fragile. Particularly if, as was often the case, he was working against the clock to avoid a delay. Ben's brand of wicked but completely non-vicious humour was his way of jollying everybody along to get a job done. These unique personalities do not seem to exist in the rail industry today. Maybe for the simple reason the dirt and filth associated with the war, and post-war years of steam, created challenges rarely known before or since. Equipment shortage and 'make do and mend' were the regular diet of life with the shed approaching a major reduction in steam power. Understandably, management were not keen to invest in equipment soon to be discarded.

Another of our well known characters was Mike Hunt. He had been a driver in the 'B1' link in the earlier 1950s before transferring to the passenger pilot link by 1955. He was a shortish gentleman, always immaculately turned out, who had a rare gift for laughter. He had pronounced rosy cheeks and always arrived in the signing-on lobby amidst much hilarity. He was never known to be miserable, whatever the time of day or night. He could occasionally get angry, but never miserable. He was a great mate to fire to and always ready for a little joke whenever the chance presented itself. A favourite trick he had in his 'B1' days was to place an engine cloth over the boiler pressure gauge as you left Southend. He then challenged you to get to London without blowing off with no pressure gauge to guide you. He expected the required pressure to time the train in the normal way. It could be very entertaining! It taught you to trust your judgement, listen to the engine and how it was being worked, note the exhaust from the chimney and to generally be on your toes. The 'B1s' were masters of the 10-car trains and going up and down the same railway day in, day out, could be a trifle boring. Mike made it more interesting with such a challenge and was teaching you some of the finer arts of enginemanship at the same time. He was a real character, even if some did find his early morning joviality, in particular, a little difficult to cope with!

Dick 'Hammer' Smith was a well known Southend driver. He was 'Hammer' to all and sundry; not because he hammered engines - he didn't. He never went under an engine to oil it up without taking a hammer to check all the bolts, springs, etc. 'Hammer' usually reported for duty at least an hour early on the early morning turns. He spent this extra time checking and re-making dirty oil trimmings to his satisfaction. He would ensure all oil cisterns in the motion were free of water and be under the engine up in the motions for a good hour sometimes. Needless to say his overalls were usually less then clean. It was not necessary to do this, but he did. The fitters would consign his personal credentials and soul to the other side of the great divide on many occasions. It was unusual for 'Hammer' not to need them. A particular favourite of his would be to have the brakes taken up, even if they were well within permitted tolerances for safe working. He required them to be just hanging off the wheels by the tightest of margins before agreeing to leave the shed. On one occasion he had them adjusted so tight, his engine came to a stand on one of the sharper curves in the shed. And there it and he remained to suffer much embarrassment while his mate was sent post-haste for the fitters to slack them off a touch. It was suggested this might not have been accidental, but nobody owned up to it! All part of the rich pattern of activity in any shed working.

Many other characters worked at the shed. Two more who jump readily to mind were real 'hard hitters' who made the sparks shoot upwards well and truly: Ted Rickard whose regular engine was 'B1' No. 61362, and Wally Allen on No. 61363.

Ted Rickard was a remarkable man, unique among footplate men within my experience. He had suffered a serious throat operation which had severely hampered his ability to speak. The surgeon had made a hole in the front of his neck and fitted a form of voice box activated by modulating the air pressure in the windpipe. Ted successfully trained himself to reproduce a wheezing type sound that re-created his ability to speak sufficiently clearly enough that he could be understood. He was eventually permitted to return to main line driving duties. He had successfully demonstrated to the company doctor that he could communicate face to face. Of far greater importance, he could also be understood when using the telephone - absolutely vital when talking to a signalman. It was a superb example of personal courage and determination to overcome such a serious handicap. He always wore a scarf, summer and winter, to protect the voice box air entry. He was always very careful to avoid dusty environments. Not easy on a coal-fired steam engine or within the confines of the shed during preparation and disposal duties. On the few occasions with him I always paid extra attention to keep the footplate clean and the coal well damped down to prevent swirling dust. When it came to engine handling he was a real hard hitter. He might have been slightly wheezy, but his engine never was - No. 61362 never suffered from carboned-up valves! He was a good engineman who would run into stations to stop a train as smooth as silk; it was always a pleasure to watch him do it.

Wally was a shortish, quietly spoken man with a Stalinesque-style moustache who loved his stubby pipe, and who always preferred to wear the old ex-LNE pattern soft top engineman's hat. He was the only driver ever to frighten me, and also himself - although he didn't admit to it until some time afterwards! We were working the 5.51 pm passenger, a heavy 10-car evening business train, booked to stop at Stratford, Brentwood, Rayleigh and Prittlewell. We had a particularly lively class 'B17', No. 61648 *Arsenal*. This engine, as already remarked upon in Chapter Three, was a good engine. By 1956 she also came complete with a pronounced rock and roll motion which got worse in direct

A Sunday scene at Southend shed in February 1955. On the left we can see the bunker of 'J69/1' 0-6-0T No. 68632 on the sandbox road. To its right is 'J20' class 0-6-0 No. 64675 and 'B12' class 4-6-0 No. 61555 on the No. 1 shed road. The concrete bin in the foreground is the sandbox.

Author

This view, taken on the same day shows the oil stores road. The locomotives are 'B17' class 4-6-0s Nos. 61661 *Sheffield Wednesday*, 61611 *Raynham Hall* and 61648 *Arsenal*. 'N7' 0-6-2T No. 69630 completes the line up.

Author

proportion to the speed. Nothing like as severe as No. 61613, but lively nonetheless. We were running five minutes late due to signals before Shenfield. As soon as we got onto the branch at Shenfield, Wally set about time recovery with a vengeance. We came up the steep rise into and through Billericay station, at a speed not much short of 60 mph. This was before we started down the 4½ miles of about 1 in 100 that is Billericay Bank. By Ramsden Bellhouse - half way down - we were well up in the 70s. The branch limit was still officially 60 mph although the track down the bank had by this date been renewed and graded ready for the new 80 mph limit for the electric services. He eased up a bit to sight the Wickford outer home colour light which came into view as you rounded the final curve to drop down into the station. As soon as I called out that we had the green aspect he opened her up again. We were still gathering speed as we went through Wickford station with the by now very lively rock and roll motion indicating our rapid progress. We hit the Southminster branch junction points and suddenly the roll stopped in mid-movement. The smokebox took a nose dive and the engine abruptly lurched back the way it had just come. It seemed as if we were about to jump the track. We had a nasty fright. Many drivers might have immediately closed the regulator. Wally promptly opened it out fully. This action pulled the engine through its frantic shuddering motion and maybe saved the day. Within a hundred yards all was back to normal. We were soon breasting the rise up beyond the Wick Lane road level crossing that existed in those days, with the rock and roll back into its rhythmic motion once more. We looked at each other with not a word spoken. We eventually arrived right time at Southend having recovered the full five minutes.

An excited passenger came up to congratulate us on a fine run and, 'Did we realise we had accelerated to 82 mph through Wickford?'

Wally composed himself, put on a dead pan face, looked the gentleman straight in the eye and replied, 'I do not think so'.

He then promptly busied himself inside the cab relighting his pipe to avoid any further discussion! He wanted to be right time to attend a meeting later in the evening. The fact that we nearly didn't make it to Southend, let alone he to his meeting, was left unspoken. A truly frightening experience that was never to be repeated - possibly another 'life' used up out of the famous nine, it will never be known!

Other frightening events did occur. My worst experience was to be thrown completely outside the cab of a 'Jazzer' class 'K3' engine. They had a peculiar '3-forward and 2-back' motion when running at speed. They were never the smoothest riding of engines, unless just ex-works after overhaul. They were rarely very violent to work on, but were usually lively machines. We were running at about 60 mph between Rayleigh and Wickford, one evening. The engine lurched as we found a soft spot in the track on a canted right-handed curve. This meant I was on the inside of the curve on the lower side of the slightly tilted cab floor. The unexpected lurch caught me off balance. Before this could be regained, she lurched again. The next I can recall was hanging onto the engine and tender handrails, completely outside the cab. These must have been grabbed by instinct while falling. My boots were dragging along the ballast, scuffing the leather toe caps. Insistence on wearing good strong boots saved me

Class 'K3' 2-6-0 No. 61951 passes Channelsea Junction in 1956.   *Author*

The unique two-cylinder class 'K5' No. 61863. This engine was rebuilt from a three-cylinder 'K3' class locomotive.   *Author*

further injury. Hauling myself back up the steps into the cab, the enormity of what had just happened then dawned. Fortunately we had just recently passed a train on the opposite line. My guardian angel was certainly on duty! It took some effort to just sit down on the 'piano' stool that was the fireman's seat. My mate saw nothing until he routinely checked round a little later to see me white as a sheet and looking decidedly ashen and trembling. He thought it was a joke until he saw the boots. It was a full 20 minutes later at Shenfield before the trembling eased, during which time he helped with the firing. Not an experience to be repeated. It was too close a call for comfort from being fatally injured - and another 'life' used up. It took a lot of will power to stay on that engine from Shenfield onwards running at the higher line speed on to London. My mate was so concerned he suggested a relief fireman be requested. By the end of the shift the jitters had more or less disappeared. It took a couple of days to overcome fully this most frightening experience which, fortunately, has never once troubled me since. Making an entry in the accident book to record the event, upon return to the shed, was not easy. The act of writing about it made me feel very peculiar. We heard later the track was checked the next morning and the ballast repacked. There had been heavy rain and the track 'top' alignment had dipped a little, which our lively engine had found. A class 'B12', being a much smoother riding inside-cylinder machine, would have ridden through it without any noticeable tremor. Lively riding machines were a normal hazard as has been mentioned, that came as part of the job. Today, trauma counselling would be considered and maybe provided for such an extreme experience, but we just had to get on with it, like it or lump it, as the old saying goes. Within a couple of days it was forgotten, there was no point in dwelling on it, although my experience went the rounds of the shed with several, mainly supportive, comments offered.

Fred Wiley was for many years our ASLEF union branch Chairman. He was one of the nicest of men you could ever wish to meet. He had a very quiet and steady manner which, though mild, did not permit slipshod attitudes from either his firemen or from management. His regular engine was class 'B1' No. 61360. He drove it so gently that the soft exhaust created a challenge for his fireman to keep a good bright fire until you got used to his driving style. With Ted Rickard, it was almost effortless to fire and maintain a good bright, hot fire, albeit at the cost of a stronger back. With Fred, until you had worked out how to manage your fire it was all too easy to create too thick a firebed and then struggle for steam. You had to fire little and sparingly but once the art was mastered it gave immense satisfaction. Mike Hunt used to be Fred's opposite mate until he went on the passenger pilot. Between them, they really used to take a pride in that engine. She didn't rattle or bang, steamed well, and the cab interior was always kept wiped down and clean.

Mention of ASLEF recalls our colourful branch Secretary, Bill Robinson, who was, like Fred, a very good union representative. He regularly covered the running foreman's duty whenever they were not available, in between his regular driving duties. He would indulge a really impish sense of fun, and enjoyed a joke or prank when the circumstances were sensible, but he could get very frustrated when problems were mounting up. Occasionally, some of the younger live wires would gang up against him for a bit of a lark, claiming their engine was a failure, when in reality it wasn't. Poor old Bill would spend, maybe 10 minutes, trying to re-organise the engine rosters in an effort to offer a replacement, only to discover the 'failure' had been repaired, as everybody else knew it would be. He usually got his own back within a few days! One ploy was to book out a known rough-rider to the culprit, making sure any other spare engine was officially booked as 'not available', when in fact they were. It was all good humoured fun, usually taken in a friendly manner.

Throughout the final period of steam, the engineer's electrification trains placed heavy demands on engine crewing. By 1955, all cleaners were passed for firing duties, there were no junior cleaners. Recruitment had virtually ceased with the impending run down of the shed a year hence. Most hands were firing full time, which meant inside motions and framing would often be covered in oil and grime. Not nice if you have to climb up into it. Most drivers carried a rag to wipe clean parts where they had to wriggle up for oiling. The rest of the underneath often remained filthy for weeks at a time, where in 1951, for example, this was less likely to happen. One simply would not tolerate such poor and frequently hazardous conditions of working today.

It was not unknown for a fitter still to be working, maybe on the donkey pump out on the footplating, while we were moving the engine. All in a desire not to have a delay off shed for the next working. Occasionally, we worked engines with one boiler injector only (all engines had two fitted) for a full shift to avoid a cancellation. It was against the rules, but done. The prime requirement in this situation was to always run with a thin bed of fire, in case the one injector packed up. Then you could dump the fire quickly to safeguard the boiler from possible damage.

Managers knew it happened, but turned a blind eye if the alternative would be a train cancelled. Officially, it was a disciplinary offence to take an engine off shed with only one injector working, as you were putting the safety of the boiler at greater risk. I cannot recall anyone being carpeted for doing so, or dropping a lead firebox plug as a result. All fireboxes are fitted with at least two lead filled fusible plugs. The lead will melt releasing steam to smother the fire, hopefully to avoid serious damage to the firebox crown sheet, should the water level get dangerously low. To burn a crown sheet and drop a plug was the ultimate crime in engine management. It could be a sackable offence, although rarely, if ever, enforced in post-war conditions. If it was due to pure negligence, as opposed to trying to keep the job running and misjudging the situation, then more serious disciplinary action would be considered. With management turning a blind eye on the one hand, they couldn't really sack a man on the other hand, but discipline had to be observed in such instances, which fortunately was a very rare and extreme occurrence anyway.

Looking back, we were all dedicated but also semi-insane to tolerate such basic working conditions, with some engines bouncing you around. Generally, from the middle fifties onwards, engine quality was over the worst excesses of indifferent maintenance. But, bruised ribs could still occur. Small wonder, then, that many left the footplate never to return, once they could see the impending run-down gaining momentum. Most of us had an on-going love/hate relationship with the demands of the job and the challenges faced and overcome every day.

In the final year of steam working over the branch we had a steady trickle of the Thompson class 'K1' 2-6-0 'Baby Bongos'. These engines were a tender version of the unpopular class 'L1' tanks. The 'K1' was far superior to the 'L1' and was complete master of our 10-car trains when needed. They proved to be versatile engines. It was most interesting to work on the 'K1s'. Working on them at Cambridge they would handle goods trains with little trouble. By comparison, the 'L1', particularly the Westo-fitted variety, frequently had difficulty stopping itself, let alone a loose-coupled train behind it. They were rarely seen on such workings in the London area, although sometimes so used in country areas. They were also very prone to slipping when starting if not carefully handled, whereas the 'K1s' were no more or less prone than the average engine. Most peculiar for what essentially was a common design. One can only presume this was caused by lack of adhesion weight on the 'L1', maybe because the rear bogie was taking some of the adhesion off the driving wheels.

The Tilbury 4-4-2 tank engines that came to the shed from the LT&S section initially did not have LNER-type boiler injectors, and were unpopular out on the road as a result. They became more or less confined to barracks, only being booked out when no other engine was available because they needed easy access to water columns. The water would get hot in the tanks which in turn caused the older Midland Railway-type injectors to be difficult to work. Some of the Tilbury's that came to Southend were re-equipped at Stratford with LNER injectors. These included Nos. 41949 and 41975, which we had for a time. They were more reliable out on the road, although never the most popular of engines, being life expired by the time we saw them. It is my recollection that No. 41936 may have retained her Midland injectors to the end. She had them at Southend Victoria, prior to going LE to Colchester on 22nd May, 1956. The LT&S line were careful to keep the best ones for themselves where they did good work for many years - and who could blame them!

Mention of the passenger pilot engine, No. 41936, recalls the two regular drivers, in addition to Mike Hunt, who worked this duty in their own pilot link, Sammy Flatt and Dick Snelling. Both were of shortish stature, Sam being a chubby-cheeked, somewhat rotund, jovial gentleman, Dick rather slimmer. Both had very precise ideas on how the work should be done. They each came to work immaculately attired in crisp, clean overalls, and shiny clean boots, Dick's especially so. Woe betide the fireman who accidentally splashed water or coal dust on them! Their footplate had to be regularly swept and kept tidy with the tool bucket always scrubbed clean, ready for washing up in. Only very rarely was it used for carrying tools. These were kept in the tool cupboard that was regularly wiped out and kept lined with clean newspaper. The 'front', i.e., the backhead of the boiler inside the cab, was always wiped over and kept clean by the firemen. When everything was done 'according to custom' then both men would smile and beam to all and sundry and be in their element. The regular rostered firemen were always ones passed for driving duties, to be easily available to the running foreman if required. This meant we, as passed cleaners, would often be sent over to relieve the fireman to take over the rest of

Ex-LMS 4-4-2 'Tilbury Tanks' at Southend shed in February 1955. No. 41975 is on the No. 1 shed road and Nos. 41949 and 41976 are on the No. 2 road. *Author*

An atmospheric view that nicely captures a typical engine shed scene - a lighting pole with standard signal post ladder; overhead electric and telephone wires; water column with coal brazier for winter use; and ashes, a fire-iron and general debris, coal lumps etc., lying indiscriminately around. Driver Mike Hunt is supervising the water crane while his fireman is recording the view for posterity! This image was taken in the week I was ordered to work on light duties following an ankle injury referred to in the text (*see page 152*). The class '3P' 4-4-2 ex-LMS Tilbury Tank' No. 41936 was our regular Southend Victoria passenger shunt pilot engine for most of 1954 to 1956. Her spacious cab made her a popular engine on this duty, but the class were not liked on running line workings when, as here, they still retained their old ex-Midland Railway-style water feed injectors - matters improved when some of the class were given ex-LNER pattern ones. *Author*

the shift. If we didn't come up to scratch, then the all world and his dog, as the saying goes, would be well aware of our failure. If you did your duties correctly, then they were pleasant mates to be with. A couple of lovely old men who took immense pride in their job. Sam was on the pilot roster having had a serious operation which required regular meals to minimise the discomfort of his circumstances. It explained his insistence on a regular routine to his working life. Dick was on light duties on doctor's orders. He was a quietly spoken gentleman, but his tongue could be very precise and to the point, when called for, but most times he was kindness itself.

It was the characters such as the ones just described who contributed so much in their respective and often unsung ways, to the warm atmosphere that generally pervaded the place. We were a happy shed where laughter was often heard, frequently amidst some ribald leg-pulling. Disciplinary action only very rarely occurred. The union staff relations with our managers rarely gave rise to other than the most minor conflict. Southend was a good shed, even when the going could be very tough. People would muck in together to help when it was. It was a sad day when the electrification altered forever the vibrant harmony we had enjoyed. It wasn't that the men altered, but working by themselves in a motorman's cab somehow destroyed the heart of the place. From 1957 only the daily goods train workings remained steam hauled, plus evening passenger excursion workings during the Southend Illuminations season, until both were converted to diesels at a later date, and the goods workings were eventually withdrawn with the loss of the traffic and closure of the station yard facilities.

It is a normal quirk of human nature usually to remember the brighter moments in life and forget the less happy ones. These reminiscences have referred to some of the men chosen to be shared with you, in a positive light as a representative selection. It is natural to recall these individuals in this way. But, there were also a few men who made life less happy and who shall remain nameless. Not every driver was a pleasure to fire to. A small number took an almost sadistic delight in making a fireman's life as awkward as they could. There were several ways of doing this. One of the worst was to treat their fireman like dirt and not give any credit for a job well done. Another was to remain aloof from a friendly relationship with their mate, which made for a very miserable partnership. Imagine spending hours together with mates like this in a cab barely eight by five feet maximum in size. Another technique was to be always demanding this or that be done and not give their fireman any credit for intelligence. This attitude, if you had to put up with it day after day from a regular rostered driver, could sap your confidence over time. The next chapter will discuss one regular mate who was like this until we had a sort out. Believe it or believe it not, it was not unknown for a driver to draw a chalk line on the cab floor and tell his fireman to stay on his own side of it! Rare, but not unknown. A very few men had poor personal hygiene habits which made life uncomfortable in a hot cab with body odours to be tolerated. Some drivers took great delight in making their fireman work unnecessarily hard by thumping the engine along. I don't mean the so called 'hard hitters' like Ted Rickard or Wally Allen who were good enginemen. There were those who handled an engine with no feeling for it, as if they were driving a run down army tank carrier. They handled the brake with no consideration for passengers, coming to a harsh stop instead of smoothly. Some drove erratically one day to the next without any predictable driving style so that you had difficulty maintaining a correct fire. A small number had no social skills at all, and while knowledgeable in rules and regulations, etc., were just downright rude individuals. A few were professional moaners with a 'man-sized chip on their shoulder' as the saying goes. Usually a perceived grievance they would continually harp on about to you. This was particularly so in the aftermath of the 1955 strike. ASLEF members refusing to speak to NUR members (who didn't strike because their union told them not to) made for very difficult working relationships. Some of these feuds lasted for months on end and caused much bitterness. This took a very long time to be slowly overcome. Life in the cab was not always 'sweetness and light'. Such occasions were the exception to the normal situation, but they occurred nevertheless.

In the 'Bongo' link, we had no workings to Chelmsford, or over the Southminster branch. We knew Southend men worked the 6.20 pm up goods, Southminster to Wickford, and an afternoon goods to Woodham Ferrers, 2.06 pm from Wickford and 2.55 pm return. When, or for how long, the Woodham workings ran, escapes my memory now, but it did so in the winter 1955/56 timetable. It was covered by Southend diagram 12, second shift. This crew booked on duty at 9.30 am to travel 'on the cushions' on the 9.45 am to Shenfield. There they relieved the 1st shift and worked the 10.46 am passenger to Chelmsford, and 12.20 pm passenger back to Shenfield. Next, they ran 1.15 pm LE to Wickford to work the 2.06 pm to Woodham and return to Wickford then went LE to Southend. The 2nd May, 1956 found me rostered for spare duties as required which resulted, very unusually, in firing to Harry Saville on this working on class 'B12' No. 61549. Two days later, with Harry again on the same working, this time with No. 61546, was to be my last trip to Chelmsford with steam. The new dc electric service commenced shortly afterwards with the new summer timetable.

The pending redundancy was already very much on everybody's mind. On 26th April, 1956 my request for a footplate pass was authorised to travel on the 7.50 am 'flyer' King's Cross to Doncaster and return on the 11.40 am up 'Yorkshire Pullman', travelling both ways with Leeds Copley Hill men. We had Gresley class 'A3' No. 60051 *Blink Bonny* down road, and Peppercorn class 'A1' No. 60144 *King's Courier* up. Doing a good proportion of the firing both ways, much to the surprise and amusement of the crews concerned, satisfied any doubts as to my ability to do this work. I had asked for this pass to find out about the work to make sure it would be a right move, before seeking a transfer to King's Cross. Speed in the low 80s for just a few minutes with only four coaches, on a lively class 'B17' from Shenfield to Chelmsford, was one thing. Doing 90 mph with 12 coaches, on a long distance express on much better riding machines, for mile after mile, was an unknown world. It was also hugely different from a class 'B1' at 60 mph with regular stops. Speed is one thing, but the endurance needed to fire large express engines on long journeys - I travelled 312 miles that day - was a concern. This day out on my rostered 'Rest Day' (!) showed such fears were groundless. It also showed how thoughtful my manager was to support the application for the pass. These were not readily granted and usually required an inspector to be present. I must have been 'wired on' (as we would say) as nobody appeared.

Footplate work could rarely be described as being dull, even if it did sometimes become routine. Special workings always made for variety and a note about a few of them will be of interest.

The Liverpool St turntable was being repaired on 7th/8th/9th January, 1956. Special plans were made to draft in seven class 'L1s' for London workings - Nos. 67709/10/20/21/33/51 and 58. Tank engines were designed to be worked either way without the need for turning them, and hence this temporary arrangement. We had No. 67709 (from Ipswich) for the 11.54 am up passenger to Liverpool St and 2.50 pm return passenger on the 7th. On the 9th, with Bill Frost we had No. 67733 on the 6.38 am up and the 9.08 am down passenger workings. We managed, which is all that can be said. Sheds do not send their better engines to other sheds, if they can avoid doing so! On the 10th we had class 'B17' No. 61605 *Lincolnshire Regiment* with an Ipswich eight-car main line corridor buckeye set to give our passengers on the 9.08 am an unusual treat. This was a reaction of the turntable repairs. My notes do not record if the buffet was working. The up working to form our train had been altered. Naturally, the class 'L1s' were quickly sent away again. If our two engines were typical, we had been sent less desirable specimens!

We were rostered 'As required' on 4th June, 1956. A duty came up at short notice to travel 'on the cushions' to Wickford with Ted Woods, one of our younger passed firemen. Bill didn't sign the Southminster branch so, quite correctly, declined to do the duty. With Ted we relieved Wickford men to work the 3.54 pm passenger to Southminster with class 'N7' No. 69725. We had been instructed to change over with Southminster men who gave us class 'N7' No. 69616 to work the 6.20 pm goods back to Wickford and then proceed LE to Southend. An ordinary working, until the reason for it emerges - we had been told at Southend that No. 69616 was to be condemned for scrapping. This was following an emergency examination of her boiler at Southminster due to poor stays and tubes, and hence our special turn to bring her back to the shed. My diary has an additional note that she would be the first 'N7' to be withdrawn. She was permitted to work the goods to Wickford, but thereafter banned from any other work. She disappeared from the shed on 6th June. Harold, our boilersmith, had done a washout and emergency boiler repairs to make her fit enough to go LE to Stratford. We had had a real struggle to maintain sufficient steam and water to work our train to Wickford, and even more trouble running LE back to Southend. There was so much water pouring down the firebox tubeplate from the leaking tubes and stays, we nearly had to stop short of water and steam - we would never have lived down the ignominy of it! She was so bad - such a circumstance was quite exceptional. We were well used to having leaking tube plates, but never did I work on any engine in such a seriously leaking state as poor old No. 69616 was on that day. Small wonder Harold had to work his magic tricks to make her fit enough to manage the long trip to Stratford! Fortune must have been with her because records reveal she was reprieved and survived, but she still became an earlier casualty in the class, being condemned in January 1959.

Class 'L1' 2-6-4T No. 67720 on Channelsea curve waiting to work forward via Stratford station.
Author

Class 'N7/5' No. 69630 at Southend shed in 1955.   *Author*

We had occasional specials over the Chingford branch. On 23rd August, 1956 with Bill, we booked on duty at 4.15 am to work the 5.51 am Southend to Liverpool St, then worked LE tender first to Channelsea carriage sidings at Stratford, to pick up the 9.58 am cars to work tender first to Chingford for the 11.18 am excursion to Southend, with our regular engine No. 61335. We worked the entire diagram without turning the engine between leaving and arriving back at Southend. This was possible because the road to Chingford formed the apex of a triangle. It was a nice sunny day with the train very well patronised. I do not know how the return excursion working in the evening was diagrammed. We worked our train from Chingford via Hall Farm Jn, Temple Mills, High Meads, and Channelsea curve, to gain the down main line via No.10 platform (as it then was) at Stratford station. Yet another routing that has long been impossible since the Hall Farm connection onto the Lea Valley route was removed. There has been talk of restoring it to permit empty electric stock working from the Chingford road to go direct to/from Ilford car sheds. This would also allow direct services once again from Chingford to East Coast destinations, such as to Southend and Clacton. Like many sensible ideas, wait until it happens!

Two days earlier with Bill Stevens, we were booked to work an officers' inspection special from Liverpool St to Southend with class 'B1' No. 61399. This was Stratford's 'special' engine at that time, always kept nicely cleaned and polished for such occasions. It all went wrong when the tenderful of dust we had on the up working with class 'B17' No. 61612 *Houghton Hall* added to the boiler water problems that emerged. We were working the 5.51 am up passenger with the normal 10-car formation. As soon as we pulled away from the first stop at Prittlewell, three minutes after departing from Southend, we knew we were in trouble. Very dirty water in the boiler was causing severe priming that we just could not stop. Priming is when the boiler water carries over through the regulator valve with the steam into the cylinders, as previously explained. The kettle was reluctant to boil and the water was like soap suds in the gauge glass, it was so frothy. We were fighting a losing battle to maintain the water level, running with the cylinder drain cocks open for frequent periods. The fire had been built up slowly and was well alight and bright and in good fettle. The heavy priming prevented normal power being applied which stopped a decent draught being created on the fire. It began to go dead on us, no matter how lightly she was fired. Because of the water problem, the regulator had to be continually eased to avoid the risk of damaging the cylinders. Control decided enough was enough and wisely terminated us at Rayleigh - our fourth stop and less than 9 miles from Southend. We struggled to work forward as empty cars to Wickford to stable in the up refuge siding, done with just 120 lb. steam pressure (full pressure was 225 lb.). It was possible to reach Wickford because of the predominately downhill gradient from Rayleigh. By not stopping in Wickford platform we had sufficient momentum to carry us through the station and on up the initial gradient of Billericay Bank. We needed the uphill gradient to help us set back downhill into the siding. But only after the vacuum brake cylinder valve strings had been partially pulled to stop the brakes sticking! We were in desperate circumstances, and Bill's report, describing this, was to be accepted

An aerial view of Southend shed on 8th May, 1955, showing the field roads to the left, respectively Nos. 1,2, 3 and 4 roads, with temporary engineer's siding provided for electrification works, to the right. *Author*

Taken on the same day this ground level view shows 'B1' class No. 61370, 'B12' class No. 61576 and 'B1s' Nos. 61335 and 61336 on the No. 2 field road. No. 3 field road is occupied by 'Tilbury Tank' No. 41952 and engineer's rolling stock. There is more engineer's stock on field road No. 4 and, on the extreme right, on the temporary additional road. *Author*

when the inevitable 'please explain' was called for. We were eventually allowed back onto the running lines a couple of hours or so later (after the Control had carefully verified our situation) to work the cars to Thornton Fields Sidings, Stratford. This was to get them into place for their rostered evening working. While the morning peak service was going by (with cock-a-doodle-do's on their whistles from our merciless colleagues!) the fire was pulled round and restored sufficiently to manage a slow ascent of the bank with water kept at a maximum of half a glass. The heavy priming still continued as we passed 'our' special being worked by Stratford men, coming down the bank as we were crawling up it. The final humiliation came when they too blew a 'cock-a-doodle-do' to rub it in! All most distressing, with details reported in the local paper as a delay of half an hour in those days was so rare, it was very newsworthy. It was confirmed later that No. 61612 was long overdue for a boiler washout. Due to a misunderstanding at Stratford she had been sent to Southend the previous evening, with the advice that this had been done, when it had not. There was a suggestion she had been sent to us to solve a problem at Stratford, something about a temporary shortage of boiler staff. Such tricks were not unknown. Coupled with the dust we had for fuel stacked the odds against us, and sadly on this occasion we lost the battle, a rare occurrence in my career (one of only three occasions). She was quickly scheduled for a washout. Because of the heavy delays we had caused, this was specially reported upon - the amount of sludge that came out was described as 'very heavy' and the boiler water sample was described as 'bad' when analysed. For good measure we retained a sample of the dust, in case it was needed for evidence - much to our relief, it wasn't required.

Such a serious loss of time would be very carefully enquired into, for obvious reasons. The fact that we were adjudged not to have been guilty of engine mis-management was vindication of our attempts to overcome the difficulties met with. It might have been decided differently, in which case the disciplinary procedure could have been invoked. How would this have been applied?

Under the Machinery of Negotiation procedures, agreements exist between management and the unions as explained in Chapter One. One of these agreements covered the administration of discipline of employees in accordance with the agreed 'Disciplinary Procedure'. This was designed to ensure as far as it was practicable to do so, that a uniformity of application was achieved on a national basis. It covered all grades, waged and salaried, throughout the industry below officer level. Very briefly summarised, the process started with an explanation being required about a wrongdoing that was alleged to have been committed. (Note: the procedure to be described will by now have been updated, especially since the privatisation of the industry.)

The initial explanation was called for on a 'Form No. 1' to which we had to reply in writing within 48 hours. Not two days, because for staff on shift work it was essential to tie it down, to avoid misinterpretation, especially if the explanation was urgently required. A specimen form from this era is reproduced here. (A subsequent revision of the agreement was to permit three days for the initial reply.) If the explanation was accepted we were told so, in writing, the matter was closed and it did not appear on our service record card. If our explanation was not accepted we were awarded a punishment appropriate to the

LNER 2971/5/45—15,000

S.A.14/3799

LONDON AND NORTH EASTERN RAILWAY

Form No. 1

B 1101

Motive Power .... Department, ... Southend .... Station, 31st January 194 52.

Memorandum to... Passed Cleaner D. Butcher,
                  Southend.

It is reported that you have committed the undermentioned irregularity.....................................

.... Failed to take duty as booked on 2.1. and 3.1.52. ......

....

....

....

Please give an explanation in writing within 48 hours.

G.A.Donald

Loco' Shed Master.

Examples of disciplinary procedure forms referred to in the text.

S.A.14/3799.   (B.1411 70)

THE RAILWAY EXECUTIVE
EASTERN REGION

DISTRICT MOTIVE POWER SUPERINTENDENT
STRATFORD

Ext. 5392   Ref. S.A.14/3799.   Date 13th February, 1952

To   Reference

Passed Cleaner D.Butcher,
    Southend.

            Referring to your reply to Form 1 dated 31.1.52,
your explanation is accepted and no further action will be taken
on this occasion.

                            [signature]

            Asst. District Motive Power Supt.

wrong doing at the 'Form 1' hearing, confirmed in writing on a 'Form No. 2'. (No specimen copy available - I never had one!) We had seven days in which to lodge an appeal against the severity of it. If this was lodged, the subsequent 'Form 2' appeal hearing would normally be taken by a person who was not the one who had awarded the punishment, and who usually was more senior to the one who had. You were entitled to union representation at, or to take a fellow employee to, the appeal hearing. A footplateman would probably wish to take another footplateman, a clerk another clerk, etc., if a union representative was not preferred. This option was available because a small minority of staff were not union members. The person had to be employed within the same BR Region, but need not be in the same grade. We could not, for example, have a private solicitor as the application of the procedure was managed entirely 'in house'. At the 'Form 2' appeal the punishment would then be either confirmed, amended, or squashed, depending upon the merit of the appeal. If adjudged to still be guilty, the outcome was endorsed on our record. Provision existed for more serious cases of wrong doing to go to a third, senior management level, for review before implementation, e.g., if a dismissal, or reduction in grade, was proposed. Generally speaking, it was a reliable and well understood system. The key objective was not to get into it, in the first place.

Footplate work is by its very nature, as has been previously mentioned, a potentially dangerous occupation. It is misleading not to acknowledge this fact. Some of today's writers are guilty by omission in choosing to ignore this important facet of it. It is all very well to be admired when in the public vision at a station platform, but the reality can be very different. The risk of a mishap occurring is ever present, and usually without any prior warning. Getting badly scalded, for example, can easily happen as will be explained. Skin burns and blisters became part of the unwritten job specification. A blow back (when flames rush out of the firehole door) could result in a serious, even fatal, outcome. Even a routine hazard, such as a gauge glass exploding, is dangerous if not dealt with correctly. Yes, our work could and did, on many days, give immense job satisfaction with successful outcomes to mainly minor difficulties - which were many! You usually had just a good, routine day with only minor problems to deal with. But, it could just as equally be frustrating as the situation with No. 61612, above, has outlined, when the circumstances got beyond us. Very rarely, a more extreme event could occur. For me, a sequence of events commenced on Friday 25th November, 1955 which triggered a chain reaction that culminated with a very serious outcome.

On this day, we were running into London with our regular engine No. 61335, with my regular mate, Bill Frost, on the 1.13 pm up passenger from Southend. Going through the London end junctions at Bethnal Green a bad dip in the pointwork caused the engine suddenly to lurch, with me giving the cab floor a wash down with the slacker pipe to tidy up before the terminus. This was a normal routine at a suitable moment with no immediate need for signal observation. We liked to arrive in London with a tidy cab, as did most crews. The severe jolt caused me to lose hold of the pipe. This immediately spun out of control (being under high pressure) very seriously scalding one ankle. Urgent treatment at Bart's Hospital and relief of me by a Stratford fireman to cover the return working had to be arranged.

The doctor said, 'Okay' to continue normal work, but not on that first day, if my promise to rest it as much as possible was complied with. The resulting severe discomfort was manageable as '35' was a very good engine for steaming, once you knew how to fire her, as previously mentioned. The following Monday, after resting the ankle over the weekend, the burns were redressed. This was organised during our turnaround time in Liverpool St between the 7.25 am up and the 10.18 am down passenger workings. Relief was arranged in advance by our running foreman, to enable me to visit the hospital. So far, so good - it was painful, but bearable, and slowly healing. The next redressing was to be on Thursday.

Fate now took a hand. On Tuesday (29th) there was a derailment at Rayleigh which caused us to be terminated at Wickford on the down working. We were instructed to return to London with emergency authority to run at restricted speed tender first as an 11.45 am special passenger, arriving at 12.45 pm. Class 'B1s' were too long to be turned on either the Wickford or Shenfield turntables, which were the only available options. The sight of such a special working running up the main line, with the engine the wrong way round, would have been unique. We then worked the 1.50 pm down passenger through to Southend, as by then the derailment had been cleared.

The ankle did not like either the extra work or the total mileage of 145, when it should have been just 85 miles. The next day it had swollen. Being on '35', I managed with help from Bill - good regular mates did this kind of thing for each other. (Bill returned to work on one occasion after a spell off with shingles down one side of his face. I did his oiling duties for a couple of days. He stayed in the warm cab doing my duties. You just helped each other, it was a normal thing to do.) On Thursday, Bill had to fail '35' during our preparation duties. The standby pilot was class 'B17' No. 61600 *Sandringham*, known to be not the best riding machine. Because of the hospital appointment we decided I should persevere and work the 7.18 am. This turned out to be an unwise decision, but too late to alter once you are out on the road. With help from Bill, we got to London. My turnaround relief was waiting as arranged, the same as on Monday. The doctor took one look at the by now seriously inflamed ankle and ruled 'enough was enough'. He signed me off sick there and then. He would not hear of any argument to the contrary. He even threatened to keep me in overnight, so concerned was he about the risk of further infection. The wound was not looking too good. It resulted in a week on the sick list (with further visits for treatment) and then a short spell on light duties on the passenger pilot before he would pass me as fit for main line duties.

Bill had therefore to work the 10.18 am with my relief fireman, who had come up from Stratford shed. At Rayleigh there was single line working in operation due to engineering work. On the single line they had the extreme misfortune to knock down two men. Sadly, one was killed. The train was travelling at a low speed on the wrong line, i.e., against the normal direction of travel. This was being done entirely correctly under procedures written for such circumstances. For a long time afterwards, a strong feeling of, 'If only it had been me on the engine, would it have occurred?', persisted. This would not go from my mind, try as hard as I might. Everybody said it was quite wrong to feel that my absence from the footplate had let Bill down through trying to keep at work. One or two even said to think like this was stupid, as nobody could have foreseen the circumstance, it was a pure chance event. But, men had been knocked down. A regular set of men together develop a close harmony of safe working practices. Each comes to instinctively rely upon the other, without having to ask for this. Bill had a strange fireman, neither knowing the other, being from different sheds - was it a factor? It will never be known.

In my later career it was necessary to attend inquiries into the events surrounding men being killed out on the track and elsewhere, fortunately not very often. Without exception they were very distressing to everybody concerned, and all were caused by the unforeseen circumstances of a momentary lapse of concentration. One incident in particular is recalled involving a track ganger who was concerned to watch the extent of vertical track movement under a passing train. He was correctly standing in a safe place while doing so, confirmed by the driver of the approaching second train travelling in the same direction on an adjoining track. After the first train had passed, he then stepped back into the path of the second train, giving the driver no warning or chance to sound the whistle again. The driver had sounded it as he approached, but with no acknowledging wave, no doubt because the noise of the passing first train had prevented it being heard. The driver saw everything and found it hard to describe to us the sequence of what had happened. He was reliving every second in slow motion as he explained it all. In those days gangers would walk their 'length' alone with no one to look out for them, and because of this, accidents to such men were rare, due to the extreme care they exercised for their own protection. Usually, accidents tended to happen when a group of men were together. Today, much stricter safety procedures have considerably reduced the occurrence of both injuries and fatalities on the track. The very high risks attached to working in the vicinity of moving trains will always be a danger than cannot be totally solved.

Having a regular engine made life more enjoyable. We kept our cab in near immaculate condition. Mr Hardy, our assistant superintendent at Stratford, arranged a supply of the special 'Derby' cleaning paste for the copperwork. This was a mildly abrasive cleaning compound originally introduced by the old Midland Railway for its engine crews, hence the name, Derby being their headquarters. This was issued from the Stratford stores where it was normally reserved for the 'Britannia' top-link crews only. He issued this special authority for three regular-manned Southend engines - ours, No. 61576, and one other whose number now escapes me.

No. 61335 had the Stone's (of Deptford, London) system of steam-powered dynamo electric lighting that was kept in good order by ourselves. It was very useful during early morning preparation and late evening disposal duties. Not many engines, after such a long time in traffic as '35' had been since her last overhaul, had this equipment still working. It was regularly used and reduced the normal everyday hazards when working about the engine in darkness. Occasionally passengers would pass a remark as they walked by the cab with us reading a newspaper with the excellent cab roof light switched on. They couldn't relate steam to electricity. One even asked if we were plugged into a ground socket! Passengers often spoke to you. We knew several by sight who would pass their discarded newspapers to us. With our more frenetic, modern, life style, such older-fashioned kindly gestures are much less usual today.

Driver Frank Edwards and his mate with their regular engine 'B12/3' class 4-6-0 No. 61576 at Southend. The previous day, 28th December, 1956, they had worked the official last train from Liverpool Street to Southend with all the dignitaries as part of the celebrations to commemorate the introduction of electric services. The special clip bracket which can be seen below Frank's hands had been affixed to carry a plate with the crew name details. The dignitaries returned to Liverpool Street in one of the new trains, which became the first electric passenger carrying service to depart from Southend Victoria. *Author*

The highly polished cab interior of No. 61576 on her penultimate day on the 'Sarfends' as we would say. The three crews who regularly manned this engine took tremendous pride in her appearance, both inside the cab and externally. *Author*

Most engines did not have the luxury of electric lighting. Normal practice during darkness required the use of smelly paraffin flare lamps which could readily fall and maybe burn you with a momentary lapse of concentration. 'Flare' was the operative word! These 'lamps' (a misnomer really, as a lamp is normally enclosed behind glass) were a flat-bottomed, oblong, oval-shaped metal container with a handle at one end and a 4 to 6 in. length spout at the other end. Into this a cotton wick was inserted to soak up the paraffin to feed the open and entirely unprotected flame. The round wick was about ½ inch in diameter providing a sizeable flare, or flame. The container had an approx. 2 in. diameter filler hole that was plugged with a matching wooden stopper secured to a short chain, which would frequently work loose and could be accidentally knocked out quite easily, with the risk of the paraffin spilling out. This would be the driver's sole source of light to be carried around as he oiled up and checked over the engine ready for a turn of duty. At each oiling point it had to be placed on an adjoining ledge - if one was nearby - to leave both hands free. When oiling the inside motions it was necessary to climb up into them by standing on the brake hanger rodding to reach the oiling points. This required the flare lamp to be first lifted up above the head to be placed on a ledge before climbing up. It was all too easy to dislodge it if proper care was not exercised, especially if the motions were dirty and covered in an oily gunge as frequently occurred when a shed was short of cleaning staff. Such hazards were simply accepted as normal. They were not even queried, let alone challenged - even though suitable waterproof and shockproof electric lamps had been around in the outside world for several years! Battery handlamps were eventually introduced in the final era of steam on BR, but only because they were necessary for use on diesels. Many drivers carried their own electric hand torch using batteries at their own expense to avoid using the flare lamps.

Walking around the average dimly lit engine shed building offered many inherent risks to catch the unwary. Manhole covers, fire irons lying on the ground, ash and clinker, boiler washout pipework projecting at face level in some sheds, washout hoses on the floor, oil spillages, random lumps of coal - the list could go on. All waiting to knock you or trip you up in semi-darkness. Limited lighting often smudged with soot, were other normal hazards. Self-safety was practised as an instinctive routine, you quickly learned that to be otherwise was too dangerous. Obvious hazards were attended to, such as a loose fire iron lying unsafely on the ground. All too frequently it was just the inbuilt nature of the workplace that one could do little about. Imagine carrying the normal engine preparation kit of a heavy bucket of tools, up to four full bottles of engine oils, a coal pick hammer and two firing shovels, for maybe a quarter of a mile at some sheds. This was a normal daily work requirement. Sometimes you had almost to grope your way alongside freshly lit-up engines churning out thick sulphurous smoke. You had little choice but to continue walking. (On ex-GE passenger engines, four oil bottles were required - engine, cylinder, Westinghouse pump, and paraffin for headlamps/flare lamp/gauge glass lamp. In other areas you had no need of the Westo oil which made life slightly easier.) No amount of lighting could penetrate the thick smoke inside, say, the Jubilee shed at Stratford, when the firelighter had been on his rounds. We accepted this as our normal life, we were fully accustomed to do so. Shed floors were regularly swept and scraped

Class 'B12/3' 4-6-0 No. 61576 on No.2 shed road at Southend.   *Author*

Class 'B1' 4-6-0 No. 61335 on the turntable at Southend in 1956.   *Author*

clean, but with on-going engine activity, disposal, preparation, shed shunting, all the time, you had to be constantly alert. Some sounds instinctively warned you to beware in amongst the general cacophony of noise that was the on-going background to any busy shed. Handbrakes being screwed off, the squeal of wheels, vibration in the rail if you were under an engine, whistles sounding, a donkey pump being started or a large vacuum ejector being blown to create brake power prior to movement of an engine, someone trimming coal, the rattle of a fire iron - all carried a potential warning message. But, it took experience to learn and to recognise these preliminary signs of a potential risk. It was an instinctive practice always to look out, then shout out, then sound the whistle and to take a second quick look round outside an engine before moving it. Looking back, in retrospect, it is amazing to recall how few were the accidents that did occur, relative to the extent of exposure to serious risk that we routinely accepted.

It is nice to see the carefully tended, usually spotlessly clean engines and generally tidy shed working areas on our preserved railways. They are a far cry from the daily reality in which we worked and overcame the normal hazards of running shed conditions. This is not a moan, just an explanation of facts to highlight the comparison of today with our daily life. We didn't have to tolerate it , we could have changed our employment. When 'steam is in the blood' (as Mr Hardy has said in his book with a similar title) we were not keen to give it up. But, and it is an important 'but', this did not justify all of the regular occupational hazards we had to endure. It is sad, but true, that very senior management in those times begrudged spending on even small improvements. Steam was going, why spend? Unless, that is, it became absolutely essential to do so. Simple improvements could have given benefits out of all proportion to the finance required. Capital investment on new facilities - as opposed to maintenance expenditure on existing facilities - was difficult to get authority for from headquarters. Management at ground level was often as frustrated as the staff were, by the severe financial stringencies imposed. In later years the purse strings had to be relaxed as stricter safety standards were introduced. But, as always, life had its brighter moments, to balance the adversities. Let me describe one such occurrence.

Shortly before the end of steam passenger workings, Bill and I came to work on 4th December, 1956, to discover class 'B12' No. 61573 rostered to us, when '35' was available. Needless to say - we asked why? Back came the answer. 'It is a special request, as you have an important person riding with you on the down road trip'. Mystified, we worked up with the 12.05 pm parcels to Liverpool St as scheduled. Backing onto our return working, the 5.33 pm, generally accepted as one of the toughest workings for a 'B1', let alone a 'B12', we spotted inspector Percy Howard on the platform and thought, 'Oh well, here goes!' Percy was always a very fair minded manager. He would not tolerate poor engine management, but always made allowances when justified. He had a realistic approach to our problems and was respected for his objective attitude. Our mount was one of the stronger 'B12s', but the wear and tear of many miles since last being overhauled was evident. A good fire, ready for the task ahead, had been built up before Percy stepped up to introduce Mr R.C. Riley, the well known railway photographer. As for the trip itself, Bill got stuck in, determined to make good progress with our heavy train. So much so, his fireman had a bit of a

Driver Bill Frost again, this time on the engine we had for the footplate trip of the well known railway photographer, R.C. Riley, as described in the text. In front of the three headlamps on the tender can be seen the wheel for working the water scoop.   *Author*

Class 'B17/4' 4-6-0 No. 61661 *Sheffield Wednesday*, seen here with a 180 psi boiler approaches Warners Bridge between Prittlewell and Rochford with an up road working just a few weeks before she was overhauled and rebuilt to class 'B17/6' with the 225 psi boiler.   *Author*

struggle to keep up, until after we had passed Shenfield! We stopped, well on schedule, at Brentwood with half a glass of water. We were down a little on steam pressure from the decent pace Bill had been setting. But, we got away very smartly up the hardest stretch of the bank off the end of the platform, on the 1 in 80 incline. The flag was kept flying, even if the white feather from the safety valves wasn't until we got onto the branch! No. 61573 was always a good engine and didn't let us down. Her regular crew didn't like losing her, any more than we had wanted to have her. It was an enjoyable run, with thanks given to the 'important person', for the experience of a trip with a difference that varied the usual routine. It was virtually unknown to have a 'B12' on this, the heaviest loading train of the steam-worked down evening services. Mr Riley duly included details of our run in the article he wrote about the final days of steam on the Southend line - my one very minor moment of public acclaim!

Mention has been made of the various classes of engine that operated from the shed. Checking back through my notes it is surprising for such a modest sized shed to realise the wide variety of classes we had through the 1950s. Let me list them: 'B1', 'B2', 'B12', 'B17', 'J15', 'J17', 'J19', 'J20', 'J39', 'J67', 'J69', 'K1', 'K2', 'K3', 'L1', 'N2', 'N7', LM 'Tilbury' tanks, and BR Standard '4s' - all, with the exception of the class 'J15' (only rare visits), regularly being seen on shed at differing times. The class 'L1s' were common in 1951/52, but had largely disappeared by 1955/56 with only occasional appearances. The class 'J17s' included, in 1956, No. 65563, a regular at the shed throughout that summer. Class 'J19s' appeared mainly in the early 1950s. Class 'K1s' and the BR '4s', unknown in 1951/52, were both regular visitors during the final months of 1956. Class 'B2s' were less common - George Morris and I even had the Cambridge reserve royal engine on 17th October, 1956, No. 61617 *Ford Castle*, all very highly polished as well (and what a good old rattler she was!). Class 'K2s' were common in 1951/52, but had gone by 1956. Other classes had visited the shed not too long before my arrival. The class 'A5', ex-GC design, 4-6-2 tanks, had worked for a spell earlier in 1951 when the Liverpool St turntable was being rebuilt; a class 'F5' 2-4-2 tank, No. 67203, was for many months the passenger shunt engine in 1950/51 and, not long prior to this period, 'Claud' 4-4-0 tender engines had been used before their transfer away from Stratford to East Anglian country sheds. The class 'K2s', with their ex-GN design tall lever reverse and spartan cab comfort with no side windows for protection from the elements, were probably the least liked of the regular visitors, although a good workmanlike mount upon which to do a day's work.

The class 'N2' 0-6-2 tanks, another ex-GN design, had a limited existence, being cast-offs from elsewhere. They were all non-condenser engines (see next chapter for explanation of this). Definitely not 'top of the range' models, and very unpopular, although I was to come to admire them, as will be revealed. The remaining classes were constant occupants at the shed, generally giving reliable service up to the very end, notwithstanding some dubious riding qualities. Details of engines in use on a typical day shortly before steam ceased are listed in the Table on page 163.

Class 'N2' 0-6-2T No. 69523 at Stratford in 1955 and since preserved as LNER No. 4744, after being one of the final batch of engines withdrawn when the class became extinct in September 1962.   *Author*

BR Standard class '4MT' 2-6-0 No. 76034 at Southend shed in 1955.   *Author*

The first time a 'Claud Hamilton' had visited Southend for many years was in 1955, it also proved to be the last such visit. Class 'D16/3' No. 62518 was working an officers' inspection special to review the progress of the electrification works. The locomotive had just been outshopped from Stratford works and was being used for this working prior to being returned to its home shed. It was one of the last few survivors from a total of 121 engines that had been built, withdrawal came in October 1958.   *Author*

A 'Skirted Lady' outside the engine repair shop at Stratford works, showing the ex-GER ornamental valances over 7 ft diameter driving wheels of class 'D16/3' No. 62592.   *Author*

The last Belpaire-boilered ex-GER tender engine to remain in traffic in 1955, No. 64676, seen here on No. 2 shed road at Southend, just a few weeks before she entered Stratford works to be rebuilt with the small round-top boiler, similar to all other members of the 'J20' class. Both designs of boiler were common to the 'B12' class engines (before many of this class were in turn rebuilt with the larger round-top boiler to become class 'B12/3') which explains the large size of the 'J20' machines with their long wheelbase, as can be clearly seen in this view. For over 20 years until the advent of Bulleid utility 'Q1' class 0-6-0s, the 'J20s' were the most powerful six-coupled engines in the country. They were capable of not only hauling, but more importantly, also being able to stop heavy trains and were very useful on the Southend road where their power on the lengthy ruling 1 in 100 gradients was put to very effective use. They almost certainly avoided the scheduling of a daily fifth goods service, by being available to handle the four booked services that were required daily Mondays to Saturdays to meet the normal traffic demands prior to the 1955 ASLEF strike. *Author*

This view illustrates the difficulties that could be experienced when the forward view was seriously hampered by steam gland packings blowing at the front end. Apart from the wasted effort to produce the wasted steam, such conditions could be extremely hazardous for the crew. This unidentified 'B12/3' class 4-6-0 approaches Warners Bridge near Southend in 1955. *Author*

Table Three - Southend Shed Engine Diagram Roster, 20th December, 1956

This details a typical day in the last full week of normal working. The following, final week, included the Christmas holiday and modified arrangements for the steam to electric changeover. The shed required a roster of about 30 engines, but, by the final week the run down had begun with spares provision being reduced. The need for a normal on-going maintenance cover was not required with engines scheduled for imminent scrapping, particularly of class 'B12', when 10 were to be withdrawn almost immediately as a direct result of the Southend line electrification.

Diagram No.	Engine No.	Class	Train Depart	Notes
71	61000	B1	1.45 Goods	A rare roster for a B1
PP	69725	N7	5.00	Passr Stn Shunt Pilot
17	61575	B12	4.53 Cars	For 5.03 departure from Rochford
18	61360	B1	5.14 Passr	
11	61663	B17	5.51 Passr	
77	68529	J67	6.00	Goods Yard Shunt Pilot
1	61921	K3	6.03 Passr	
16	61335	B1	6.14 Passr	
73	64769	J39	6.30 LE	To Wickford
12	61602	B17	6.38 Passr	
22	61516	B12	6.50 LE	To Shenfield
20	61600	B17	6.59 Passr	
13	61609	B17	7.10 Passr	
14	61362	B1	7.22 Passr	
19	61654	B17	7.38 Passr	
21	61553	B12	8.17 Passr	
15	61361	B1	8.35 Passr	
76	64676	J20	9.18 Goods	
23	61000	B1	10.44 Passr	
71	64677	J20	1.00 LE	Hockley, etc. Shunt
24	61516	B12	5.06 Passr	
72	64675	J20	5.30 Goods	Standby spare until 4.00
25	61558	B12	6.25 Passr	Standby spare until 5.00
Pilot	61519	B12		Standby spare, kept in steam
Wash Out	61578	B12		
	68636	J69		
Blow Down	61335, 61361, 61558 - done at night before engines entered traffic			
Stopped	69616	N7		Under Repair

Unusually on this date, no class 'K1' engine was at the shed. The previous day, No. 62015 had worked the 5.51 am, and the following day, No. 62033 worked the 6.03 am. The smallness of the remaining class 'B12' fleet will be noted. Most had been progressively moved away in the preceding days, for re-allocation elsewhere or to be withdrawn for scrapping. From our long time normal allocation of up to 12 engines, only half survive on this list - Nos. 61516, 61519, 61553, 61558, 61575, and 61578.

It was the job of the late turn running foreman to compile the engine working list for the following day. Throughout most of 1956 a lot of these were saved from the waste bin. These records provide a silent commentary recording the locomotives working from the shed during the final year of full steam working. The record is by no means complete, but a sufficient number were saved (about 50 per cent) to give a fairly accurate picture of the power provision. An unexpected bonus is that most were written on the reverse of discarded engine diagram workings, unfortunately incomplete, but still of interest. A specimen sample is reproduced here which also gives a sample text layout of how our diagrams were advised to us.

SATURDAY, 10th MARCH 1956.

SOUTHEND DEPOT

No.101.

	Loco	5. 5pm L
	Southend Vic.	6.20
8.44pm	Goodmayes	9.54
12. 3am	Southend Vic.	
	GP	3.30 L SUN
	Loco	

1st Set Cancelled.

2nd & 3rd Sets as booked

No. 103.

	Loco	5.45am L
6.10am	Wickford	6.50

and as booked

1st Set On duty 4.45am

2nd Set As booked.

No. 102.
Engine of No.102 dgm FRIDAY.

	Stratford Loco	3.45am LA
	Outlet	3.55 LA
4.22am	Goodmayes	4.48
8.20	Southend Vic	L
	Loco	9.35 L
	Southend Vic.	9.50
1.23pm	Goodmayes	2.34pm
4.40	Southend Vic.	L
	Loco	8.45 L
	Southend Vic.	9. 0
11.52	Goodmayes	12.20amL SUN
12.43am	Stratford Loco	

1st Set (Stratford Men) On duty 2.45am
Home passrs. per 9.45am to Shenfield,
thence per 10.45am.

2nd Set On duty 8.35am
Relieved on arrival Southend.

3rd Set (Stratford Men) On duty 5.30pm
Passrs. per 5.53pm to Shenfield, thence
per 6.30pm to Southend.

**Engine works as per No.102 dgm.
MONDAY.**

===

Issued at Shenfield.
Monday, 5th March 1956.

G.F.Fiennes,
Operating Superintendent,
LIVERPOOL STREET.

An example of a typical Engine & Men's Diagram Working Notice to alter normal rostered
workings. These workings covered special engineer's trains in connection with the electrification
work.

On Saturday 29th December the odd one or two, and on Sunday all, up trains were steam hauled and down trains dc electric worked, to a pre-planned programme which cleared the shed of nearly all passenger steam engines and the line of all locomotive-hauled passenger rolling stock. It positioned the new dc electric stock ready for Monday morning. At 3.00 pm on the Sunday, the remaining passenger engines on shed were Nos. 61335/61/62, 61576, 61600 *Sandringham*, 61610 *Honingham Hall*, 61672 *West Ham United* and 61942. The very last passenger engines went LE to Stratford late on the Sunday night. I did not ascertain which was the last down passenger train to be steam hauled on the Saturday. Bill and I worked together on '35' for the last time on this day when we worked up with the 6.14 am to Liverpool St and returned with the 9.10 am down service. The last steam-hauled up passenger working was the 8.50 pm on the Sunday, worked by driver Fred Tomlinson and fireman Mick Bonham with '35'. Fred was chosen for this honour as the senior driver who had worked for the longest period at the shed. Mr Hardy could not miss such an occasion and was on board as the inspector, after having spent the afternoon helping to give our old girl a clean up for the final trip. He kindly invited me to join them in the cab at Wickford for the run up to Liverpool St. This was not without its moments, but a final signal delay precluded a right time arrival, one minute late was booked to the engine, the balance being booked to signals - he said he would settle for that! The trip home in the new electric unit was a sad occasion for the few of us who had ridden the up train for old times' sake. I used the new service to report for duty at 9.00 am at King's Cross shed, the following morning. It was a peculiar experience to be sitting with passengers whom we had for so long past been taking to work.

Table Four - No. 61335 8.50 pm Southend (Victoria)-Liverpool Street, 30th December, 1956*

		WTT	Actual			WTT	Actual
Southend	dep.	8.50	8.52	Shenfield	arr.	9.36	9.38½
Prittlewell	arr.	8.52½	8.54½		dep.	9.37	9.40¾
	dep.	8.53	8.55	Brentwood	pass	(9.41½)	9.48
Rochford	arr.	8.57	8.58¾	Romford	arr.	9.50	9.56
	dep.	8.58	8.59¼		dep.	9.51	9.57
Hockley	arr.	9.03	9.04¼	Ilford	arr.	9.59	10.04
	dep.	9.04	9.05¼		dep.	10.00	10.04½
Rayleigh	arr.	9.10	9.11	Stratford	arr.	10.07	10.10½
	dep.	9.11	9.12		dep.	10.08	10.10¾
Wickford	arr.	9.17	9.17½	Bethnal Green	pass	10.14	10.16
	dep.	9.18	9.18½	signal stop 10.18¼ - 10.19½			
Billericay	arr.	9.28	9.28½				
	dep.	9.29	9.30	Liverpool St	arr.	10.17	10.22

Notes
i)   The locomotive was eased approximately 1½ miles before Billericay station.
ii) The WTT gives no passing time at Brentwood. The time shown has been interpolated from standard start-to stop timings for Southend line trains in the same WTT, i.e. Shenfield-Brentwood trains 5 min., Brentwood-Romford 9 min.
iii) There was a slack through Maryland station.
iv) The WTT specified Liverpool St arrival in platform 13, actual arrival was in platform 11.

* Supplied by Ken Butcher, the author's brother.

Class 'J69/1' 'Buckjumper' 0-6-0T No. 68636, the final member of this very numerous class of 160 engines to enter traffic in 1904, being built for working the inner London area suburban services. During the final months of steam on the Southend branch she became the regular passenger shunt pilot at Victoria station, being recorded here after the overhead wiring is complete and waiting for trial energisation just eight weeks before the changeover to the new traction. *Author*

The final day of down road steam workings on Saturday 29th December, 1956. With my regular mate, Bill Frost, we have just completed our final working together on our long time regular engine, class 'B1' No. 61335. It was a sad day to realise it was all over for us, after 15 very happy months together. On Monday Bill went 'electric', '35' went to the shops for a long overdue overhaul, having covered 91,000 miles since her last general overhaul with no intermediate overhaul since, and your author began a new life at King's Cross shed. *Author*

Within days, our old faithful was admitted to Stratford works for a complete general overhaul, having covered 91,000 miles without an intermediate repair. This had been permitted following our request to Mr Hardy to keep her until the end. He agreed we could, knowing we looked after her, and that she still rode tolerably well, although getting rough. He very kindly had her photographed after the overhaul and sent us all a copy. It was suggested this may have been the highest mileage ever reached by a class 'B1' engine without any works overhaul being undertaken (the trailing axleboxes had required a brief visit to the works when an oil feed pipe broke causing one box to run hot, but no other repairs were done). He wrote personally to both the regular drivers, Fred Tomlinson and my own mate, Bill Frost, to compliment them on this achievement.

Mr Hardy was a manager who cared - he took a considerable interest in his men, both footplate and workshop, and spent as much time as he possibly could being among us. He would often be seen out and about, riding with his enginemen, or just pausing for a quick chat as he walked along the platform, perhaps to a meeting somewhere. Stratford was a very large district and yet most enginemen could recognise him by sight, or if not, certainly knew of him. This was no mean achievement, as I was to discover. There were many who had reason to thank him for some little kindness he had taken the trouble to organise, or some detail attention to the working arrangements he had adjusted following a comment to him. The GE section was fortunate to have him during the many upheavals that occurred as the entire East Anglian area was progressively modernised. When you are working at ground level on shifts you often could not name, let alone recognise, your senior officers who were just faceless bosses. Mr Hardy was one of a very few managers who would climb on an engine, entirely unannounced. He could do our job, either driving or firing, and was greatly respected for this. He knew most of our roads, which again was very unusual. Drivers would offer him the chance to have hold of their engines, knowing he was fully competent to do so. Like most managers he could not tolerate fools very well, but if you had a genuine concern he would always listen and, often as not, give you an answer. You may not have liked his reply, but he was direct and straightforward.

The ASLEF union was the main one at the shed, but the NUR had members as well. There were about 150 footplate staff in the line of promotion, when at full strength, of whom about 15 were NUR, the remainder being ASLEF members. We were under this overall total in the final months, as was to be expected. Secret ballots were held to choose our union representatives to sit on the Local Departmental Committee (LDC). They were our shop stewards, if you prefer to quote from outside industry. Unlike some of their outside (to the industry) namesakes they were very rarely militant. Our industrial relations were normally conducted in an atmosphere of co-operation, not confrontation. The LDC was the formal means for discussions between management and staff at our local, i.e., shed, level. Our representatives were not nominated according to membership of a particular union or being in a particular grade. We chose representatives entirely at local level, whom we thought would be best able to represent our points of view. There was little direct, or even indirect,

The final up Southend steam working on Sunday 30th December, 1956. Standing in front of the cab of 'B1' class No. 61335 are, *from the left*, your author, R.H.N. Hardy, Fred Tomlinson and unidentified.   *Author's Collection*

A 1,500 dc electric train waits to leave Southend Victoria on the newly electrified line.
British Railways

'L1' class 2-6-4T No. 67731 shunts Southend Victoria electric set at Goodmayes yard on 13th March, 1962. *M. Edwards*

interference by union HQ. The local meetings were a two-way process between management and the staff whereby each side could raise, and hopefully resolve, issues. This committee did an excellent job throughout the many problems that arose with the demise of steam.

If a matter could not be resolved at the local LDC meeting level, a procedure existed for our shedmaster to refer his point of view upwards to Stratford (the location of the district motive power superintendent's office). Our representatives would refer our point of view upwards to Union Headquarters. Both sides would then bring the matter forward for discussion and decision at the Sectional Council level. Half a century ago it was not generally realised or understood outside the rail industry how well our industrial relations procedures were structured. They permitted full and democratic discussion between employees and management. This was in sharp contrast to many other large organisations' procedures at the time. Very few had such effective means of formal discussion available. The excellent procedures that had been developed over time within our industry explained the comparative freedom we enjoyed from industrial disputes. There were pockets of industrial unrest, mainly in large goods depots, but these were the exception. When we did have a general dispute, it achieved media headlines, being such a rare occurrence. A key part of our procedures stemmed from the fullest possible involvement of the employee representatives, at local and national level, in the management decision process. Such principles have now become more widely introduced by industry.

Long before such requirements were established through government intervention, the rail industry had two primary methods of formal communication between employee and manager. These were the 'Negotiation' and the 'Consultation' procedures. Under the negotiation procedures, general matters discussed would include local working arrangements. It might, for example, be management seeking agreement to diagram a working shift of extra time on duty above the normal national agreement limits. Under the negotiation procedure our representatives had the right to refuse to agree, but not a right to refuse the management wish to negotiate. Under the consultation procedure, management would advise their intention to pursue a policy that was, in principle, not negotiable, such as the decision to electrify the Southend line. The two procedures frequently worked in tandem alongside each other at the same meeting. The consultation matter would be advised at an initial meeting as a proposal being considered and a response invited from the staff representatives. At subsequent meetings the progress of the proposal into a firm decision and how it was to be implemented would be advised, i.e., consulted upon. The core decision usually created residual queries. These in turn would be discussed between the two sides to agree the best option for each query. Depending upon the individual matter it would be dealt with by the relevant procedure. By structuring the discussion meetings in this manner, we, as employees, were kept in the picture, which was sound sense. We had the right, through our elected representatives to have our input considered before 'tablets of stone' were created. Having been both an employee and a manager, I can say with clarity, it was a well structured system. It worked and made a huge unsung but very positive impact on the whole spectrum of our industrial relations. These principles are now incorporated into industrial relations arrangements in most industries (other than maybe by some smaller employers), when previously no comparable structure of formal management/staff liaison arrangements were in place. Obviously, some larger employers had their own arrangements, but this was not always so.

About 55 of us on the footplate lost our jobs at the shed. All who desired it were found positions at other sheds, with most transferring to Stratford. It was a period of considerable upheaval. The close-knit camaraderie that working together with a mate on a steam locomotive encouraged was to be severely tested. In the final weeks men who retained their jobs were working with others who were to lose them. Most accepted and understood the position. A small minority of drivers were tactless enough to say they were looking forward to being by themselves. This didn't endear them to their firemen. In the event matters came to a peaceful conclusion. There was little rancour and a very great amount of sadness and regret at the passing of the old order.

There was one general criticism voiced of the process through which we had gone over the preceding months. The majority of us leaving the shed for good, did so on the Saturday. Nobody from the management side was on hand to speak to those being made redundant as we completed our final turns of duty on the Saturday morning. It was a major scheme to reduce the staff numbers. Our own representatives were there, but management created the impression of ignoring the issue, whether or not this was the intention. Engines and men came on shed to complete their final disposal duties. We said 'cheerio' to our drivers, were met by an LDC member for a brief chat, and went home just as if we would be returning again the next day. Southend had always been a happy shed, and the lack of such a gesture was not typical. A short general letter of appreciation addressed to us individually could have been sent out - it wasn't. All we had received, was the strictly official letter of redundancy advice in accordance with our conditions of service, stipulating in impersonal terms what was to become of us.

It was a lesson in staff relationships that left a lasting memory not forgotten when, in my later career, I was the management. I made a special point of seeing our clerk, Tom Jackson, to thank him, but not everybody bothered to do this for a man who had been a real friend to us all. It was a final antipathy partially because of the apparent local management indifference. Mr Hardy made the effort and visited the shed to spend Saturday afternoon and most of the final Sunday speaking to as many of the men as he could meet. Being a Sunday, there were fewer at work, but his interest was appreciated by those of us whom he met. It was an action entirely typical of him, even though he had obviously forfeited time at home with his family to be with us instead.

Some men, particularly amongst the more senior ones, found the change difficult to come to terms with. Most welcomed the cleaner environment, but some found the loneliness of the motorman's life difficult to accept. They missed having a regular mate alongside them to share their working day. A small number really missed the daily rough and tumble that was the steam engine, but the majority did not. I still regularly met many of my former drivers.

These views are a summary of their opinions expressed over the following couple of years travelling with them. Regular invitations were extended to ride in their cabs when travelling between King's Cross shed and my lodgings in Ilford - they welcomed the chance to have someone to ride with them. If another person was already there, the invitation was always declined. The driver plus myself only was my own, purely personal, firm rule. Being correctly qualified, and knowing the road, you fully understood when not to distract the driver. They were always interested to hear of my progress, especially when the move came on to main line work. They wanted to hear of the overnight fast goods, and the expresses to Newcastle, etc. Dare it be said, they could become very nostalgic talking about 'the old days' although usually agreeing their new life style had definite advantages!

And so ended the long history of steam passenger working on the former GER route to Southend. The shed did not finally close to steam until much later, as the goods workings continued with steam haulage until the eventual change to diesel power. My records do not cover this era, having moved to King's Cross, to be described in the next chapter. But, before we continue the next phase of our journey together, does Rule 0 require attention?

'L1' class 2-6-4T No. 67735 at Liverpool Street ready to haul an electric set to Gidea Park after a derailment at Bethnal Green had cut electric services on 17th June, 1962.

Leslie Sandler

Chapter Six

The Footplate Years - King's Cross Suburban

Reporting for duty at an entirely strange shed inevitably created a feeling of apprehension, leaving the Great Eastern section behind to venture upon new territory. The Great Northern section (GN) embraced different working practices. The 1923 Grouping may have amalgamated separate railways into the one LNER company, but the individualistic operating ways of the former companies still survived to a considerable extent. Not least, the inbuilt suspicions towards staff transferred from another section. Every section had practices and prejudices that were jealously safeguarded - a culture not universally agreed with by everybody. The spirit and inbuilt pride engendered by the former pre-Grouping companies, not only survived, it thrived. Generally, this encouraged positive attitudes. The surprise was to experience a negative prejudice of an intensity and initial bitterness that was totally unexpected. It came as a shock to discover that such an attitude could still survive after 34 years since the Grouping. Events were to confirm the proverbial 'short straw' had been drawn and prove my experience to be an almost, but not quite, isolated exception to the rule. By far and away most staff were very helpful in explaining the different working practices. But, a small hard-core of hostility existed towards 'foreigners', as we were called, that had still to disappear.

In 1957 a significant proportion of the drivers at King's Cross were original GN men. Many had 1919 seniority dates, from when the eight hour working day was introduced. This had required a large number of extra staff to be employed. Unfortunately, the early post-Grouping era witnessed an influx of transfers to the shed particularly from the Great Central (GC) section. This had caused much resentment because the promotion prospects of the ex-GN men were seriously retarded as a result. Many of the foreigners at that time had higher seniority and therefore secured earlier promotion to the detriment of the existing ex-GN men. This created serious conflict. Prejudices also developed against the different working practices the ex-GC men brought with them. They initially tried to get these accepted to the detriment of the established GN practices. Their greater willingness to work overtime, for example, inhibited additional staff recruitment and thus promotion prospects. The brush once tarred, was thereafter applied to all strangers from elsewhere, even though there was little on-going justification for this. Prejudices, once established, have a habit of creating cultures and attitudes that can take many years to overcome. Foreigners, i.e., any non-originating GN section staff, all suffered as a result, and particularly so in the earlier years of the new LNER. But first a comment on some of the different working practices it was necessary to learn.

On the GN section, footplate crews did not do their own coupling to trains. Shunters were provided at every station to undertake this duty where trains were booked to start or terminate. At King's Cross we never disposed of our engines upon arrival on the shed. There were separate staff to do these tasks. All

A 1953 view from the North London line of the Great Northern main line and King's Cross goods yard between Caledonian Road and Camden Road.

R.E. Vincent

trains were vacuum braked, without a Westinghouse pump to be seen (or heard!). It was quite simply the way it always had been. These circumstances were taken as normal, because that was the way the old GNR had structured its working arrangements. In contrast, on the GE section, passenger train shunters and engine firedroppers were a rarer breed - footplate staff had always done these duties and thought nothing of it. This was how the old GER had decided to structure its working arrangements. To a GN engineman firedropping at the larger sheds was unknown; at the smaller ones there was no alternative and men accepted these duties were part of their normal work. King's Cross was very definitely a larger shed! In the eyes of some men, we who came from sections that did this were treated almost as 'blacklegs', because the practice deprived people of employment. With coupling duties this did create employment. We, who had always performed these tasks, knew no different because this was how we had been trained. You can imagine the reaction that occurred when initially attempting to perform these duties, not knowing otherwise. It was a steep learning curve! The old GNR management looked for fuller productivity from enginemen, and had decided disposal duties would be carried out by less skilled staff. Hence, why ex-GN section enginemen jealously safeguarded such working practices. And why the later managements - LNER and BR - expected, and generally achieved, more productive train workings within the basic rostered day, although this was always an arguable situation.

My first week was occupied working on the North London shunt trip workings - 'occupied' because working on the 350 hp diesel-electric shunters did not require a shovel. A fireman was required to work over running lines, unlike on engines confined to yard working limits only. The learning of new roads began again! Our duties included the steeply graded North London incline. One of the fireman's jobs was to walk alongside the locomotive (remember it is a diesel we are discussing) to spread small ballast on the rails by hand to supplement the normal sanding, which might also need 'encouragement' with the use of a hammer to tap the sand box discharge pipe. In this manner we would gradually slip and grind our way upwards towards the Maiden Lane exchange sidings at the top. Being in January it was bitterly cold and damp, or raining, to add a touch of unwanted realism to the proceedings, with no hot firebox to dry you out We also shunted, each day, the Caledonian coal yard that was located high above the Copenhagen main line tunnels (the second set of tunnels after leaving King's Cross passenger station). This yard has long since gone and the land redeveloped for other uses. It was reached via a long and very impressive steeply graded curved viaduct (more sanding of the rails by hand!) that, much to my surprise, still partially survived, with no track, in 1996. Seeing this remaining structure still standing 40 years later, readily brought back the memories now being described. Working on these turns allowed me to become acquainted with the goods yard workings and practices, of which more in a later chapter.

The second week was spent out on the main line on goods transfer trips between the inner London area goods yards of King's Cross, Ferme Park, East Yard and Clarence Yard. Yet again more road learning, knowledge that was soon to be useful as my drivers began teaching the various signals and road

Class 'N2/4' 0-6-2T No. 69585 waits to depart from the notorious platform 16 at King's Cross with an empty stock working to Finsbury Park from Moorgate. It required keen attention by enginemen to ensure a clean start from this location on a steep uphill gradient with trap points located in rear of the last coach to safeguard the Widened Lines route to St Pancras behind the train. In adverse weather conditions engines would occasionally stall and require assistance. Towards the end of steam with the ageing 'N2s' beginning to cause concern, regular assistance began to be rostered to avoid delays with the heaviest loading trains. The train engine would stop short of the platform end to leave room for the assistant engine to gently back on, couple up and work double-headed to Finsbury Park where it would be detached. The very light haze from the chimney and the white feather at the safety valves indicate a fireman in full control to give his driver the maximum steam pressure with a good white hot fire without blowing off, which can be very distracting in such a situation when the driver is concentrating to achieve a trouble-free departure. I always planned to be about 5 psi below maximum pressure with the water level clearly visible in the gauge glass to offer a margin if required to prevent blowing off and to ensure the engine did not 'pick up' the water by priming - an absolute requirement to be avoided at all costs.

Author

names, etc. Engine preparation duties brought me into contact with my first main line engines as we got them ready for the main line crews. These included the various 4-6-2 Pacific classes, the 2-6-2 class 'V2' (always known as the 'Green Arrows', after the first one of the class. This had been given this name to publicise the introduction of a pre-war express goods service that carried the higher rated and guaranteed delivery 'Green Arrow' traffics). The 2-6-4 class 'L1' tanks were also on the shed roster, and as equally unloved on the GN as they were on the GE, unless they were just freshly overhauled and the rattling and banging had not yet commenced.

On 7th January, my diary reminds me of the sad accident that occurred that morning at Welwyn involving the up 'Aberdonian' sleeping car express. One person was killed in this mishap. Such events are an exceedingly rare occurrence. When they happen, railway staff throughout the country would frequently feel a sense of personal loss that their industry had slipped from its normally very high standards of safety. It is an intangible thing, but staff in all grades from the lowest to the highest would discuss such feelings, with considerable sympathy for those involved.

During this second week, advice came through agreeing to my move into the then new hostel recently opened alongside the Ilford station Aldersbrook sidings, named after the Aldersbrook stream that bordered the site. The building of this very comfortable and modern hostel, called 'Aldersbrook House', was a drastic measure taken by management in their desperate need to overcome the acute staff shortages still prevailing in the London area. With the reducing levels of general goods train workings at many country sheds, following the 1955 footplate strike and with the resultant growing competition from road transport, men were offered an alternative to redundancy and discharge if they were willing to move. Many did so and everybody benefited. With the eventual closure of the entire M&GN system in early 1959, the existence of the hostel helped Stratford and the LT&S section to ease their near insoluble recruiting problems. Being qualified to apply for a room (through being made redundant at Southend) made life a lot easier. Travelling to and from my own home each day was taking far too long. It was to become my new home for four years before moving out prior to getting married. Becoming a clerk meant my residency qualification ceased, but, until the room was needed for a shift worker, the hostel manager allowed me stay on well beyond any entitlement to do so. This gentleman, Bill Horsefield, was to receive the MBE for service in the community - a very well deserved recognition to a man who was a most public spirited and genuine friend to many people. His kindness in allowing me to stay on for as long as he could, was much appreciated.

During my second week at the shed, a peculiar and quite unexpected scenario occurred. The true extent of the occasional prejudice towards foreigners that still existed began to emerge. My name had been posted up in the notice case to be rostered to a regular mate in the No. 5 Link, known as the 'Regular Met. Link'. Met. was abbreviated from Metropolitan referring to the work in this link over the underground Metropolitan Lines between King's Cross and Moorgate. From the moment this posting appeared, totally unknown men began seeking me out. In all, at least a dozen or so over the ensuing days - a most unusual

Class 'N2' 0-6-2T No. 69593 approaches Potters Bar with the 10.54 am King's Cross-Hatfield train in January 1955.   *P.J. Lynch*

Class 'N2/4' No. 69582 departs from King's Cross with a Hatfield train in 1953. The indifferent post-war maintenance is evidenced by the leaking steam glands at the front end and the injector clack valve blowing through badly with the steam seen under the cab footstep. As the 1950s progressed matters did improve, but such sights as this could still be seen.   *Author*

situation. Their concern was to warn me about my new mate. By the Saturday, my own concern was becoming very real. All 'advised' of the need to be aware of his tantrums; his bullying tactics, and that several of his previous firemen - I was assured this was not an exaggeration - had left the job because of him. All claimed he treated his fireman like a 'nobody', and that he was a very difficult man to get on with. When one of the running foremen, to whom pure chance gave me an opportunity to speak about all this, said in effect that it was all basically about right, then clearly my life was about to be rudely awakened! This foreman also added that if life became impossible to first seek him out before taking any precipitate action - an unheard of suggestion.

My new mate was to be driver Fred Nuthall, and my new regular engine the class 'N2' No. 69512, an 0-6-2 ex-GNR design suburban tank engine, similar to the machines we had seen briefly at Southend. She was equipped with the steam exhaust condensing system for use on the London Transport lines when working through their tunnels. The engine was also fitted with the train brake 'trip-cock gear' equipment, as fitted to all tube trains. She had been built for the GNR by the North British Locomotive Co., Glasgow, and entered traffic in early 1921. The initial batch of engines to this design were built by the GNR Co. at its main Doncaster works (known throughout the GN as the 'Plant') but as more were urgently needed an outside order was also placed at the same time. By pure coincidence, No. 61335 had also been built by the North British in 1948 because the self same Plant was once again too busy to do so. Limited numbers of 'B1s' were built by the railway workshops at Gorton (ex-GCR) and Darlington (ex-NER), but most were constructed by private contractors. In each post-war period, railway workshops were busy, following the respective world wars, on other new construction and with overhauling the arrears from the wartime lack of regular repair.

Our first turn of duty together was on Sunday 13th January (a poor omen this!) working on diagram No. 300. We were on duty at 10.50 am, prepared the engine (not our own, but a similar one, No. 69593) to work the 12.40 pm passenger, King's Cross to Hertford North, and the 1.51 pm return passenger to King's Cross. Arriving for work, a silver-haired thickish-set man in his fifties was waiting who had a gruff attitude, declined to shake hands and after looking me up and down, just said 'follow me'. This was after he had checked with the duty signing-on clerk, in my presence, to confirm me as his 'new stoker'. We walked round to the oil stores without a word being spoken. A brief request by him for our tool padlock keys, oil and sponge cloths and, still in silence, we proceeded to our engine in front of the Met. shed, with me carrying the oil bottles, etc. And, this is how it continued. Our brief conversation covered my unfamiliarity with the workings ('Yes, I know that'), likewise of the road ('That's your problem'), and with the class of engine ('You'll learn'), summarised our exchanges up to departure time. We each brewed our own can of tea. Normal practice was to alternate with each sharing the other's can to give a fresh drink on the outward trip and another for the inward trip. Not this time! Giving him the tip to start the train from a platform, or anywhere else with a signal he could not see, he crossed the cab to check before doing so. A suggestion that he teach me the road was met by a stern rebuff - 'Teach yourself'. At the end of the shift we booked off without hardly a word. During the shift he briefly enquired about my background. He made it very plain he didn't like foreigners. Coming from the Eastern Section (as the GE was known on the GN in the London area; elsewhere it was called the 'Sweedie') was my misfortune, and, 'Don't expect me to help you. Your arrival has stopped one of our own passed cleaners being made up to a regular fireman'. This was enough justification for his attitude. He was certainly living up to the forward forecast! The whole day was a most miserable experience, eased only by returning home to Southend to organise my move to Ilford later that evening.

The next day we had our regular engine, whose cab was less than spotless and the brasswork only wiped over, not polished. It was tolerable but not clean, like '35's' cab had been. Our turn on that Monday was to work diagram No. 256 - on duty at 2.45 pm, prepare the engine, work 3.30 pm LE to Bounds Green Sidings (north of Wood Green, now Alexandra Palace, station), for the 4.15 pm empty stock (not 'cars' on the GN, but 'stock' - another difference to learn!) to Moorgate, before working the 5.22 pm passenger to Hitchin, returning with the empty stock at 7.30 pm to Welwyn Garden City, stable it, then LE to Hatfield to work the 8.35 pm passenger back to King's Cross. This was, without doubt, the hardest day's work in the link, and fate had decreed it to happen on our second day together! There were 48 turns in the link, with 24 regular-manned engines, each with two crews, so the odds against this happening were high! Sufficient steam pressure was just barely managed on such a difficult working, receiving no guidance and not knowing the road. 'N2s' are not the easiest of engines to fire to, and do not steam so freely as the similar GE class 'N7s'. The 'N2s' did steam, contrary to claims that are sometimes made, but they had to be mastered first. To be faced with working a heavily laden eight-coach set on a journey of some 35 miles (not so much shorter than Southend to Liverpool St), with a moderate-sized suburban tank engine, with no help from the driver over a new road with such a totally strange engine, was a daunting task. The trip was tough going and very miserable. (In later timetables the service was to run only to Welwyn Garden City, because it became too much to expect the ageing class 'N2s' to be relied upon.)

Grudging instruction was given on how to set the trip-cock gear. 'Been one of our own lads, this wouldn't be necessary', was the comment made. This was always done as you came to a stand in the King's Cross York Road platform (it had no platform number). The cock was located on the fireman's side below the coal bunker. It is designed to stop the train immediately, should the engine inadvertently pass a red signal, and is a mandatory fitting for all trains, passenger and goods, that work over any London Transport Executive (LTE) railways, as they were then called. As you moved away from the platform a test sign lit up, worked by a trackside contact, to prove the trip gear arm was correctly aligned. Fred worked a lever in his corner of the cab before we departed from York Road, which it was later learned, not from him, operated the condensing equipment fitted in the smokebox. This diverted the exhaust steam into the side water tanks by means of two large size diameter pipes, one each side of the engine to each side tank. This condensed the exhaust steam to avoid it filling the tunnels. When we had stood in the Bounds Green sidings he said 'Get a good fire on, and make no smoke on the Underground', but not why. This was learned by later observation, as he would not explain what happened or why it was necessary. Sufficient to say we ran all our workings to time, but only just. My struggle for steam continued, but in the process it was emerging that whatever else Fred might be in terms of his wish to discredit me, he was a very good engineman. He successfully managed with the limited steam and boiler water levels he had on offer.

The next day, Tuesday, we worked into Broad St, formerly the main London terminus of the old North London Railway (NLR), which became part of the LMS at the 1923 Grouping. There was a four-track main line into this station. The No. 1 lines were not electrified and were steam worked; the No. 2 lines were electrified on the dc 4-rail system. This was later altered to the 3-rail system in the 1960s, before final closure of the tracks into the station from Dalston Jn in 1986. Again, a similar negative response when trying to ask about signals, gradients, and so on. By this time it was becoming very obvious his fireman was an unwanted necessity that he had to tolerate. Debating in my mind whether to provoke a confrontation was resolved by deciding this was not the best way forward. Equally, that he would not have the satisfaction of beating me became my guiding creed. Come what may, this was not going to happen. Instead, the tables were going to be turned, although with little idea of how this might come about. Opting to play his own game back at him, all my effort was concentrated entirely on learning all that it was possible to teach myself. Help with this came on the odd occasion from other drivers if Fred had a rare day off. Without exception, they all took an uninvited pity on me. Enquiries asking: 'How did you get on?', earned guarded replies such as 'We are getting there'. I had no wish for any opinions to be reported back. He was denied this possible satisfaction.

My first move in this game of playing to win (for this was the best way to approach it in my mind, to look upon it as a game, or battle of wits) was to produce a tin of 'Brasso' to commence buffing up the brasswork on my side of the cab. After wiping over his half with a slightly oily rag as a normal part of the fireman's preparation duties, my side was given the extra attention, but not his - no way! The fireman's half of the cab was in fact two-thirds of it. Thus, the polishing covered both water gauge glass frames but no further towards his side. Likewise the insides of the cab and roof - my two-thirds were shone up with a thin smear of engine oil, with no comment from me, nor by him to me.

By the end of the week a fair standard of shiny cleanliness for my two-thirds had been achieved. And still he made no comment! He continued regularly to cross the cab to check the guard's 'Right away' to depart from each station stop and to check any signals on my side, such as the smaller ground signals. These were usually called 'Tommy Dods' or 'Dods' on the GE, and 'Dollies' or 'Dummies' on the GN - the origin of the terms is not known. Then, after a few weeks came a return for two weeks to normality - he went sick with a suspected gastric ulcer. The road learning was completed with the help of the various relief drivers during this unexpected rest from Fred's ill-disguised hostility. My life became easier as a result, as he soon noticed after his return.

While he was off sick, the remaining brasswork and cab roof was buffed up for the benefit of the drivers who were proving so helpful. By the end of his fortnight off sick, the complete cab was looking a real picture. Once you got it clean, it was not too difficult to keep it like it. Our opposite crew began to take a keener interest in it too! When he returned we were on the early shift that week, so rather than return to the former two-thirds, the full 'treatment' was continued thus benefiting our opposite crew on the late shift. Giving him a day to settle back into his routine, produced his acceptance of my tip for the 'Right away' without checking it. Progress! He was still entirely indifferent, but at least the atmosphere lost a little of the 'edge' to it. A couple of days later he made a cutting remark about me being a 'foreigner'. Further progress was made by replying that the choice was his, as this fireman had no intention of bowing to him. We had to work together and it was up to him to accept a foreigner who could not alter the fact of being one. He did not like it, but thereafter the tension eased a slight nudge more and he began to acknowledge me as a human being. Cleaning the brass and cab was continued and his gruffness and general attitude were deliberately ignored. At all times my attitude remained polite, but unbending. By doing this it was possible to keep one's sense of humour. To get all het-up would only make the day together totally, instead of mainly, unbearable. It was a long way from being enjoyable as it was, without provoking matters further.

This totally disjointed and fractured relationship continued for almost three months. It was sheer misery, despite my attempts to treat it as a challenge. The one good point in his defence throughout this time was that he let absolutely nobody, not even the running foremen, interfere with his 'stoker'. When he sent me to report a defect, it was quickly acted upon. Other firemen went to the foremen and then waited for a response before returning to their engines. He would not allow this - 'Report and do not to wait' was his edict. My strict instructions were immediately to return to the engine. He argued, not with me, that my preparation work had to be completed. In this he was entirely correct, but the foremen hated him for it. He was totally intransigent and treated most people with contempt. He was universally detested - it was a very tragic situation. If ever a person had an outsize chip on the proverbial shoulder at this time, it was Fred Nuthall. Behind his back some even parodied his surname by claiming he was 'Not all there', which was entirely untrue. He was a first class engineman. He was entirely consistent in his driving style, never working the engine any harder than absolutely necessary. His braking was as smooth as silk. The guard's hated him and loved him - they hated the way he treated them, but loved him for his considerate handling of the train. He was a total paradox - until the day.

When it came, as inevitably it had to, despite all my effort to avoid it, the balloon went up well and truly with no holds barred! By this time a routine had long since developed to accommodate his awkward ways. He had more or less accepted he wasn't going to beat me, although it never emerged if he thought this, or not. By keeping my own counsel and just doing my work day in, day out, we had reached a kind of accommodation. One of our unspoken routines involved the morning fry-ups on the firing shovel. A perfectly burnt through body of bright hot fire was insisted upon, and the shovel had to be cleaned ready for his use. After his fry up, mine was permitted. On the fateful day, we were taking our break in Finsbury Park carriage sidings. He was cooking his fry-up on the shovel when disaster struck. Losing my balance while reaching to adjust the blower valve handle (which controlled the draught on the fire) it got accidentally turned full on when trying to save myself from falling into him. This immediately increased the draught on the fire and with it his bacon and eggs were sucked into the firebox! The immediate apology with the intention of offering him my breakfast to replace it, was cut off in mid-sentence.

The verbal eruption that occurred did neither of us any credit. It was like a tightly wound up spring breaking. He accused me of totally unprintable things and metaphorically sent my soul to the devil and back in the space of maybe, two, perhaps three, minutes. That was it! - enough was enough, having taken more than was justified. To his utter amazement, after three months of docility, he got it, lock, stock and barrel, with a few selected assessments of his character. Summed up, my remarks pointed out very forcefully how much he was detested, how stupid was his insular attitude, and it was about time we worked as a team, rather than as two individuals in constant unspoken conflict. The whole episode lasted barely five minutes. He lost his breakfast and mine stayed put in the bag. Eventually the siding signal came off, the shunter called us forward and we resumed the rest of our working without a word being spoken, apart from the few that were strictly necessary to do our job. We booked off duty and went our separate ways. I was not at all proud, or even remotely pleased, about what had been exchanged between us. He, as the driver, would have been entirely within his rights to have reported my behaviour towards him. He did not do so. What it did do, though, was to lance the long festering carbuncle that had grown between us. My quiet tolerance of his insular attitude had certainly frustrated him. His repeatedly sarcastic remarks and his intolerance of me had obviously built up, for the reasons explained. Our next duty together was approached with deep foreboding.

Then came the amazing metamorphosis! Arriving early for work the next morning gave me the chance to be busy getting '12' ready when he climbed up into the cab. He put his 'traps', as we called our personal bits and pieces, into the cupboard, turned round and held out his hand for me to shake. For a second or two, I was stunned. Several possible reactions had been mentally debated, but not this! He gave a genuinely warm handshake and not a word was said.

From that moment life between us began anew. It would have been difficult to have asked for, or desired, a better mate to work for and be with. Fred became a person transformed. Presumably no fireman had ever spoken to him so frankly. Several had fallen out and called him unprintable names, but it seemed nobody had spelled out to him, without calling him names, how much he was detested. We neither of us ever referred to the 'incident' thereafter. He never verbally apologised and neither did I, but somehow his handshake said it all. For a day or two it was prudent to be cautious, but any fears were proved entirely groundless. He still treated others in his old cavalier manner, but over the following weeks even this gradually mellowed. Not a lot, but a bit, sufficient for others to begin remarking upon it. 'What have you done to him?', was sometimes asked to which might be added the odd saucy suggestion such as 'Have you put bromide in his tea?', or similar observation! It took a few days,

Driver Fred Nuthall in the cab of our regular engine, class 'N2/1' class 0-6-2T No. 69512. The cab interior was usually maintained to a high standard with all brasswork polished, bright steelwork emery-clothed and paintwork rubbed over with a thin smear of engine oil. It took us half-an-hour each morning to do it, and what a difference it made to the comfort of our time together. If ever another crew were given our engine, Fred would raise hell with the running foreman, with the result that we nearly always had her, except on scheduled shed days for boiler washout, etc., and if possible these were arranged for our rostered rest days - it was not worth the upset for them to do otherwise! This photograph was taken on 18th May, 1957 in Holloway carriage sidings. *Author*

but within a week we were sharing our tea cans. He began to clean the brasswork and his cab sides and roof, and also to talk about his World War I experiences in the trenches. These were an edited version of what must have been a very disturbing time for someone in his late-teens. He had volunteered under age, by lying about this, although he never admitted to it. He never discussed the gruesome details, but you got the positive feeling he had experienced them. He began talking about his main line firing days prior to World War II, and how he had been a fireman for 23 years and 4 months - very important, the four months! It partially explained why he bore such very deep grudges against the 'foreigners' who had retarded his promotion. Bit by bit he slowly opened up. Some of the reasons for his gruffness became apparent, although it was impossible to agree with his earlier attitudes that had developed as a result.

It became a pleasure to come to work. Our little fracas was not mentioned to anybody else, preferring to obey the old adage, 'Least said, soonest mended'. It worked, so much so, that for the next 25 years after we ceased to be regular mates, we continued to exchange Christmas cards until one year in the middle 1980s his never arrived. A follow up letter received no reply.

He was always the driver, with me the fireman. Never once did he allow me to touch the regulator, not even in the shed. Only once did he ever pick up the shovel to do the firing. This happened on my first day back at work after a long absence due to a hernia operation. He noticed me struggling and in his gruff way, told me to stand to one side. Whereupon he fired half a dozen rounds into the box to give me a breather. My thanks were acknowledged by being told, 'Forget it'. By now it was easier to understand his personality, and he meant no offence with his remark. His gruffness hid a shy man, although he would not have agreed with this, thinking of himself as a 'real' man. He never again queried my instruction to move; if I said a signal was 'off', i.e., clear to proceed, he took my word. And, from my point of view, best of all, nobody was ever allowed to interfere with his 'stoker' - never his fireman, always his stoker. I was absolutely bombproof in his eyes from any outside interference. We had many happy hours together.

The work in the Met. link was rarely onerous. We worked a regular two shift pattern with no full night shifts, although with some very early morning starts at any time from about 2.00 am onwards. Table Five (*overleaf*) gives some sample details from our 48 week roster cycle. Aside from running the frequent suburban services, we also worked most of the empty main line stock movements into and out of King's Cross passenger station, apart from the heaviest trains, 13 coaches and upwards, considered beyond our engine's capability. It was a regular occurrence for trains to stall on the initial climb out of the terminus inside the Gasworks tunnel, but Fred never did, his engine handling technique was superb. By quietly observing him, it was possible to learn a lot. We would work these trains to Holloway down sidings, Waterworks sidings (between Hornsey and Wood Green on the down side), Bounds Green sidings, Hornsey sidings (two yards - one south of Wood Green, and one north of Hornsey, stations), Ferme Park yards (both sides, down and up) and occasionally to East yard (south of Finsbury Park on the up side). We would

A brace of class 'J50' 0-6-0Ts Nos. 68981 and 68966 on Hornsey shed. The foreground shows the typical underfoot conditions that were to be seen at many sheds in the post-war era of steam operations; there were honourable exceptions, but at most sheds, sights like this were all too common, particularly in the larger conurbation areas where staffing was often a problem. *Author*

Class 'N2/4' 0-6-2T No. 69586 pulls away from Wood Green with the 9.24 from King's Cross to Hertford North on 20th July, 1952.   *A.R. Carpenter*

pull stock out of Holloway down sidings forward to Clarence yard (south of Finsbury Park on the down side) to run-round and then work via the dive-under the main lines to climb up the steep gradient to Holloway North Up signal box and thence down into the terminus.

Table Five - King's Cross No.5 Link - Extract of Work Roster, Winter 1956/57

Week	On duty	Diagram No. and Working
1	2.45 pm	256 - 3.30 LE Bounds Grn; 4.15 ecs M'gate; 5.22 Hitchin; 7.30 ecs WGC; 8.05 LE Hatfield; 8.35 KX; LE Top Shed; Off duty 10.45.
2	4.40 am	262 - 5.25 LE HCS; 5.40 ecs KX (for 6.45 Grantham); 7.24 Hert. Nth; 8.33 M'gate; 9.53 ecs Fins. Pk; LE Top Shed; Off duty 12.40.
3	1.35 pm	262 - 2.20 LE Fins. Pk Western Sdgs; 3.0 ecs Fins. Pk; 3.07 Hert. Nth; 4.31 M'gate; 5.50 New Barnet; Shunt yard; LE Top Shed; Off duty 10.30.
4	6.39 am	261 - 7.24 LE KX; 7.54 Hert. Nth; 9.01 Fins.Pk; 10.35 ecs KX (for 12.00 nn Hert. Nth); 12.45 ecs HCS; 1.20 ecs Bounds Grn; LE KX; Rel. at 2.24 by 2nd set; Off duty 2.39.
5	1.15 pm	252 - Rel. KX 1.40; 1.44 ecs HCS; 2.40 vans KX; 4.53 ecs Bounds Grn; LE Hornsey CS; 6.20 ecs KX (for 8.20 Aberdeen); 8.35 ecs HCS; LE Top Shed; Off duty 10.00.
6	4.00 am	272 - 4.45 LE Fins. Pk Western Sdgs; 5.20 ecs Fins. Pk; 5.31 Hert. Nth; 6.31 KX; 8.59 WGC; 10.29 KX; Rel at 11.45 by 2nd set; Off duty 12.00 nn.
7	11.40 am	276 - Rel. HCS 12.30; Steam Heating as req. for C&W staff; LE Top Shed; Off duty 7.40.
8	5.41 am	263 - 6.26 LE KX; 6.56 WGC; 8.30 Broad St.; 10.20 LE Fins. Pk; dispose* & prepare eng. for 2nd set; Rel. at Fins. Pk ; Off duty 1.41.
9	1.42 pm	260 - Rel. 1st set at KX 2.07; 2.51 ecs HCS; 3.55 ecs KX (for 4.50 Newcastle); 4.55 LE Fins. Pk; 5.23 ecs Broad St.; 6.32 Cuffley; 7.37 ecs Fins. Pk; LE Top Shed; Off duty 9.42.
10	5.50 am	253 - 6.50 LE KX; 8.15 ecs Hornsey; 10.25 ecs KX (for 12.20 Newcastle); Rel at KX 1.25 by 2nd set; Off duty 1.50.
11	11.05 am	267 - 11.30 passr to Fins. Pk; Rel. 1st set 11.45; brake testing for C&W staff to 3.30; 4.00 ecs Broad St.; 4.56 Gordon Hill; LE Top Shed; Off duty 7.05.
12	6.20 am	268 - 7.05 LE New Barnet; 8.39 M'gate; 9.43 ecs KX; 10.00 Hert. Nth; 11.31 KX; Rel at 2.05 by 2nd set; Off duty 2.20.
13	10.25 am	257 - Rel. KX; 10.54 Hert. Nth; 12.35 KX; 3.30 Hert. Nth; 5.01 Fins. Pk; Rel. by 3rd set; Off duty 6.55.
14	1.35 am	255 - EP1.50 LE KX; 2.20 Hert. Nth; 4.44 KX; 6.30 WGC; 8.40 ecs Hatfield; 8.54 M'gate; Rel by 2nd set at York Road platform at 9.33; Off duty 10.00.
15	12.29 pm	266 - Passr to Fins. Pk on 12.54 KX; Rel 1st set; LE Bounds Grn; 2.45 ecs KX (for 4.12 dep); LE Fins. Pk.; 5.05 ecs Broad St.; 5.54 Gordon Hill; LE Top Shed; Off duty 8.29.
16	4.05am	256 - 4.50 LE KX; 5.20 WGC; 6.45 KX; 8.00 Pcls Gordon Hill; 9.06 Broad St.; 10.20 LE Top Shed; Off duty 12.05.

Notes
The full work roster covered 48 weeks in this link.
* one of the rare occasions when we disposed of an engine, i.e., cleaning the fire etc., required in this case because we were not booked back to Top Shed.

C&W = Carriage & Wagon; ecs = empty coaching stock; EP = Engine prepared; Fins. Pk = Finsbury Park; Hert. Nth = Hertford North; HCS = Holloway Carriage Sidings; KX = King's Cross Passenger Station; LE = Light engine; M'gate = Moorgate LTE; Pcls = Parcels train; WGC = Welwyn Garden City.

When working stock via Bounds Green this entailed climbing up over the Wood Green flyover. With a full 12-coach main line train on the draw hook, this could be a severe challenge for an 'N2'. Only once did Fred ever stall on this incline, caused by a sticking brake. The normal routine was to stop a good quarter mile up to a half mile back towards Hornsey from the Wood Green gantry stop signals south of the station for this flyover. Then to wait for the distant signal underneath it for the next section to be pulled off to confirm you had a clear run at the steep climb up onto the flyover. Sometimes we stood for a half hour or more. As soon as the first signal cleared, the fireman turned the blower full on to get the fire white hot, and corrected any thin spots in the fire. Once the lower, distant, signal was cleared, the driver usually asked his fireman if he was ready, before commencing the headlong rush at the incline. You quite literally 'went for broke' - there were no half measures! People on Wood Green station waiting for a train rarely failed to turn round to watch the spectacle. Fred was a master at surmounting this regular challenge to his engine handling skills. Came the day, when it was my turn to do it when working with a young driver, by handling the engine as Fred did, we surmounted the stiff climb with minimum fuss. He didn't think he had shown me! Following the same technique starting from the extremely difficult platform 16 at King's Cross, got me safely away, soon to be described. Today's younger drivers get very few chances to watch senior hands at work and thereby to learn the required skills based on experience. It has to raise queries about how this weakness should be addressed. They are fully and competently taught via the medium of training modules, but these cannot teach experience, the development of that vital sixth sense that is so necessary for maximum safety.

Needless to say, life in the link inevitably produced its lighter moments. One incident that remains very clear occurred one morning in New Barnet down carriage sidings. We had a diagram where we were booked to run coupled with another engine as LEs to New Barnet to work two separate up passenger trains. You arrived in the downside sidings, uncoupled and dropped onto the respective sets of stock prior to each drawing forward in turn. We stood alongside the other engine exchanging pleasantries with the crew. As we were to be the first departure, Fred was concentrating on creating the vacuum brake to check all was in order. The yard exit signal came off, conversation ceased, the shunter gave us the tip to draw forward, and Fred opened the regulator. We had gone barely two yards when there was an unholy noise and the brakes came violently on. The other driver, Tommy Spicer, was a shortish, very jovial man with a very corpulent deportment. Suddenly he started laughing so much that he gradually subsided from view behind his cab side door, being unable to continue standing. A quick check soon discovered the reason for his mirth. Our shunter had connected the vacuum pipes, but forgotten the coupling! It is surprising how much re-enforcing wire there is in a vacuum bag (our term for the connecting flexible pipe). We had come to an abrupt stand, probably three yards from the train with the bag broken but the uncoiled wire still physically attaching us to the stock. The resultant shambles was bouncing up and down with the tension! Poor Tommy just could not contain himself. Fred was not amused. He just would not see the humour of the situation. It was the only occasion since our 'incident' when his former frostiness towards me briefly returned. It was serious, because many passengers were inconvenienced that morning. Fred just went purple with rage at the shunter, which unfortunately made the humour of the situation even more poignant! Tommy's continuing laughter didn't help the cause, either! Our train working was cancelled as nobody could locate a spare vacuum bag in time. Fred's anger arose because of the shunter's oversight and especially was he infuriated because many passengers had been delayed. He had a finely developed sense of commitment to our customers, gruff man that he was. To cause them unnecessary delay was simply forbidden in his code of ethics.

On the GE section, guards' brake compartments always carried spare bags as standard issue, but this, apparently, was not the routine on the GN section, except on main line stock, much to my surprise that morning. Between the four guards' compartments available in the two sets of coaches, not one spare bag was found, neither could one be located elsewhere in time.

Contrariwise, as awkward as he was, he always followed one particular working routine, accepted by everybody. It was entirely against the rule book, yet regularly practised every single weekday. He was a real tartar for the rules, but even he would not oppose this regular breaching of them. We had a turn which included a LE departing the shed to run to Gordon Hill (on the Hertford Loop) in the wee small hours of the early morning. The rules said a maximum of four in the cab; this was almost always very rigorously enforced by everybody. Except on the Gordon Hill LE. If you only had four you were running lightly loaded! As many as 10 would be in the cab some mornings, rarely less than six. It was a recognised get-men-home taxi service. The fireman made sure to put on a good fire, as it would be impossible to use the shovel once you were underway. The practice was never queried, let alone challenged. Definitely one of those occasions when management knew how to develop a need to be elsewhere! As you dropped down to the shed outlet signal to ring out, shadowy forms would begin appearing to seek the driver's 'OK' to hitch a lift. It was the unwritten rule never to assume, but to always ask first.

The one other occasion when we had a difficult time, occurred upon his return to work from holiday to discover he had not got his beloved '12'. It was not easy to explain 'we had bent her', when the motion fell apart at speed. He went straight after the mechanical foreman, Harry Billings, to enquire how long before she would be repaired. The reply put him in a lousy mood for the day. The next day he was worse - he had discovered what had happened.

Knowing Fred was to be on holiday for a week, Harry saw his chance to get a full valves and pistons exam done, which required '12' to be stopped for a couple of days. He then planned to get her back in traffic with time for any minor problems to be sorted out before Fred returned - good thinking. Except that on this occasion his fitter omitted to insert a crucial split pin in a motion bearing pin nut. My driver for the week was Len Lacey, a senior passed fireman. Len, during his preparation of '12' on her first day back in traffic, on the Wednesday, unfortunately failed to spot the missing pin while up in the motions oiling up with his, probably smoking, flare lamp. An all too easy error, if you are not paying sharp attention.

Class 'N2/1' 0-6-2T No. 69512 at Hertford North in 1957.   *Author*

Class 'N2/1' No.69538 working a Hatfield-King's Cross inner suburban service in 1958, passing
Red Hall, south of Hatfield.   *Peter I. Paton*

Fortunately, we were working the last down road early morning passenger not booked to stop at Bayford on the Hertford North loop line, the 5.31 am Finsbury Park to Hertford North. Len had just got '12' swinging along nicely after departing from Cuffley when at about 45 mph there was an almighty bang from the front end and obviously something very seriously wrong as evidenced by the severe vibration and gruesome noises. We were approaching the 1¼ mile-long Pondsborne tunnel. Len managed to stop just a few feet short of the tunnel entrance. A quick examination soon revealed the right hand set of motion to be broken and entirely useless. Len wasn't sure what to do. Grubbing around in the ballast I found a rusty nail - absolutely ideal. At my suggestion, he gave her a breath of steam with the cylinder drain cocks open and with the engine set in mid-gear, the piston valve was centred by hand to shut off the right-hand cylinder to all steam. Because the valve had just been overhauled, it moved freely making this possible. Loosening the valve spindle gland, the nail was then tapped into the spindle packing and the gland retightened unevenly so as to deliberately cant the packing to lock the valve spindle solid. My hours of voluntary attendance at the Southend Mutual Improvement Class were proving their worth. Watching the bent motion parts from the footplating through a couple of wheel revolutions confirmed we could not break anything more and the remaining pieces were safe enough to be left *in situ* at slow speed. Officially, the remaining parts should have been dismantled, but by proceeding slowly it was possible to leave it still connected *in situ*, thereby avoiding further delay to following services.

Our guard had started walking back to protect the train with detonators to prevent possible collision from the next following train, as required by the rule book. With a long blast on the whistle he quickly rejoined us. Len then gently entered the tunnel on the downhill gradient to keep us rolling forward on the remaining good, left-hand cylinder. Never, had 1¼ miles seemed so long! With the old girl waggling from side to side, we eventually emerged from the tunnel, carrying on through Bayford to arrive at Hertford. We delayed the train running half-an-hour behind us by just five minutes. We were thereafter a total failure. Much later two engines arrived coupled together, complete with a fitter. One was to work our empty stock away, the other to tow us back to shed for repair, after the fitter had added his bit to what we had done, including taking down the connecting rod, to ensure the safety of the engine for the much longer trip back. How Len subsequently explained his failure to check the motions properly in the first place, never emerged.

What can be recorded is that when we came to work the next day, he insisted on making me the driver for the rest of the week with him firing. This was his way of saying 'thanks' for enabling him to move the engine to clear the main line. Our decision to move our crippled engine, with its makeshift repair, avoided what would otherwise have been very serious delays to the rest of the morning service. He was probably able to mitigate his failure in his report because these delays had been avoided by our prompt actions. Obviously, at the time we were unaware of the cause - this emerged during the investigation after getting back to the shed, and when the offending bearing pin and nut were later discovered - about half a mile apart - on the ballast after not being found on the engine. On the Saturday our diagram took us into Moorgate and out again, and hence the challenge of driving up the notorious steeply graded, sharply curved, Hotel Curve Tunnel into platform 16 at King's Cross. My GN section driving prior to this week had been very minimal. We managed, our engine No. 69575 and me, without any untoward problem, by applying Fred's methods and with encouragement from Len not to be frightened of it. This was to be my only opportunity to have hold of an engine into Moorgate, but it gave me considerable confidence to know I could do it.

When Fred learned of the split pin, Len's name became unmentionable; when later still he learned of how we had minimised the delay, he did offer a friendly comment - praise indeed! If he learned of my extended three days' driving experience, he never mentioned it. Eventually, a week after his return to work we had '12' back, but not for long. The replacement motion parts supplied from the Plant did not fit properly and her steaming and general running were very poor. He failed her upon return to the shed and we never had her again during my remaining time with him. She did eventually return after a complete main works overhaul, possibly at Stratford, who were by this time undertaking GN section repairs to fill spare capacity created following the Southend electrification. By this time my promotion to the No. 4 Main Line link had occurred. I believe it was to be '12s' final major overhaul before being withdrawn for scrapping in July 1962 - the end of a delightful old lady who had served me very well during our time together.

Other minor highlights during my year in the Met. link included the introduction of Welsh coal, already mentioned in Chapter Five. We struggled for most of the first day. Fortunately, being a Saturday, we were not pulling fully laden trains around, and also Fred was on a day off. Ernie Sellwood, with my inept help as we struggled for steam, kept the show on the road, but only just, with not too much time lost. My opposite fireman, Peter Lacey with his regular mate, Bill Jones, also struggled and again just kept the kettle boiling, as we later learned. We did not have '12' that day, which would have helped us both. She was booked for a shed day, and hence why Fred took a day's leave owing to him - very clever as it turned out. When he returned '12' was still stopped with valve rings to be renewed, and we had another unknown engine No. 69576. This was when he showed me how to fire with Welsh coal, not very long after our 'incident' and our now improved relationship. Under his guidance, the firebox received a good lumping, but leaving the coal level well clear of the brick-arch. With this we ran light to Broad St, letting the coal 'cook' gently to get it well warmed up before working the 4.35 pm throughout to Hertford North without touching the shovel again. Cracked it - Welsh coal? - no problem! How quickly are the mighty fallen! The fire was too thin for the return journey and we had a struggle to get back. The lumps went in, but there was not a big enough bed of fire left to properly catch them alight in time. Another lesson learned. Fred said not a word, but was certainly smiling to himself! Being post-incident my lack of the necessary skill was alright. To contemplate what the outcome might have been pre-incident, did not bear thinking about.

Then came the morning when Fred slipped up in his engine preparation on 10th June - a unique event in my year with him. At Hertford North, after buffering up to the train, the shunter quietly beckoned me down from the cab. He pointed to the lack of a front coupling!

'Got him!', was his reaction.

My face was apparently quite a study, as he remarked later.

'I've waited a long time for this to get one over on him', came his next pithy comment.

It was too good an opportunity to miss!

'Fred', called our shunter, 'Can you come down from the cab? We have a small problem'. He reluctantly agreed with us that the lack of a coupling was, when all was said and done, not a large problem! He had failed to notice it was missing while doing the preparation duties. We had run LE to Hertford where our stock was stabled for the up road working. We had some fun and games transferring the remaining coupling from end to end throughout the shift. Engine screw couplings are very heavy items to lug around, heavier than their carriage or vacuum-fitted wagon counterparts. They have to be lifted up to shoulder height before tipping them up and over sideways-on to achieve removal from the coupling draw hook shank. It is a two man job, most times, to lift them. We could have used the carriage coupling, but Fred said, 'No, it's my error, and we use the engine coupling', as required by the operating instructions.

One true moment of humour came when we were spotted by two drivers walking nearby, carrying it later in the shift. Their priceless observations and Fred's powerful replies would, sadly, if included here, prevent this book from being published! It was pure 22-carat gold quality and worth every second of our combined efforts throughout the shift, just to listen to that verbal battle of words. Discretion on this occasion was definitely better than valour, to paraphrase the old saying. Keeping a wise silence took some effort, believe me! The story quickly went the rounds, no doubt from the Hertford shunter. For several days afterwards there were regular enquiries asking if we had both our couplings with us, and what had Fred done with the absent one! Much to my surprise, he took it in good humour which was a reflection of the progress we had achieved since our upset. In an odd way, this episode also helped him to mellow just a little more, as other enginemen began to realise he could be human after all and began speaking to him more regularly.

Saturday 6th July found me on my rostered rest day riding with Old Oak Common Royal Train driver Walter Harris, at his suggestion. We had met earlier in the year. My application for the required footplate pass caused consternation when it arrived at the shed. Called in to explain why it had not been requested through 'the proper channels', it soon became clear the lack of an adequate explanation would prevent it being issued. The rules were the rules and had to be obeyed, as the stern faced authority was forcefully explaining - a jumped up 'jobsworth' in the office. When he had said his piece, my quiet explanation that Walter was personally known to our Regional motive power officer, Mr T.C.B. Miller, abruptly stopped him in his tracks. To press home my rare advantage it was further explained that the pass was being issued on Mr Miller's personal authority. Rapid retreat of 'jobsworth' from his hostile attitude! Short of bowing and scraping, he did not know what to say by way of extricating himself. It was entirely unintentional on my part, not realising the implication, but the ability to pull rank was delightful to experience, once the reality of the situation had dawned! It was rare for a humble fireman to have his superiors apologising, particularly when, realising the intended withholding of the pass was not going to plan, the next higher ranking 'jobsworth' had joined in. Walter had suggested my request be sent direct to Mr Miller, without realising it would upset delicate sensitivities. The pass was promptly released after they had checked my day off was being correctly taken.

We had a memorable trip. Departing from Paddington on 'Castle' class No. 5099 *Compton Castle* with the 7.30 am to Bristol we were running at 70 mph past Dolphin box, approaching Slough, when a front cylinder cover completely blew out. Stopping immediately, Walter could see no other damage, so decided to continue on at reduced speed to Slough. Here he commandeered '6100' class large prairie type 2-6-2 suburban tank No. 6146 with which we worked forward to Reading, running at 60 mph in the process. While exchanging No. 6146 for the standby main line pilot, 'Hall' class No. 5956 *Horsley Hall*, the carriage examiner, making his routine check round the train, discovered the cylinder cover had damaged the underneath of the second coach which had then to be removed, causing more delay. Walter's mate was meanwhile busy building up the fire to discover this was very dirty. Walter checked it, agreed with his mate, but there was little that could be done about it. Reading shed received a roasting for this failure to provide a pilot engine fit for the task, as Walter was to explain afterwards when we next met. We struggled on to Bristol to arrive with barely enough steam to release the brakes when stopped by signal in the approach to the station, and with hardly any water in the boiler. We arrived with just minutes to spare before our booked return working to Paddington was due to depart.

The engine bringing this train in from Plymouth was scheduled to come off, having done a full day's work, and the fireman had run the fire down ready for disposal. Walter immediately organised with Control to exchange footplates. Thus, we took over No. 7019 *Fowey Castle* for the up journey. It was an object lesson in firing technique for me to watch, fascinated, as his fireman overcame the problem of a low, and dirty fire, using their standard Welsh coal. My similar efforts at Hertford came flashing back! The difference being my total lack of experience compared to the master craftsman it was my rare privilege to observe at work (and from whom I unwittingly absorbed how to do it - to be revealed in Chapter One of Volume Two). We had departed immediately with no time to build any sort of fire first. Walter's mate immediately set about doing this after the 'Right away' from our guard who quickly scrambled into the front brakevan, to save precious time. A working firebed was gradually built up in small and frequent stages, with help from Walter who nursed the engine, losing time, while this was done. It took about 20 miles before he got the nod from his mate that time recovery could begin in earnest. We had departed about six minutes late, and then lost another five minutes at least. We passed Wootton Bassett about 11 minutes down on schedule. No. 7019 proved to be a good engine. Walter was soon giving her 'the treatment', as we would call it, so much so that we eventually ran into Paddington almost on the minute of right time, helped by some very smart station work along the way, without doubt urged on by our guard - a classic example of good teamwork by all concerned. It was the first time Walter had smiled since before Dolphin on the down road! Not the day out that he had hoped to give me, but a most interesting one for all that. His own regular mate was on holiday, and his replacement was not fully familiar with Walter's driving technique, but no matter, they worked as an excellent team. It was an unexpected bonus to observe at first hand some very skilled footplate work. To watch how Walter actively did all he could to assist his fireman to recover from such an adverse situation was a superb example of real teamwork.

On 1st September my first booked main line turn was rostered, to Peterborough with Jack Thompson on class 'A3' No. 60059 *Tracery*. My day out with the Leeds men now paid dividends, as the wide firebox and the basic knowledge of how to fire them had been learned. Jack realised my road knowledge north of Hitchin was non-existent, but had no anxieties about my ability to produce steam. He was considerate and helpful, which was an enormous help and we had a good day out together. Fred was not amused to have a temporary mate and pressed me not to volunteer for lodging away work on main line duties - a non-committal reply was the wiser course of action, coward that I was! We had long since achieved a happy relationship and there was no sense in aggravating it. He was strongly opposed to lodge work, saying it was all wrong to spend time away from home. My trip only whetted the appetite for more main line work. His reply? 'You'll learn!'. The old Fred was still alive and kicking beneath his newly relaxed demeanour!

A spell in one of the excellent Railway Convalescent Homes in the October following the operation already referred to, took me to the Dawlish Home for a fortnight. The good work these homes undertake to help railway staff of all grades to recover after illness is superb. The six homes then in use have been gradually reduced to reflect the contraction in rail staff employees over more recent years. It was a very helpful and enjoyable break. We were walking most days along the seafront in open-necked short-sleeved shirts, when the folks at home were reporting cold weather and the wearing of overcoats! Staff of all grades from the Chairman downwards can be members of this excellent organisation. It was, and still is, entirely classless and everybody, irrespective of their job status, gets treated in a similar manner. Each Home has a matron in charge with a small staff who dedicate themselves to your welfare. To join, we authorised a small amount to be deducted every payday towards the cost of running the Homes. They were, and are still, managed on a non-profit making basis.

Soon after returning to work, a little birdie whispered that promotion to regular main line work was shortly due. A couple of weeks later this was confirmed with my name in the notice case allocated to a new regular mate, Joe Denley, in the No. 4 link. This link covered express workings, passenger as far as Grantham, vacuum-fitted goods as far as New England, Peterborough, and the Cambridge branch workings. Joe had a brother, Ernie, driving on main line duties in the No. 3 link, which covered the non-lodge top main line work as far as Doncaster. No. 3 link also had an unusual summer Saturdays only turn to York and back - a round trip of 377 miles for one day's work! (Or, to put it another way, just 17 miles less than working throughout from King's Cross to Edinburgh. The difference, of course, being the short rest period at York between the outward and homeward trips). Every year this roster had to be specially negotiated by management to seek the required approval from the LDC before it could be issued, as it infringed, by a few minutes, the normal maximum of a nine hour shift.

My final day with Fred came on Saturday 28th December when we worked into Moorgate and out to Hertford North on class 'N2' No. 69581. Although looking forward to my new work, a very definite pang of sadness was experienced to be leaving Fred, who had become a real friend after our disastrous start together. He was an engineman of the highest calibre and the initial period had long since been forgotten between us. We were to still occasionally see each other, either in the signing-on lobby or while out on the main line. He never failed to acknowledge me. Little did either of us know then that our paths would again cross some years later in totally different circumstances.

Thus ended a more than usually memorable year. Our relationship working on the Met. trains had become a most enjoyable period. We ran between the four London area starting points of Moorgate, Broad Street, King's Cross, and Finsbury Park, to Welwyn Garden City on the direct main line northwards, or to Hertford North, on the diversionary main line that ran from Wood Green to south of Stevenage, and to intermediate terminating points as well. These, together with the evening train to Hitchin, and the many main line empty carriage stock workings 'round the houses' as we called it, between King's Cross and Bounds Green, comprised the Met. No. 4 link roster. All the roads had been thoroughly learned to know my way around the inner London area with total confidence. Occasional trips doing the driving, mainly with the younger men, provided much useful experience, all tucked away inside 'the little grey cells', as the late Agatha Christie's fictional Belgian detective, Hercule Poirot, would say.

One cheeky wag wanted to know, 'How had the taming of the shrew been achieved?', to which a very innocent smile seemed the best reply. Even the aforementioned running shed foreman was a mite curious, saying it had been thought impossible, which goes to prove that minor tremors in life do occur. The reality rested with Fred himself, who had done the changing, not me.

It had become a most interesting and, in so many ways, a very rewarding 12 months. The time had come to move onwards and upwards on the promotion ladder to wider horizons of both scenery and experience.

Chapter Seven

The Footplate Years - King's Cross Main Line

Unlike a year earlier with Fred, Joe was to welcome me with a hand shake. We could have started off on the wrong foot. Fortunately for me, although not for him, he was on the sick list for the initial few days of our being rostered together.

Travelling to work by motorbike on Sunday 29th December, 1957, ample time had been allowed. Turning sharp left, correctly, into a narrow one-way street, a car coming out of it in the wrong direction caused a collision. The front forks were bent but just rideable and, being a Sunday, worth the risk with little traffic around. Fortunately, a phone box was nearby. After sorting out the accident details, a call to the shed explained matters.

'If you can get here by shed departure time, do so. We will get your engine prepared', came the hopeful response.

This was just managed - not the ideal way to meet a new regular mate!

If you are to do something new, there's no better way than to do it in proper style! I found myself climbing up into the cab of one of the famous class 'A4' streamlined Pacific engines for our first outing together. Except that it wasn't Joe in the cab! John Hill sat in the driver's seat with a huge grin to welcome me aboard No. 60033 *Seagull*. We had shared several trips in the Met. link together. In my hurried arrival to book on, knowing time was short, checking the driver's signing on duty signature had been overlooked. His temporary mate was disappointed to lose out on his expected trip, but after thanking him for doing my work, he accepted it and departed. We were to work the 12.15 pm express to Peterborough, the first stop, come off, and go LE to the New England shed to turn before working the 5.12 pm up express back, again non-stop, to King's Cross. It was an odd curiosity that at both New England and Grantham sheds, instead of using a turntable, we turned our engines on a tightly curved triangle track layout, provided within the shed complex. *Seagull* was one of the few engines of the class fitted at that date with the 'Kylchap' twin chimney exhaust system, installed from new when she had been built at the Plant in 1938. (This equipment had been originally developed by two famous overseas engineers, Mr Kylala and Mr Chapelon, hence the name.) It made my job to fire to her so easy. She was such a free steaming engine, that my limited experience of wide firebox engines made no difference. To have such a beautiful, smooth riding, and sweet running engine on this first trip as a full main line engineman was pure bliss!

We had a superb day out together on *Seagull* and thoroughly enjoyed ourselves. Also, as with Fred, neither of us on that memorable day could possibly have foreseen how our paths were again to meet in the future.

The 'A4s' are rightly well known through the exploits of the most famous one of them all, *Mallard*, now preserved for the nation at the National Railway Museum, York. They rode like a carriage, generally steamed very well, and were much admired by their crews. Paradoxically, they could be dirty engines

A busy scene at Top Shed, King's Cross. The locomotives on view are, *from left to right*, 'A4' class Pacifics Nos. 60010 *Dominion of Canada* and 60014 *Silver Link*, 'K3' class 2-6-0 No. 61852 and 'A4' No. 60033 *Seagull*.

to work on. This was due to the air smoothed action of the rubber sheeting between the engine and tender causing a wind tunnel effect as some air was sucked into the firehole via the tender coal space. This brought dust into the cab if not regularly damped down using the tender spray provided.

Around the time of starting my main line career, authority was given by our Regional management to alter all ex-LNE design Pacific engines to the twin chimney exhaust arrangement. The improvement in performance and fuel efficiency, related to the stiffer train schedules being introduced for diesel traction, was out of all proportion to the minimal cost incurred, even at this late stage in the limited life span left for steam traction. There were stories at the time claiming the East Coast regions had to overcome some determined opposition to get these improvements introduced. The British Transport Commission (BTC) were also understood to be less than keen to start hearing of the magnificent steam haulage exploits made possible with the transformed engines! The Regional managements could, and did, sanction the small cost per engine from within their own budget limits, said to be as little as £160 per machine, recoverable within the remaining engine life required. The much improved operating benefits obtained far outweighed the cost, and proved of real benefit during the early, less reliable, days of diesel operations when steam had frequently to take over, often at short notice. As diesel reliability improved and fleet numbers built up, so the need for steam ceased, but until this happened, the rebuilt engines proved to be a real asset.

The next day was like old times again, spent firing to Charlie ('Duke') Ellington on class 'B1' No. 61075, working to Hitchin and Baldock - my first trip on a 'Bongo' for over a year. We returned from Hitchin LE with class 'A3' No. 60108 *Gay Crusader*, to bring her home after an earlier failure. She was one of the original batch ordered by the GNR before 1923, although not entering service until the early months of the new LNER Company. She was initially constructed to the larger GNR loading gauge dimensions with higher cab and boiler mountings, and was driven from the right-hand side of the cab. Eventually she was rebuilt to fit the smaller LNER standard loading gauge profile, and converted to being driven from the left-hand side. This was better for the driver more easily to observe the trackside signals. Altering the loading gauge enabled her to work over the principal Scottish routes when required, with their tighter loading gauge profiles.

Such new found pleasures couldn't last! It was back to the class 'N2s' and 'L1s' working 'round the houses' as explained in the last chapter, except that our link normally worked the heavier 13-coach and upwards trains. Then a set-back occurred. A bout of flu laid me low for 10 days. Finally, on 23rd January, Joe shook my hand warmly to welcome me aboard as his new mate. We were to have a very happy year together. A typical selection of the duties covered by No. 4 link will be found in Table Six.

'L1' class 2-6-4T No. 67785 crosses Woolmer Green viaduct with the 11.21 am to Baldock on 20th August, 1956.   *R.M. Newland*

Table Six - King's Cross No. 4 Link - Extract of Work Roster, 1957/58

We frequently did not work the same diagram duty for a full week. A representative selection of typical diagram workings is therefore listed in the weekly order as they appeared on our link roster.

Week	On duty	Diagram No. & Working
1	1.50 pm	230 - 3.10 LE Fins. Pk; 3.40 ecs Broad St.; 4.39 Hitchin; 6.05 Baldock; LE Hitchin; Work as req. back to Top Shed.
2	7.23 am	237 - EP; 7.38 LE KX; 8.08 Cambridge;12.50 KX; dispose & prepare engine at KX Passr. Loco. for 2nd set; Off duty 3.23.
3	10.00 pm	? diag. no. - EP; 10.20 LE KX Goods; 10.40 P'boro New England; LE Top Shed or work as req.; Off duty 6.00.
4	5.15 am	254 - Rel. KX 5.40; 5.42 ecs Hornsey; LE KX; 8.13 ecs Hornsey; LE Hornsey Shed; work as req. to Control orders; Off duty 1.15.
5	7.25 pm	285 - EP; 7.50 LE KX Goods; 8.20 P'boro Westwood; 12.45 KX Goods; LE Top Shed; Off duty 3.25.
6	5.23 am	232 - 6.23 LE KX; 6.53 Cambridge; 11.25 KX; LE Top Shed; Off duty 2.20.
7	3.15 pm	237 - 4.15 LE KX; attach to 4.24 Hitchin (double headed wkg.); 5.50 Cambridge; 8.50 KX; LE Top Shed; Off duty 11.59.
8	3.15 am	19 - EP; 3.30 LE KX; 4.00 Grantham; passr Doncaster; 8.49 KX; Rel. on arr.; Off duty 11.58 (this was a No. 3 link roster wkg coverd by No. 4 link men as required).
9	10.20 pm	279 - No. 1 Passenger Shunt Pilot KX Passenger Stn. Off duty 6.20.
10	4.20 pm	51 - EP; 4.35 LE KX; 5.05 Grantham; LE or As req. Top Shed; Off duty 12.20.
11	6.25 am	280 - 7.10 LE KX; No. 2 Shunt Pilot; Rel by 2nd set 2.00; Off duty 2.25.
12	12.01 am	As required - we could be booked to cover any duty during this week.
13	9.00 pm	? diag. no.; EP 9.15 LE Clarence Yard; 9.45 P'boro New England; 3.10 Fins. Pk East Yard; LE Top Shed; Off duty 5.30.
14	5.15 pm	20 - 6.15 LE KX; 6.45 P'boro Nth; Relieved; walk to New England Westwood Yard; 10.48 KX Goods; LE Top Shed; Off duty 2.05
15	12.10 pm	235 - Relieve at KX; 2.16 Cambridge; 5.21 KX; LE Top Shed; Off duty 9.05
16	7.50 am	251 - Relieve KX 8.15; 8.43 ecs Hornsey; LE KX; Carriage Pilot; 2.34 ecs Holloway; LE Top Shed; Off duty 4.20.

Typical rostered Sunday diagram workings were:

6.50 pm	95 - 7.50 LE KX; 8.20 Grantham; 11.58 KX; Relieved 2.35; Off duty 2.50.
6.51 am	293 - 7.51 LE KX; 8.21 Cambridge; 11.50 KX; LE KX Passr. Loco.; Off duty 2.51.
7.36 pm	291 - 8.36 LE KX; 9.21 Royston; 11.20 ecs Baldock; 11.50 LE Hitchin; 1.00 ecs Fins. Pk CS; LE Top Shed; Off duty 3.36.
11.50 am	90 - 12.50 LE KX; 1.20 Grantham; 5.28 KX; Relieved 7.40; Off duty 7.55.

Notes
The full roster covered 36 weeks of work in this link.
ecs = empty coaching stock
EP = Engine prepared
Fins. Pk = Finsbury Park
KX = King's Cross Passenger Station
LE = Light Engine
P'boro = Peterborough
Rel. = Relief

'9F' class 2-10-0 No. 92042 leaves the Hertford Loop at Bounds Green with a New England-Ferme Park freight on 5th February, 1955.   *S. Creer*

Class 'N2/4' No. 69589 on a down ballast working approaches Wood Green in 1958. My main line regular mate, driver Joe Denley and myself leaning out holding the firing shovel. This was a special Sunday turn where we had relieved the early morning crew in the platform at Finsbury Park immediately before getting the 'right away'. The incorrect headlamp code (for a light engine) and headboard display were only discovered upon arrival at Hitchin, but by this time our sins of omission had been recorded for posterity by my brother!   *Ken Butcher*

Our first day out was very low key, doing two trips clanking 'round the houses' on an 'L1' tank No. 67793. A couple of days later, it was back on the main line, this time to Grantham and back on another 'A4' No. 60006 *Sir Ralph Wedgewood*, named after a former Director of the LNER. The first 'A4' to carry his name had become a victim of Hitler's bombs and was scrapped as a result of an air raid on York shed in 1942. We worked the 8.20 pm express (for Edinburgh) down and returned with the 11.58 pm express from Grantham back to King's Cross.

The following day gave me my first trip on a 'Spaceship'. These were the hugely successful BR Standard design heavy freight engines, class '9F', with the unusual 2-10-0 wheel arrangement with the flangeless centre driving wheels. We had the most modern version of this design, with a twin chimney exhaust system, but built to a different design to the 'Kylchap' type. They had wide fireboxes, similar to the Pacifics, and they could not only pull, but also run! Speeds in the 80s were common, despite their small-sized driving wheels, designed for heavy goods train haulage. Not only could they pull heavy loads, more importantly, they could also stop them, with so many coupled driving wheels to provide excellent braking capacity. Our steed for the trip down was No. 92184. We worked the 666 down express goods, 8.20 pm from King's Cross. We were soon turned out on to the main line to follow in the wake of the 8.20 pm express passenger. We worked back with the 1321 up express goods, 12.45 am from New England yards with class 'V2' No. 60889. During these early runs together Joe was teaching me the route knowledge so necessary to make our trips together more satisfactory.

On the GN section all trains were given a reporting number in the working timetables (WTT). Down trains usually had even numbers, up trains usually had odd numbers. We rarely referred to main line workings by their time, but instead used their reporting number. When we said, for example, that we were working 666 Dn, everybody immediately knew which train we were talking about. If we were to have said 8.20 pm goods, a blank reaction would have been the probable response. With each new issue of the WTT, trains were often marginally retimed to accommodate altered services. It caused little disruption to the daily working language using the reporting numbers, which were not altered. An excellent system, although it suffered a hiccup when the new four character BR-style headcodes were introduced, until we learned the new identity codes. Regrettably, the new BR codes were less respectful of the odd and even number practices, although most principal workings retained the old pattern. To aid clarity of understanding in this narrative, I will use the clock times to describe our workings, although the reporting numbers will creep in occasionally as background as we continue our journey together.

The third of my three failures to produce the required steam occurred soon after the above trips. Joe and I had booked on to discover our rostered working was cancelled. Instead we were sent 'on the cushions' to Peterborough to pick up a special train of ballast hoppers required urgently in London. During our preparation of class 'WD' 'Austerity' No. 90158 Joe noticed an ominous remark chalked on the cylinder casing, to say she had been water tested. This suggested trouble.

It was the only trip we had together with one of these engines as King's Cross men very rarely worked on them. We soon discovered the kettle wouldn't boil.

'9F' class 2-10-0 No. 92174 approaches Finsbury Park with 40 vacuum-fitted 16 ton mineral wagons for King's Cross Loco. on 8th May, 1958.

We struggled along from one goods loop to the next on this particularly dark and stormy Saturday night. In each loop we had to pause for breath - in our parlance a 'blow-up' (already explained in Chapter Four) - to regain boiler water levels and steam pressure. It was a long and frustrating journey! Eventually at Knebworth, to do even this proved impossible. Joe advised Control to terminate us, before we stopped short of steam on the main line. South of Knebworth there is only double track through the Welwyn tunnels and over the long Welwyn viaduct. We would have caused chaos. We were surprised when Control suggested we took the Hertford Loop line - which was open that night - but Joe declined, as this would have meant returning to Stevenage first. There are two long tunnels and some stiff gradients on this route which would almost certainly have been a problem, plus the absence of any goods loops to escape into. We had rocked and rolled and rattled our way slowly forward for most of the journey at barely 20 mph. Joe decided we had had enough of it, fighting against ever lengthening odds. We were not the first crew to fail her, as witnessed by the need for a water test. This was only done to check poor steaming engines. We tried every trick in the book that we knew. Joe thrashed her, worked her lightly, tried long and short cut-offs, all to no avail. I had white hot thin fire all over the box, thick fire at the front and thin at the back and vice versa, thick fire all over, but no matter what we tried the end result was not forthcoming. She beat us. Our coal wasn't too bad, but she just would not produce the results. The exhaust beats weren't good, but still tolerable. We could detect no blows in the smokebox, she was just a lame duck. Joe in his report, suggested checking the blastpipe alignment with the chimney. In one loop we said to the bobby (signalman in railway language) to 'keep us inside' until we popped the whistle. I set to, to partially clean the fire, but it made little difference. We even had a struggle to get her home over the final mileage, LE. New England had certainly worked one into us that night, to get rid of a dud engine. A rough trip like this helped put the rest of the daily action into a better perspective. We often had to struggle, but rarely like we did that night. My ribs were bruised and aching, something that had not happened for some time.

Regular workings to Cambridge, usually on 'B1s', but sometimes with a Pacific, such as when we had 'A3' No. 60108 again, became a normal part of our lives. These workings were usually nice little numbers, with relatively light loadings, particularly on the Buffet Expresses.

Sometimes, I would pop round to visit my former landlady, Mrs King, during our layover at Cambridge. She had retired after being a district nurse for nearly all her working life. It was always a pleasure to have a chat and cup of tea with her. During these visits I came to know her better than when living with her. Her stories of attendance at childbirth could be very entertaining. When lodging with her, aged 17, she hadn't been comfortable talking about such a subject, but now being aged 23, she felt able to talk more freely. Remember, 50 years ago, female conditions were very much more considered to be non-male areas of conversation. Her greatest disappointment in life was not to reach 1,000 births - she got to 984. She could tell a tale or two! One of her favourite stories concerned a very highly strung mother-to-be who had absolutely no idea that twins were about to be born. The first baby arrived, and the mother began to relax, thankful that the ordeal was over. Mrs K, who had her suspicions of a

'A3' class Pacific No. 60066 *Merry Hampton* on King's Cross shed with 'A4' class Pacific No. 60028 *Walter K. Whigham* to the left.   *C.R.L. Coles*

twin, had to gently explain she was sure another was waiting! Both babies were quite small, and the mother claimed her doctor had not told her - Mrs K thought the doctor might have done this deliberately in case the news would un-nerve her completely. She never met that particular doctor, who was a temporary locum, so she never found out. Whatever the facts of the matter, the mother, upon news of the second one, promptly passed out! Mrs K had therefore an unconscious mother about to give birth, with the first child bawling merrily away alongside her while she did so with no help, and unable to leave the mother to summon any. This had occurred in her earliest days as a district nurse, long before today's modern pre-natal care became a feature of working class mothers' pregnancies. She had retired at age 65, after over 40 years as a mid-wife, and was then a widow into her 70s when we first met in 1952. She was a kindly, warm hearted lady, who would help anybody if she could.

On one of my trips to Cambridge with Harry Brown, when Joe had a couple of days off, we had a 'B1' No. 61200 just new out of works, and she ran absolutely silently. We could easily hear the rail joints, most unusual on a 'B1'. She steamed so freely, the fire nearly got too low. Harry had noticed this and when we stopped at Hatfield with our down semi-fast working surprised me by saying, 'Come on young David, its time for you have hold! I feel like a little exercise', he announced. So off we went with me doing the necessary, for the first time on the Cambridge road, and offering a silent 'Thank you' to Joe for insisting I learn the road properly.

'Do you know your way round Cambridge station?', he asked as we pulled out of Harston, the last stop before Cambridge.

'Yes' I replied, 'I will be alright'.

He gave me a quizzical look, but made no comment, and left me to it. Later, sitting in the shed messroom, one or two of my former mates recognised me and had a chat. Harry wanted to know, 'How came they knew me?' One of them explained we both used to work on the yard pilots! That let the cat out of the bag, amidst a very wry smile from Harry. He enjoyed the leg-pull.

We were booked to work a Buffet Express up road, and naturally it was assumed he would resume the driving, as I went to slip out to build up the fire.

'Put a good lump into her' he said as I left the room.

Odd, I thought, but did as requested and then returned for a final brew up. As we walked to the engine, he turned to me.

'OK, clever clogs (remembering the leg pull), have you driven a fast express before today?'

'No, not really, only our Southend semi-fasts to Liverpool St.'

'Want to have a go then?'

Seeing my hesitation, he said, 'Go on, get on with it, I'll keep an eye on you'.

And so off we went, first stop Letchworth, then Hitchin, Welwyn Garden City, and King's Cross. At Hitchin, Harry had a 'cuppa' while his driver slipped half a dozen quick rounds of coal into the firebox. Then off we went away up the GN main line. It was a very stimulating experience. As we ran in through Finsbury Park normal practice was followed when running into a terminus, to offer him control, but he said, 'No, you've done alright so far, you had better finish it off'.

It was a very cautious final run in and probably a minute or so dropped, but the guard came by the cab window to say, 'All OK driver, right time'.

So ended my first main line express driving experience. Harry was to let me do the driving occasionally again. Well into his fifties, he enjoyed the physical exercise that firing gave him. He will appear again in this narrative, in a later chapter.

Another memorable event early in my main line career occurred when I was booked to be with a shed shunting driver, Dick McArthur, down at the Bottom Bunk as it was called. This was located alongside the turntable at the shed. Our function was to clear the fire-dropping pits of engines after disposal and examination by the duty fitter. It was normal practice for the crew to split up with one driving the shunting 'mike' or pilot, and the other working the point handles and controlling the shunting from the ground. It was always a bit of a 'hit and miss' type action to get the shunting done, in between the other engine movements departing the shed to drop down to the shed outlet road. Our 'mike' was the ex-GN class 'J52' 'Donkey' 0-6-0 saddle tank No. 68846. This was unusual because she was normally a Hornsey engine. Probably, she had come to Top Shed for attention in the workshop and was booked on this duty for a day or two to check she was alright before being returned - she nearly didn't make it! The origin of the 'Donkey' nickname was never discovered. Perhaps the connection was their rugged pulling and staying power as a maid of all work.

Top Shed was so called, not because it was the best shed, although our biased partisanship would claim this, but to distinguish it from the Bottom Shed, or 'Passenger Loco.' as it was known, located alongside the King's Cross station track throat. This could be a very busy place which took a lot of pressure away from the hectic cauldron that was Top Shed. The volume of LE movements between the station and Top Shed, and within the station area to and from the Passenger Loco. was very considerable. The function of the Bottom Bunk crews to keep the disposal pits clear of engines was a vital component in the smooth working of Top Shed, and in turn of the passenger station, by avoiding a backlog building up of engines requiring to come to it. If we couldn't receive engines for whatever reason, then the passenger station would soon be in dire difficulties. The Bottom Bunk shift was an interesting turn of duty that only very rarely came my way if rostered spare duty as required and no main line work was available.

We had done a couple of shunts when one movement caught me out. Dick was supervising from the ground with myself driving the 'Donkey'. To save time two Pacific engines were being shunted - my decision to do this as the cabin foreman was getting concerned about the backlog of clearance shunts. Their combined weight nearly caused a nasty collision with another movement. Even with the sands open to increase adhesion and braking, on the slight down grade, our little engine was beginning to lose control. Dick could see this and as we came closer to a collision ordered me to abandon ship. This was reluctantly done with the regulator left full open intentionally so the engine was trying to push the movement back, away from the other engine that had so unexpectedly stopped foul of our line. Having started to draw slowly forward on Dick's signal to do so, he had assumed the other engine was going to move clear of us. At the critical moment it could not because of another engine preventing this. Thus, the braking distance Dick had assumed, was lost. We barely had time to watch the inevitable mishap as the movement slid towards the final two or three feet. A heavy glancing blow at slow speed with 350 tons of weight doing the pushing, can do some mighty damage, quite apart from the loss of the engines being available. The sand pipe was still running while we stood powerless, when at the final second the wheels got a grip and the old girl began oh!, ever-so-slowly, to start going the other way. It was like watching a Keystone Cops' sketch from the era of silent movies, being played out in slow motion. We had come within inches of disaster. The moment the wheels gripped immediate action was taken to climb back up on board and the day was saved. It was my fault moving two engines when one was the normal practice. We could take such a risk a thousand times, and then the unforeseen would happen with no warning. We afterwards discovered oil on the rails - not a real excuse, the circumstance should not have occurred in the first place.

Looking round, it was surprising how many onlookers had gathered as if by magic to watch events unfold. Even the Bottom Cabin foreman who directed our activities, had emerged from his little brick building to see what was going on. He subsequently, and rightly, gave me a dressing down for not moving the Pacifics one at a time.

'You are a main line fireman and should know better', is a much censored summary of his blunt words.

But when you are scrambling about to avoid possible delays, you take the occasional risk. This one turned into a risk too far, for it very nearly put the shed out of action. Then it wouldn't have been a verbal dressing down, but probably the full book opened up, with a disciplinary charge and for Dick also, as the driver in charge of my actions. By such slender threads - in this case with barely six inches of distance remaining to catastrophe - do you retain an unblemished record. The foreman did acknowledge he had asked us to 'look sharp' as congestion had built up during the shift changeover period which was why I decided to take the risk to speed matters along. It might have just saved our skins. Fortunately, this was not put to the test!

No. 68846 was to be later repainted, organised by our shedmaster Peter Townend for a special exhibition at Wood Green, to be referred to again in Volume Two. This act was eventually to lead to the engine being purchased for private preservation and its survival today as GNR No. 1247. The odds would have been strongly against this happening if the old girl had been bent that day. The damage would probably have caused her to have been scrapped instead, being at the end of her working life, as the cost of repairs would probably not have been authorised.

Those magic few inches of track were to make their contribution to the growth of the steam engine preservation movement. No. 68846 became the first engine to be sold by BR out of traffic, in full working order, into preservation, in May 1959. *Flying Scotsman* was to be sold likewise out of service, in 1961, to be followed by several others as the final years of steam drew to a close. Authority at BTC level were not keen on 'live' engines entering the private domain, wanting to see them disposed of as scrap to avoid all non-diesel publicity as they promoted the new image. No. 68846 created the crack in their armour by establishing the precedent that it could be done - and a good job too. Funny old world, the way an unknown minor event can contribute towards later more important developments. We didn't damage her, and thus she survived to be specially repainted to carry the full BR lined black livery for the Wood Green exhibition. But for this decision, it is extremely unlikely she would have been selected for sale and thereby make a pioneering contribution to the preservation story!

A couple of days later, more road knowledge was gained with a trip to Doncaster, pushing my boundary of experience ever further northwards along the East Coast route. This trip found me firing to Len Pibworth, as Joe did not sign for the road beyond Grantham. We worked the 4.00 am express from King's Cross to Leeds as far as Grantham, with class 'A3' No. 60039 *Sandwich*. After relief and travelling forward 'on the cushions' to Doncaster, it was our turn to relieve the incoming crew on class 'A1' No. 60148 *Aboyeur*, to return with the 7.50 am Leeds express departing at 8.54 am non-stop over the 156 miles to London. Most of the ex-LNER Pacific class engines were named after famous racehorses and hence the sometimes peculiar names, such as that carried by our engine. We had two good runs. My mastery of the skills needed for high speed express work was steadily improving with each trip. We ran to time throughout with Len having all the steam needed - occasionally too much, which is bad practice. Lack of road knowledge north of Grantham was a handicap, but he kept an eye on matters with friendly encouragement and advice.

It was very demanding work, both physically and mentally, but usually very satisfying. Some engines, particularly the 'A1' class members, could be very lively riders at the higher speeds, and occasionally, very rough-riding machines. Sometimes, one came home black and blue with bruises from 'A1s', but never from 'A3s' or 'A4s', which were far smoother-riding machines to work on. Main line trips on 'A2s' never came my way, rather surprisingly, so a knowledgeable comment of what they were like cannot be offered. We had none on our shed roster, and fate decreed that although I occasionally prepared them for other crews, a main line run on one never occurred. The 'A3' could be a hard riding engine, but never a rough-rider. A rough- or even a hard-riding 'A4' was never known. They were exemplary riders and very comfortable engines on which to work - this opinion is based upon having worked on nearly all of Top Shed's 'A4' fleet as 1958 progressed. Few drivers took the 'A1s' much above 90 mph because of the way they could waggle their back ends quite severely without warning for no obvious reason. The 'A3s', within my experience of them, were rarely driven much above 90 mph, although capable of it. With the 'A4s' we would often come down Stoke Bank approaching 100 mph, and sometimes a bit above this speed. My own personal highest was about 105 mph on a trip with Ben Oakton to be described in Volume Two. Other crews went higher, but a twist of fate was to deny me such opportunities, except for one memorable journey as a passenger behind Bill Hoole on his 'swansong' RCTS trip with 'No. 7', when we reached 112 mph, with a special authority to allow this to take place.

On 21st February came a footplate trip with a difference. Travelling home on the Circle Line, as we ran into Liverpool St, quite by chance there standing alongside his steed in the bay platform was a friend from the Dawlish Home. John Jackson was a Met. line electric loco driver based at Neasden LTE shed. We hadn't met since being together at Dawlish although we had kept contact. The chance to say 'hello' was too good to miss. What was not intended was to find myself riding with him to Rickmansworth and back on his Met. line electric locomotive! A most unexpected pleasure and a very enjoyable experience. These trains were LTE-owned vacuum-braked stock worked on LTE tracks, operated by LTE locomotives, as a through service worked forwards from Rickmansworth by BR steam engines to Amersham over BR-owned tracks at that time. No. 6 *William Penn* and her sisters were air-braked machines, similar to all other LTE passenger rolling stock. She was not fitted with an air/vacuum proportional valve, or, if she was, it was out of use. As the train came to a stand with the vacuum brake coaches, the locomotive could bounce back and forward on the coupling drawhook, if John did not also separately apply the locomotive air brake as well. His technique was to run in on the vacuum with the locomotive air brakes just rubbing the wheels. As we came to a stand, he applied the air brake fully, which then held the train while he recreated the vacuum ready for departure, when the air brake would be released. Two vacuum exhausters were provided. On this trip John had one with a fault, not working. It was interesting to see how he overcame the slower release of the vacuum brake and avoided delay to the train, by relying on the locomotive air brake to save time. This was to be my only ride on one of these very interesting and unusual machines. One has survived - *Sarah Siddons* - preserved in working order by London Underground Lines (as the successor to LTE) for special operations.

Two days later, back with Joe again, we had a gallop to Grantham and back on class 'A4' No. 60032 *Gannet* working the same diagram as on our first Grantham trip together - 8.20 pm down and 11.58 pm back. Joe had taught me the road, and was now testing my knowledge of it. Without warning he began to ask. 'What is the next signal that we are approaching?', or 'What is the permitted speed?' Later on, as my knowledge increased, he would quiz me on the location of facing trap points, trailing catch points, where water column and lineside telephone facilities existed, and countless other details that the keen engineman took the trouble to learn, such as the incline of the gradients. On today's vastly modernised railway so much of this knowledge is no longer needed with the much greater provision of power signalling, cab to base radio links, and the elimination of most catch and trap points, for example. In steam days we relied very heavily on oil-lit mechanical signalling with long distances between signal boxes. There were very few intermediate phones available. This vital road knowledge was required at our fingertips, if faced with an emergency situation. An engine breaks down in fog - which way should we walk for assistance, once the immediate emergency protection arrangements have been complied with? Many locations, such as on the remote Stilton Fen south of Peterborough can be very lonely places on a wild winter's night. If the failure occurs, say, two miles from one box and five from another, valuable time could be saved by knowing our location and going to the nearest one. Such knowledge builds up the finer arts of enginemanship that a keen crew teach themselves, just in case.

Knowledge of catch point locations was vital. If our engine failed in the section and it became necessary for the driver to issue a wrong line order 'Form

'A3' Pacific No. 60039 *Sandwich* accelerates towards Copenhagen tunnel with the 'Yorkshire Pullman'.

Eric Treacy

B' to authorise the assisting engine to come back wrong line onto the front of our engine, details of these had to be entered on the form as a double safeguard to remind the assisting driver. There were four different forms for wrong line working - 'A', coloured pink, issued by the guard to the signalman, controlled movements onto the guard's train from the signal box in advance of the train - used if the train was divided, either accidentally or intentionally and the train engine had worked forward to the signal box in advance; 'B', coloured green, served the same function, but was issued by a driver, to control movements back to that driver from the signal box ahead of where his train was at a stand - used if the engine was unable to move due to failure; 'C', coloured white, issued by a guard to a driver to set back to rejoin two halves of a divided train within the one block section between two signal boxes; and 'D', coloured yellow, issued by a signalman to a driver to control a movement back to that box from the section ahead of it - used to return a failed train/and or engine back to the box in rear. The choice of which form was appropriate depended upon which direction it was decided the assistant engine should come from and in which direction the crippled engine/and or train was going to be moved to clear the line. Throughout my footplate career, I always carried a green 'Form B' inside my Rule Book, together with a spare red flag, and a vacuum pipe rubber ring, in the breast pocket of my issue serge jacket - neither form nor flag were ever needed, but the rubber ring was useful on several occasions.

Joe kept me 'on my toes', as the old saying has it. It became a point of honour never to admit he had caught me out. It meant studying the Sectional Appendix fairly thoroughly. He did this with all the roads we ran over. With increasing proficiency, he started to ask, 'Where is the next road bridge located ?' - all vital knowledge that enginemen were, and in some respects still are, required to know in the darkness. Today, catch points especially, with rare exceptions, are just a memory, following the abolition of loose-coupled goods trains.

A 'Catch Point' is a trailing set of spring worked point blades inserted in up hill track to catch runaway vehicles; a 'Trap Point' is a signal box-worked facing set of point blades inserted into any track to trap, i.e., prevent a train fouling another track, if it fails to stop in time when it should do.

The 31st March found me working my first lodging turn. This was to Leeds and back with Harry Newland, on 'A3' No. 60059 *Tracery*. (Throughout most of the 1958 summer timetable, two engines - this one and No. 60039 *Sandwich* - worked turn and turn about, each alternate day, on this diagram). We had the heaviest daytime passenger train, at that time, booked out of King's Cross, the 5.20 pm 'Yorkshire Pullman' loading to 11 Pullman cars (Pullmans were never called coaches) weighing about 440 tons tare, say about 460 tons gross. The irony being it was rostered for the least powerful Pacific class, the 'A3'! They could handle it without much difficulty, it was just a curious anomaly. We worked the 10.00 am up from Leeds the next morning. It was harder work for me between Doncaster and Leeds, not knowing the road, with the odd fierce gradient to contend with. Harry was very good with his helpful guidance over this stretch. It was to be my only trip over the West Riding main line.

The amusing aspect of this turn was the lodge we were booked into at the ex-Midland Railway/LMS shed at Farnley Jn. This was a real old fashioned relic of a building. It was by far the worst lodge we had to use. It was a large dormitory divided by wooden partitions that neither reached the floor nor the ceiling, rather like a public toilet cubicle. If one person snored, we all suffered with him. A poor arrangement for the latter half of the 20th century. The ornate style of the wooden partitions suggested it had been built back in the 19th century. Washing facilities were equally as spartan, reminding one of military style barrack arrangements. Our other lodges were far superior to this primitive left-over from a long-gone age. It was very comparable to the dormitory building that was located right in the middle of the Stratford shed complex. This was surrounded by the smoke emissions and noise of steam engines. Very difficult to maintain a semblance of cleanliness within. Windows, although provided, could not be opened with all the sulphurous fumes. The aroma of sweating bodies could be smelt unless the penetrating aroma of smoke blotted it out. The Farnley Jn version was similar. Harry's practice was to buy fish and chips, maybe have a pint or two, before taking the long walk to the lodge. This is what we did. We had a good wash on the engine before leaving it. It was too late to consider going to the pictures, so the meal and the social pint made a pleasant evening before turning in for the night. The next morning it was back to Copley Hill to prepare '59' for the homeward trip. The lodge was not good, but the engine and the trip home were.

We had other lodges at Hull, Newcastle, and York. The Hull working never came my way. This was always rostered for class 'B1' engines, due to bridge weight restrictions beyond Doncaster. It was one of the longest distances scheduled for this class of engine anywhere in the country, almost 200 miles, working one train throughout with one crew.

Saturday 5th April went from the sublime to the ridiculous, being booked to work my first lodge turn to Newcastle. This was altered at short notice to working on the Passenger Station No. 2 Shunt with Bill Brindle on 'N2' No. 69516! A very leisurely afternoon was quietly spent reflecting on what might have been. The following week with Joe, we were running to Cambridge and back. The Monday was interesting with my first trip on a BR Standard class '5' No. 73159. She was a decent engine. It was unusual for us to have one of this type. Joe was not keen on them, claiming the draughty cab was uncomfortable. This was a regular complaint, particularly by drivers who had little choice but to sit down on all Standard tender engines, being denied the fireman's physical activity to help blood circulation.

All BR Standard designs had modern equipment - self cleaning smokeboxes, rocking fire grates and ashpan hoppers. Both boiler water injector controls were on the fireman's side, which avoided distracting the driver, as could occur with the traditional layout of one each side of the cab. The driver had all his gauges and controls comfortably at hand, as did the fireman. The tender shovelling plates were at a sensible height and made the task of firing more comfortable and less back-breaking than some of our older design engines. The one big complaint was the draughtiness of the cabs on the tender engines. Efforts were made to alleviate this but with only limited success. Although we had the hot fire hole, the cold draughts would swirl around our backsides and could be very uncomfortable at times, particularly in the winter.

An unusual trip came shortly after this when, with Sam Trigg, we worked a naval special express non-stop to Grantham. We returned LE for 105 miles back to the shed. We had the original class 'V2' No. 60800 *Green Arrow* for this day out with a difference. It was unusual to travel so far light engine, as normally Control would find a train for us to work.

At the end of April a week on the Cambridge Buffet Expresses with various class 'B1s' was rounded off with a Sunday run to Grantham and back on 'A3' No. 60062 *Minoru*, down with the 1.20 pm express for Leeds and back with the 5.28 pm non-stop restaurant car express. This was an unusual working as we were booked to run 'block and block' (as we called it) throughout to London just 10 minutes behind another similar train. The 'A3s' were a fireman's engine and with the open-backed cab we did not get so dusty as with the other Pacific classes. Most were still equipped with the old single-chimney equipment which required a more exact firing technique than with the double-chimney engines, to achieve the best results. They really were a very satisfying engine to work on, if one took the time and interest to understand them properly.

Many years later, long after leaving BR, the opportunity came my way to have a go on the shovel on *Flying Scotsman* southwards from Banbury. The years had passed, and likewise my age had advanced since last firing an 'A3' - it came as something of a surprise to realise the extent to which the back had lost its strength. The skills required to fire right into the back corners of the wide firebox had not diminished one little bit, but the stamina definitely had! Passing Bicester it was prudent to acknowledge the obvious and hand back the shovel to its rightful owner with grateful thanks for his kindness in letting me have a spell reliving a past life that it had been assumed would never come my way again. To be riding a main line engine, working hard at speed, and to experience the familiar movement, noise, and smells, recalled many memories of these most successful engines upon which the daily bread had once been earned. This had included this particular one, separated by a span of almost 30 years between the two trips. It was great to be on board her again. My wife had even foregone our planned day out together (it happened to be on Mother's Day!). Not only that, the dear lady even drove many miles through unknown countryside to collect me afterwards. She said that when we married, she married BR as well - not completely true, but her sentiment does have validity!

So life and my increasing experience, together with improved road knowledge, steadily gathered momentum as the weeks went by. Main line work was regularly interspersed with carriage trip duties 'round the houses', usually with class 'L1s', working the heavier trains out of the terminus. These would often load up to 15, sometimes 16, and even, occasionally, 17 bogie vehicles, off incoming up expresses. Such passenger train weights and lengths do not exist in today's era of fixed train formations. Steam specials rarely exceed 12, although up to 14 has been known, but this is exceptional. Today, one might see an empty stock or parcels working reaching such loadings, but precious little else.

The No. 4 link provided spare men for the top links, and hence the number of trip turns in the link. This enabled the duty roster clerks to cover these, utilising passed cleaners/junior firemen and passed firemen/junior drivers to replace us

'L1' class 2-6-4T No. 67779 at Red Hall, immediately south of Hatfield, in 1958 with an up Baldock to King's Cross outer suburban working, with your author on board as the fireman.
Peter I. Paton

'A4' Pacific No. 60022 *Mallard* waits to leave King's Cross with 'The Elizabethan' in September 1953.
R.H. Clark

when required for working on top link duties, which regularly occurred. I worked many of the top link turns, mainly to Newcastle, but not the prestigious non-stop 'Elizabethan' turn to Edinburgh. This turn was jealously guarded by the regular No. 1 link crews who hardly ever failed to maintain their roster to work it! The 'Elizabethan' was the longest regularly scheduled non-stop steam-hauled train in the world, at 393 miles distance. The Edinburgh, Haymarket, crew and the London, King's Cross, crew changed over north of York, via the unique corridor tenders specially built for this service. King's Cross shed also crewed the longest regularly scheduled non-stop steam-hauled goods train in the world, of which more in Volume Two.

One trip merits a special mention, when 5th May became an unexpected surprise. Rostered with George Crutchly on 'A3' No. 60110 *Robert the Devil*, to work to Grantham and back with the (371 down) 12.20 pm and 5.48 pm up special expresses, seemed a normal duty. We booked on and walked round to check the late notice case for any last minute advice of altered speed restrictions or other working arrangements, then headed for our engine. This had already been prepared by another crew, waiting for us to climb aboard. We were soon dropping down to the outlet signal. For a duty like this, we booked on 45 minutes before station departure time; for this diagram, at 11.35 am, to ring out at the outlet signal to the Goods & Mineral box signalmen, at 11.50 am, ready for departure from the station at 12.20 pm. It will be realised from this description, we had little time to hang about. It was also essential to comply with Rule 0, which, you know by now, takes precedence over almost everything else. For a fireman to be letting his driver depart from the shed without obeying this is the ultimate unofficial disciplinary offence! As we were dropping down to the outlet signal, George casually remarked, 'Do you realise we are booked to Grantham at an average speed of just over 60 mph, start to stop?' Not exactly just another routine trip on our 'A3'! Clearly a little bit extra was going to be required from the fireman, who was at that moment far more concerned to pour the freshly brewed liquid.

Experience of high speeds on the (20-year-old) streamlined 'A4s' had become a regular pleasure. To suddenly realise we were about to do it with an engine approaching twice this age, sent a real tingle up the spine. *Robert the Devil* was another of the original GNR-designed machines, ordered by them for building, and delivered in the early days of the LNER. In common with the rest of the class, she had been modified over the years. In her case this had included recent alterations to her single blastpipe in an early attempt to improve the steaming qualities, only partially successful. It was not until the decision to fit the full double blast pipe system, to all class 'A3' and 'A4' Pacifics and some 'V2s', that these engines really began to surprise us with their much improved steaming abilities, already referred to. The run to be described was done with the single chimney still installed.

Our guard advised we had 'nine on'. Sharp at 12.20 pm we got the 'right away', but then a slight delay had George muttering, before we actually moved off one minute down due to a late passenger scrambling aboard the train. This was a regular hazard we always kept a good lookout for. Once we had slogged away as usual through the Gasworks and Copenhagen tunnels to the top of the steep climb past Holloway, we began to gather speed towards Finsbury Park, steadily building up into the 50s. Watching points very closely to see how the old lady was performing proved the fire was in good shape - a normal routine. By Wood Green, after the short stretch of favourable road through Hornsey, George had her going really well, with a nice crisp bark from the chimney while the fire was now entirely to my liking. The steam pressure gauge needle was hovering almost on the red line. The boiler water level was nicely towards the top of the glass, and clearly visible.

It can be very annoying for a driver with the safety valves blowing off if he is using the brake. The loud noise masks the quieter noise of the brake application. When braking, especially coming to a stand, apart from maybe a quick glance at the brake gauge needles, a driver is looking outside the cab, he doesn't want to be checking inside the cab. It is important to avoid unnecessary distractions at such times. He relies upon his mate instinctively to understand his needs, and blowing off is not welcome. Apart from being good practice to keep water levels in sight in the upper part of the gauge glass, it ensures a margin is available to operate the water injectors to avoid blowing off. With known stops and speed reductions requiring the driver to close the regulator, you planned your engine management accordingly in advance, but adverse signals could not be forecast.

By New Southgate we were really into our stride in the 60 mph speed range. We continued like this all the way up the long grade to Potters Bar. George's driving style wasn't hurting her at all. She just sounded good. Over the top and speed quickly increased before he had to ease down a touch while we traversed the long sweeping reverse curves past Red Hall box and on through Hatfield. (This was the site of the tragic 2000 Hatfield mishap, when a shattered rail was to initiate a major review of track maintenance procedures. It also sent tremors throughout the industry with the resultant operating problems for many months afterwards.) Increasing the output again, we carried on in grand style through Welwyn Garden City, then the double track section over the high viaduct, through the North station, and the two tunnels - and on towards Knebworth, by now back on quadruple track. After easing back to around 60 mph to scoop the water troughs at Langley, speed was then quickly built up again as we continued through Stevenage and on down through Hitchin. It was customary to blow a long blast on the whistle as you approached this busy junction station, rather than the more normal shorter blast, to give good warning of your approach at high speed - we were up into the high 70s. After Hitchin commences one of those marvellous racing stretches for which the East Coast route is so famous. With speed now well up to the permitted 90 mph, we hurtled on past Cadwell, Tempsford, and Three Counties - George, 'Robert', and yours truly were all on form! We were motoring, with a positive, but not too loud, exhaust sound coming from the chimney. The engine was riding well with a smooth even motion, and steaming well. It was a beautiful experience - one that you really did not wish to end. Even the weather was obliging with a nice sunny day.

In this manner we continued, on through Biggleswade, Sandy, and St Neots. Past the Barford automatic signals alongside the electricity power station, until it was time to come down to 70 mph for the second set of long sweeping curves, this time through Offord station, before accelerating again on down through Huntingdon. Before this station we passed over the viaducts spanning the River Ouse and also the Cambridge - Kettering single line, mentioned in Chapter Four. George was soon opening 'Robert' out again to surmount the three mile climb up past the lonely Stukeley signal box and on to Abbots Ripton. Here, my steady work with the shovel could ease off, ready for the lengthy crossing of the Stilton Fen at the permitted 65 mph, before we rolled on through Yaxley, past the extensive brickworks, to slow down for the severe 20 mph limit required through Peterborough North station. This restriction, like so much else along the East Coast main line today, is now a distant memory since the large scale modernisation in more recent years to upgrade and electrify the route.

As the tail end of the train cleared the station area, and with the engine now approaching the Westwood box, one mile north of the station, George opened up again in earnest. Before this, as soon as the chimney had cleared the overhead station roof canopy, he had eased open the regulator a touch to keep the train under way while we cleared the station. This was the moment to quickly slip a round of coal into the box, before resuming my seat ready to sight the Westwood signals, out of George's sight line until we regained the straight main line again under Spital bridge. Once the Walton box distant was sighted in the cleared 'off' position under the Westwood home signal, located on the long gantry that spanned the tracks here, firing was resumed to prepare for the final long climb up to the Stoke summit, 20 miles away, five miles south of Grantham. The fire had been allowed to run down over the easier dozen miles or so prior to Peterborough. We were booked to come off the train at Grantham, so a balancing act was now required. Enough fire was needed for the gradually steepening long climb that started soon after Werrington, but equally the fire had to be run down low enough ready for disposal by the Grantham shed staff. Accelerating past the New England Yards with a good positive exhaust rhythm from the chimney as we gathered speed against the grade here, the fire was built up with single rounds using the 'little and often' firing style. This ensured a white hot fire bed was maintained. Then came a short down hill stretch, with a quick wave to the Walton signalman. He was looking out over his unusual interlaced track on the up goods lines through his road level crossing. Then, a final couple of rounds into the box were sufficient for a while.

Approaching Werrington Jn the boiler water injector was turned off. This had been on continuously since Holloway on the journey from London (apart from over the Langley troughs south of Stevenage) backed up as required with use of the second injector. We never, ever, left injectors on while scooping water. After scooping, we allowed the tender water to settle for a mile or so if we could, to minimise the risk of sucking any foreign matter into the tender water sieves. By waiting you allowed time for any rubbish scooped up to fall to the bottom of the tender tank. Scooping the Werrington troughs required teamwork between the driver and fireman to ensure no mishaps. Speed over troughs, because of the always well-soaked ballast beds, and to minimise possible damage to other trains, was limited to 60 mph. It was always a carefully judged operation at this location as the troughs started immediately after the junction trackwork for Spalding and Lincoln, and had a road level crossing just beyond the far end -

not good! Drop the scoop too soon, you could damage it on the junction trackwork, leave it too late and you underfilled the tender. It was all too easy to wreck the scoop on the road crossing if you were not quick enough winding it back up. On a run to Grantham, filling up at these troughs was not critical, so we dipped late and tried to lift early if we could. On a longer run a good tankful would be vital, to safeguard against the chance of the next troughs at Muskham, north of Newark, being low on water. A good fill at Werrington when working through beyond Grantham could mean less difficulty later on - not required on this trip.

Once clear of Werrington, it became a case of keeping up with George's working of the engine as we proceeded ever onwards and upwards through Essendine, Little Bytham, Corby Glen, and on under the M&GN Leicester main line overbridge, towards Stoke summit. Once past Essendine, the law of diminishing returns was practised. The gradient was getting steadily steeper but the fire bed thickness was gradually run down by just firing lightly as required. It was always music to my ears to listen to any engine barking away strongly up this bank. With No. 60110 and her single chimney, the steady roar was echoing back perhaps a little more strongly than was normal. She sounded magnificent as we steadily and surely reeled off the miles. Speed was built up after Werrington into the high 70s, before gradually dropping back into the 60s as George left her alone to make her own pace. She was working hard, but not struggling in any way. We were well to time and there was no need to thrash the old lady along. Our load of nine coaches was within the capability of the engine on the fast schedule we were maintaining.

Soon Stoke box came into view in the distance, to be followed a short while later by the tunnel entrance as you approached the left-hand curve into it. A quick wave to the bobby as he watched our progress past his box, and we were into the final tunnel for this trip. Throughout most of the climb the needle was hovering near to the red line on the pressure gauge, with the white feather from the safety valves flying nicely. Towards the top as the fire became thinner, the injector was now turned off and the water level mortgaged to save firing again. We entered the tunnel with just over half a glass after George eased the regulator back. Out the other end, with the reverser now brought back nearer to mid-gear, the injector went back on. Down past the High Dyke iron ore traffic exchange sidings, we were now running under easy steaming. Through Great Ponton station with speed back up in the 70s, it was soon time to shut the regulator for the final run into Grantham. With pressure now dropping back for the first time, we had made a good climb from Peterborough. The trip had gone well - it also boosted the ever growing confidence!

The gentle ringing noises from the motion echoed back to us as we ran into Grantham. These gradually eased off as we came to a stand with the shunter ready and waiting to uncouple us. We had run in a minute early, having gained two minutes on the 100 minute working time schedule for the 105 and a bit miles, with the minute late start. We had had a completely clear run with no signal checks. This, my first mile a minute scheduled working, had been a most rewarding experience. To have successfully accomplished the trip, on one of the very oldest Pacifics on the system (although modified since first constructed), somehow added a little extra sparkle to it all. Our return working on class 'V2' No. 60983, the last member of the class to be built in 1944 (21 years after 'Robert'!), was a kind of 'after the Lord Mayor's Show' sort of experience. It was good, but the sparkle was missing! The 'V2s' were an excellent all-round general purpose machine. They nearly always steamed well, ran well, and most importantly, they pulled well. We had a nice gallop down Stoke Bank in the 80s, and arrived back in London in good shape, although a couple of minutes down on our booked 7.59 pm arrival due to signal checks inwards from Finsbury Park.

The following day was out with George again, this time on one of the early single chimney 'Spaceships', No. 92039, working 264 down, the 12.20 pm express goods, King's Cross Goods to New England. The single-chimney '9Fs' did not run quite so freely as their twin-chimney sisters, but were still very good machines. Most unusually, there was no return working for us, so we enjoyed a ride home 'on the cushions', leaving others to take the strain at the head of the train. A total contrast in two days - in this respect the No. 4 link was always interesting as you never knew from one week to the next what might be in store. To ensure life didn't pale, it was back with Joe the next day on No. 60800 *Green Arrow* on the Cambridge buffet car trains. We could rarely complain of being bored, with the ever changing variety of work.

To give some idea of the staff problems that regularly had to be faced in running a large shed, the week commencing 19th May offers an indication. My booked working for this week (not with Joe who was rostered to cover main line work) was to work the 5.10 am parcels King's Cross to Baldock and the 10.45 am parcels Hitchin to King's Cross, each day. On the Monday, my booked driver rang in to say he was sick; on Tuesday my roster was altered on arrival for duty to work the 5.15 am parcels to Grantham and the 8.26 am express back with Joe, because his fireman had rung in to say he was unwell. We had 'V2' No. 60862 down, and 'A3' No. 60062 *Minoru* again, up road. On Wednesday with Joe because his fireman again failed to report for duty. On the Thursday my booked driver again failed to report for work; on Saturday I was changed to fire to John Hill because his mate had failed to turn up - we had BR Standard class '5' No. 73158 to Baldock and home 'on the cushions' from Hitchin. Granted, this was an exceptional run of late changes, but they were just the ones affecting myself. The shift running foremen had, perforce, to sort it all out in between their other duties organising engines to cover diagram workings, monitoring engine repairs and so on. Staff reporting sick were problems they didn't need.

The 27th May finally provided my first lodge trip to Newcastle firing to Bill Baines.

'No need to worry, my boy', said Bill when explaining my lack of knowledge north of Doncaster.

We booked on at 9.35 pm to prepare our own engine, class 'A1' No. 60128 *Bongrace*, to work the 11.35 pm express due into Newcastle at 4.45 am. My diary note says this train was 'The Night Scotsman', but this may have been 'The Tynesider'. We were relieved by Gateshead men on arrival and booked off duty at 5.15 am. Bill was an exceptionally light driver with our train, limited to 60 mph throughout, as it conveyed sleeping cars. It turned into a very comfortable

'A3' Pacific No. 60062 *Minoru* powers a Newcastle-bound train up the bank between Gasworks and Copenhagen tunnels. A 350 hp diesel shunter can be seen in the right background.

Eric Treacy

trip with Bill explaining a fair bit of the road to me as we progressed - ambled would maybe better describe it! - steadily northwards. It was all very relaxed .

Unlike the meagre facility at Leeds, our Newcastle lodge was at the Tyne Temperance Hotel, near to the station. This was the regular lodge for London men. It seemed to cater mainly for commercial travellers and the like, judging by our fellow diners. We were always given rooms on the top floor to avoid being disturbed by others. A light breakfast snack of cornflakes sufficed before turning in, to awake, fresh as a daisy about 1.00 pm in time for a light lunch. An interesting stroll round the Geordie capital occupied the afternoon before returning for an early evening meal.

The ease of the down trip proved to be the exact opposite of the return working on the 28th. No. 1 link firemen planned their holidays to avoid this train, if they could, which resulted in my working it on other occasions. We booked on at Newcastle station by phone to Gateshead shed at 6.55 pm to relieve the Gateshead men who had prepared *Bongrace* for us and brought her onto the train. Bill had warned me we had a full night's work - he did not exaggerate! The 7.25 pm was essentially a mail and parcels train that was advertised for passengers if they wished to use it. To call it an express, in the normal sense of the term, was a little grandiose. We were booked into King's Cross at 3.05 am, on a schedule some 50 per cent longer than with a normal express working. It was a tough turn of duty. We usually left Newcastle with 13 bogies on. We stopped for up to 15 minutes each at Durham, Darlington, York, and Selby, before arrival at Doncaster a few minutes early if possible, at about 10.45 pm to be relieved by a set of men who did any shunting required. This gave us the chance to slip out for fish and chips - very welcome. Also to slake the thirst with a quick pint before closing time. In those days such practices occurred, so long as one did it in moderation; it was an accepted part of the normal working. A couple of bottles of Newcastle brown were purchased for later consumption, after we had drunk the fresh brew of tea. We relieved our relief crew, and got ready to continue, departing at 11.15 pm. If we had a good guard he would limit the load to the rostered 15 bogies; if we didn't, Doncaster would try to sneak more on. It was not unknown for a 17, even 18, buckeye vehicle formation with a gross trailing weight of maybe approaching 600 tons, with the heavy volume of mails carried, to be worked southwards from Doncaster on this working. If we had adverse weather, particularly a strong side wind, it could become a very long night. Keeping an 'A1's' 50 square feet of grate area up to the mark with sufficient coal kept me well occupied on this arduous duty! On this occasion we had 16 bogies on, I can recall. Being my first trip with this train, rather more interest was taken in such matters than was to occur afterwards!

Leaving Doncaster the tender was checked to see if the relief crew had topped up the tank and pulled any coal forward as they were scheduled to do. Most times we were lucky, occasionally we were not. If not, then a harder trip lay ahead. By the time we had reached Doncaster from Newcastle the coal would be barely within reach if the Geordie preparation crew had built a decent fire and then gone under the coaler to fill the hole they had made. If they hadn't, then one was in the tender by York to start the process of pulling it forward. If Gateshead had and the Doncaster men hadn't, then I was about to start. If the Doncaster men had, we might get through Retford before needing to go into the tender to commence pulling coal forward. If the tank had been filled we gave Scrooby troughs (10 miles south of Doncaster) a miss, if not then we scooped. After Retford it was against the collar up to Askham tunnel, then a short breather down through Tuxford to Crow Park before the work began again in earnest to get the fire built up before pausing from my labours for Muskham troughs, just north of Newark in the Trent valley. As soon as we had scooped here, it was continuous work then up to Stoke summit as we climbed out of the Trent valley, with a brief respite at Grantham for 10 minutes, always occupied in pulling coal forward. On this trip Bill swung a few shovelfuls in the box for me in the station while busy with the coal pick. Most drivers in the top link were approaching, or in their sixties, and we could not expect them to do very much to help us. By the time we had got to Peterborough, the coal would be well back into the tender - it was physically demanding work. One had to be fit to have the stamina required. At Peterborough, a fireman was rostered to assist with pulling the coal forward. It was a duty they detested, but most made a fair attempt during the booked 15 minute stop. Occasionally we got poor help and only the minimum work done. The lengthy stops were required for the large volumes of mail and parcels being transferred at each station. It also meant the fire would cool off, which was not helpful. Too much use of the dampers created excess clinker on the bars, if we didn't watch matters. It was essential to avoid blowing off in the stations during the night hours, which meant careful management of the fire.

The final 76 miles were the killer. We had been stopping and starting, the fire had got hot and cooled down several times, and the clinker was building up. On the 'A1s' we could rock the fire grate rocker bars to break it down a bit while standing in the stations. 'A4s' did not have this useful fireman's aid. The rocker bar mechanism had two positions - one for limited rocking, used out on the road, and one for full travel to drop the fire when disposing of the engine. Rocker bar-fitted engines would also have rocking ashpans to dump the fire straight through. These could not be opened out on the road, and you never, never, used the full travel position of the rocker bars out on the road either. This was for two reasons, the hot clinker would buckle the ashpan hopper doors, and we could jam the bars in the open position, which would cause a total failure. Even worse, we might break a bar trying to force it closed when still very hot at road running temperatures.

The 'A1s' were a very free steaming engine. They had the largest size of firegrate permitted for manual firing - 50 square feet. They could digest inferior quality fuel better than the 'A3' and 'A4' engines which had only 41 square feet fireboxes. With the 'A3s' and 'A4s' in their single-chimney form, it was essential to manage the fire far more carefully on the longer journeys than with the 'A1s'. In their double-chimney form they were almost as good as the 'A1s' for steaming, smaller firebox notwithstanding. The double-chimney increased the volume of draught on the fire without pulling it about too much which gave a more even draw over the firebed. This aided fuel combustion particularly with the poorer quality coals. With the single chimney engines we would have to work the engine harder to achieve similar draughting strengths, and not necessarily achieve the same draught volumes. The resultant fierceness with the engine working hard could pull the fire about very unevenly once clinker started to build up as primary air being drawn through the firebed would obviously go to the cleaner areas of the grate which offered easier access through the firebed. The secondary air entering via the firehole completed the fuel combustion process started by the primary air coming up through the firebars and firebed.

Most of this was far from my mind when endeavouring to keep the white feather flying south of Peterborough! We were climbing against the grade with only a few level or downhill stretches for most of the next 50 miles until Woolmer Green, south of Knebworth, apart from the short gallop down through Huntingdon. We were always struggling, not for steam, but for coal from the back of the tender, with little respite - we had by then been on the go for six hours, with over 200 miles behind us! Southwards from Peterborough the routine was always the same - fire up, in the tender to pull coal forward, fire up, into the tender again, and so on. It was a solid physical slog with little respite. Such work made me fitter than at any time, before or since. As we passed Stevenage it was essential to remember the final scoop over the Langley troughs. It was important to remember to drop the scoop fully down at Langley on this train. With minimum coal left, and the water level lower in the tender than normal owing to the hard steaming required, meant less weight on the springs and therefore the tender would be riding higher than usual. A difference of 1 inch in height could be critical to a successful scooping. After Woolmer Green we had a five mile respite through Welwyn Garden City before the final uphill length of 7 miles through Hatfield to Potters Bar. Then, at long last, it would be all over.

The final bottle of the well known brown ale was retrieved from the bucket of water that had kept it cool. The first one had been drunk as we descended Stoke Bank. The driver might have a cupful in the tea can lid, or he may not. Bill didn't, from memory. Occasionally on this turn it was not unknown to whistle the code passing Cadwell box, north of Hitchin, to ask to be turned slow road into Hitchin platform, if extra coal was required from the shed. We were in dire straits to do this as Hitchin did not have a tower coaling plant, only a simple mechanical hoist. I can recall relieving one crew on arrival at King's Cross when they explained the tender had been swept clean after passing Hatfield, and there was not over-much fire left in the box for us to get back up to Top Shed! Normally, one would hope to have perhaps a ton left, but never more, in my experience on this particular working.

This then, gives a summarised description of the heaviest up road train from Newcastle worked by King's Cross crews. It was a challenge, but, as one learned the road, it became progressively that little bit easier each time. It was still very hard work for all that!

Getting home to Ilford in the early hours could be another challenge, depending on the time one finished work. There was an LTE staff bus over to Liverpool St which called at King's Cross at about 3.20 am. There was also a staff tube train on the Circle Line a couple of hours later, that ran before the public service commenced. On one occasion the first trolleybus to Moorgate provided the means. If it was a decent dry night, I would sometimes walk the four miles to Liverpool Street - it was a relaxing way to gently unwind before turning in for a decent sleep. On most turns we did get relief on arrival off a main line working, but if the foreman didn't have a set of men immediately available, we had to stay with the engine either until he did, or were released when the empty stock departed to let us go LE to the shed. On lodge turns relief was always arranged, but on other workings we could not rely on this. Generally we didn't do too badly.

On 29th May, true to form, it was back to the station shunting pilot! This was livened up when, on our very first shunt, the engine became buffer-locked with a coach on the sharp curve in the milk dock opposite the former No. 17 platform. Before we could stop, the coach had become derailed blocking the access to the station loco. Chaos! Eventually the breakdown gang arrived and after two hours of skilled juggling in the very confined space available for them to work in up against the milk dock platform face, finally unravelled it all. A huge sigh of relief from the station loco. foreman as we had trapped a couple of engines urgently required for outgoing trains.

Then the next night, it was off to Newcastle again, this time with Arthur Davis on his regular engine, class 'A4' No. 60033 *Seagull*. This was with another non-stop sleeping car train, the 11.20 pm, and another gentle 60 mph journey, running into Newcastle at 4.20 am. This engine ran like a well-oiled sewing machine, it was pure pleasure. On the return working on the 31st, Gateshead had used '33', much to Arthur's extreme annoyance, owing to an engine failure earlier. We had 'A1' No. 60122 *Curlew* which had just worked down from London. It was quickly serviced by Gateshead. As their crew were doing the disposal duties, we were preparing it. We had booked on at 3.40 pm, to work the 5.05 pm departure from Newcastle to arrive in London at 10.10 pm. The engine had worked the down 'Flying Scotsman' from London at 10 am, into Newcastle at 3 pm. This was maximum utilisation - 12 hours London to London! My principal memory of this lively riding machine was being thrown across the cab straight out of my seat and crashing into Arthur. I had no choice, the sudden violent lurch of the engine caught me completely unawares as we rounded Aycliffe curve at about 50 mph. Usually an 'A1' would throw you around on straight track; for this to happen on this relatively low speed curve was out of character. She really waggled her back end at speed. Arthur was not inclined to run her above 80 mph anywhere after that little episode. Severe bruising quickly developed from crashing into the upright metal back of his bucket seat. (When the doctor heard how it had occurred he was surprised a rib or two hadn't been broken.) She also gobbled a lot more coal than '33' would have done. This was the other side of the coin, when we had a rough engine, then 268 miles was a very long way. She steamed all right, but made hard work of it. One felt more like a navvy, rather than a fireman. My back didn't like the punishment it took on this trip after the earlier severe bruising. Arrival at King's Cross, aching all over with the bruising making breathing less easy, could not come quickly enough. It took a week for the bruising to go down. Luckily, it being a Sunday, there was a chance to rest up before returning to the treadmill on Monday afternoon after seeing the doctor for a precautionary check over in the morning. This was a day out with Joe to Cambridge and back on a BR

Standard class '5' No. 73158 - not the smoothest riding machines, but definitely better than an average 'B1' which might have been our steed instead. It was welcomed in the circumstances!

In an earlier chapter mention was made of our rates of pay structure. Moving up onto main line work meant I qualified, for the first time in my career, for 'proper' mileage allowance payments. With the more demanding and onerous duties associated with working the longer distance expresses, agreements had been negotiated by our unions to provide for enhanced payments for the generally longer mileages entailed. We therefore earned pay based on both 'time' hours, and 'mileage' hours. The 'time' hours were paid as already described at the rate applicable to the time of day, night, and Sunday, i.e., flat rate, time and one quarter, etc., related to the times at work each day. For 'mileage' hours the datum for a standard working day was set at 140 miles. Below this figure there were nominal enhanced pay allowances which commenced at 70 miles with small incremental increases up to 140 miles, which, in 1958 varied between 3d. and 1s. 9d. that need not concern us here. For 'proper' mileage worked, i.e., above 140 per day, we were paid at the additional rate of one hour's pay per 15 miles, with fractions calculated at one half hour's pay for up to seven miles, and one full hour's pay for above eight miles. Up to the odd half mile was ignored, the odd half mile up to one mile was rounded up to one mile, calculated on the total mileage for the day. Thus, a diagram to, say, Grantham and return, was 211 miles (105½ x 2). Deduct the basic 140, divide 71, by 15, gives a division of equal to 4 hours plus 11 miles, which therefore earned 5 hours payment at the basic hourly rate being paid to the individual to supplement the basic 'time' hours paid for the guaranteed eight hour day. A one way trip to Newcastle, was calculated at 268½ miles, less 140, gives 128½, divided by 15, gives 8 hours plus 8.5 miles, which rounded up, earned nine hours 'mileage' pay, plus the basic eight hours 'time' pay. We described the Newcastle trip as a 'two day one', meaning two days pay plus one additional hour, or a total of 17 hours pay per single trip. This is a basic explanation summarising the essentials. All agreements, that covered a major subject, such as pay, included 'small print' clauses to clarify detail interpretation, but these did not alter the basic description given here. (For example, rostered time to travel passenger 'on the cushions' was ignored in calculating the 'actual train miles worked' mileage payment and did not qualify to be included in the overall mileage payment for the day.) Today, totally different arrangements apply.

A very interesting week's holiday was spent in June with my lifelong friend from school days Peter Paton (to whom this book has been dedicated) who had originally been responsible for getting me interested in railways in the first place. We travelled the length and breadth of the Isle of Man 3 ft gauge system and the parallel tram systems. This was before the large scale closures occurred. It was a proper busman's holiday, travelling the trains, but very enjoyable. We also hired a Morris Minor 1000 for three days to see the non-rail sights as well. This was at the time when the special limited edition lilac-coloured Minor 'Million' version of the 1000s, to celebrate a million production models made, were coming out, one of which we saw on the Island.

Class 'A4' Pacific No. 60007 *Sir Nigel Gresley* north of Selby heading south with the 3.52 pm Newcastle to King's Cross on 7th September, 1958 - see text opposite for the remarkable co-incidence that lay behind this picture.

Peter I. Paton

Mention of Peter recalls a remarkable co-incidence that we both experienced. He and his family were heading northwards up the A1 road to Scotland on their annual holiday in 1958. They decided to turn off onto the byways of Yorkshire as a break from the monotony of the A1 - this was in the pre-motorway days. In due course they found themselves approaching a set of level crossing gates shut against them across a minor road north of Selby. Being interested in railway photography, out came his camera to take a shot of the passing train, while they were held up at the crossing. Who was working the train? By this entirely random chance, a copy of his photograph as we came up to the crossing with an up express was later received. Looking out of the front cab window caused me to doubt my eyes for a moment to see him there - a blast on our 'A4's' chime whistle acknowledged our surprise at seeing each other! A totally unexpected experience in the wilds of Yorkshire, 200 miles from our homes - he had no idea of my working that day, nor likewise myself that his family were heading north on holiday. The resulting photograph appears opposite.

My regular mate, Joe Denley was one of just four drivers at Top Shed who signed for the road beyond Cambridge to Newmarket. We therefore also worked the occasional race special from King's Cross. These trains were a nice little perk. The restaurant car crew fed us during the long layover in the sidings. We cleaned ourselves up before joining them in the restaurant car and sat on a newspaper to avoid any risk of marking the seats with our overalls, having first thoroughly cleaned the soles of our boots. Some engine crews enjoyed the racing, but we preferred a decent meal with the remaining restaurant crew members and our guard. Neither Joe nor myself were much interested in horse racing so it made for a lengthy and most relaxing interlude. Such trains must have been a very profitable operation. They rarely ran with empty seats and were primarily run for the high proportion of first class passengers that would be carried. Racegoers were known for their generous spending in the restaurant cars. The alcohol consumed was considerable, especially on the homeward journey back to London. These trains were marshalled with at least two restaurant vehicles and sometimes a buffet/bar one as well. The good humoured and often inebriated state of the passengers as they came past our engine at King's Cross was always worth observing! Special race day restaurant car trains no longer operate to Newmarket. The horse box specials that once made this a very busy place at which to work, are likewise a yesteryear memory, long since lost to road and air transport. We turned our engine on the Ely/Bury St Edmunds lines triangle using the now closed direct route between Newmarket and Ely.

An incident occurred on 12th July when, for the only time in my career, it was necessary to refuse to work an engine. It was also the only time Joe and I had a difference of opinion, throughout an otherwise very harmonious year together. We were working the 10.40 am summer Saturday express as far as Grantham with 'A1' No. 60125 *Scottish Union*. We had a real struggle right from the off and it was a battle all the way trying to keep a decent water level in the boiler, due to poor injectors which kept stopping without warning. At one point it briefly looked as if the fire might have to be dumped, the water level had got so low, but just in time one injector decided to work again, and thus saved the day.

'A1' class Pacific No. 61025 *Scottish Union* pulls away from King's Cross with a train for York.
Eric Treacy

A spectacular departure from King's Cross from 'A3' Pacific No. 60103 *Flying Scotsman* on the occasion of her last departure on a BR timetabled train, the 1.15 pm to Leeds on 14th January, 1963. *British Railways*

Eventually at Peterborough, with the long climb of Stoke Bank ahead, Joe said enough was enough, and failed her. We had lost time during our efforts to keep the show on the road. Peterborough turned out their standby pilot a 'V2' No. 60826. This was only an average machine, which clearly they wanted to be rid of. Of more concern to me, the tender shovelling plate was worn out and lifting. Thus, shovelling became a very difficult task. I was repeatedly jarring my left elbow as the shovel jammed under the split shovelling plate.

When we got to Grantham, it was my wish for Joe to fail the engine and ask for a replacement. To my surprise, he declined, saying we could manage. We were booked to work the 1.58 pm Parcels back to London. Initially, his decision was accepted until the elbow was badly jarred while building the fire up as the shovel became firmly wedged in under the plate. That was it! It was a new engine or a fresh fireman. Joe grudgingly said, 'Alright, go and tell the foreman'. He declined to go. Needless to say, this caused an upset. This gentleman initially claimed he had no replacement engine, so he was requested to examine the problem. He was reluctant to do so, but eventually did and tried to say it was all right to carry on. Upon my request to be relieved, he suddenly 'remembered' there was another 'V2' available, No. 60864. With this machine we completed the turn of duty, without further difficulty. My report on arrival back at the shed explained the reason for my actions. These were never queried. It is wrong for a fireman to go against his driver, but in this one rare instance I was fully justified in doing so. It gave me no pleasure, but the absence of any follow up action, disciplinary or otherwise, confirmed my report had been accepted. The more so as my refusal had caused a 20 minute delay on departure from Grantham. Joe was not happy, and said so. In fairness to him, that was the end of the matter - he had said 'his piece'. He never again referred to it.

On 24th July, firing to Jack Anderson, we had the engine already mentioned earlier, and which has since become world famous - the class 'A3' No. 60103 *Flying Scotsman*, as she was then known. Today she normally runs with her old LNER number as 4472. She was built by the GNR as No. 1472, but actually entered service as an LNER engine a few days after the grouping in 1923. We had a nice little gallop down to Peterborough with 382 down, the 1.30 pm summer extra express passenger. We were booked to return LE to King's Cross, but she was wanted for another working by New England shed. She was eventually to work her last train in BR ownership and, amid a blaze of publicity, to be sold out of service direct into preservation. After a complete overhaul at the Plant she re-entered traffic with a signed contract allowing her to work private charter trains. She has since travelled the world to America and Australia - a much admired engine and probably the only steam engine ever to work revenue earning express passenger trains on three continents. A truly grand old lady who is still working steam specials on the national network today. Her years in preservation now exceed her original working years - a remarkable record.

The ex-GN design class 'K3' 'Jazzers' were very rarely seen south of Peterborough on the GN main line by the mid-1950s and never on a passenger train if they did venture southwards. Imagine our surprise, therefore, when on 12th August, with Joe, we had No. 61887 on an all stations 'stopper' both ways to Cambridge and back. Where she had sprung up from, we never found out.

Joe became quite nostalgic! Her peculiar 'three forward and two back' motion, and her hard and fairly rough riding qualities at speed, brought back forgotten memories. Tales of how in his younger days these were 'a prime machine', cut little ice - he was welcome to her! It is most peculiar how enginemen the world over develop loyalties to their 'own' railway and the products it produced, irrespective of their faults.

Mention of rare engines, recalls the class 'K1' 'Baby Bongo' No. 62008 from Darlington shed, which, with Harry Taylor, we shared on 22nd August. No. 62008 is a sister engine of the sole preserved example in private ownership today, No. 62005. We worked up with her from Peterborough on 261 up, the 1.38 am express fish train to King's Cross - this train started out from Aberdeen and was always formed up with the insulated 'blue spot' long wheelbase roller bearing-fitted wagons. A 'K1' was a very rare engine on the GN main line - indeed I personally never heard of another working so far south. She had replaced a failed engine further north. We had a good run up with her and maintained the normal timings with no difficulty. Normal power was either a '9F' or a 'V2'. We had worked down with a single chimney '9F' No. 92169, on 1016 down, the 9.35 pm from Clarence yard to New England yard. This was in the days long before Clarence yard became better known for the modern diesel depot that was located there throughout the 'Deltic' diesel era, to replace the King's Cross and Hornsey sheds as steam was phased out in the early 1960s period. Harry had never handled a 'Baby Bongo' before, and enjoyed the experience. Like the larger 'Bongos' they could be noisy and rough, but were always good steaming machines. He was interested to hear me relate some of my past experiences of them.

Returning home on a Newcastle lodge turn with Harry Birkett on 'A4' No. 60007 *Sir Nigel Gresley* on Sunday 7th September while working the 3.52 pm up express passenger, we were diverted by engineering works to travel via Bishop Auckland. This was a regular diversionary route that London men had to learn and sign for, so we did not need a pilotman. It was a curious piece of road to work over through some very beautiful countryside. Unfortunately, this was to be my only trip over it. We had worked northwards with the 11.35 pm 'Night Scotsman' sleeper the previous evening with another of those gentle 60 mph runs that were so enjoyable when you had a good engine, such as with 'No. 7', as she was known to us. She was the 100th Pacific engine to be built at the Doncaster Plant, all of which were to designs by Sir Nigel Gresley, and was named after her famous designer, in honour of this.

Saturday 13th September was the final weekday of the 1958 summer service. It was also the day Abbots Ripton and Great Ponton stations lost their passenger services (apart from one down direction only service stopping 'as required' at Great Ponton on the Sunday morning - hardly ever used). In those pre-Beeching days, main line station closures were unusual. To work the last down road 'Parly' rostered to King's Cross men to stop at these stations was a sad experience. All-stations main line stopping trains were known as 'Parly' trains on the GN section. This name was a legacy from the days when Parliament required a stipulated minimum number of trains to serve each station, usually, but not necessarily, four per day each way. This was to ensure the old private companies did not 'cherry-pick' all the better value business to the total detriment of the less valuable business. With Alf Kistruck we plodded on with 'A4' No. 60015 *Quicksilver* which was anything but, calling at all 'halts and telegraph poles' as we used to describe it, King's Cross to Grantham, taking some four hours to do so. It was like a death sentence, although we did miss out a few of the inner area local suburban stations. A far cry from the trip at a mile a minute described earlier! Our return working with an up express got us back to King's Cross in well under half the time. This working came my way because Alf's booked mate had phoned in sick. It made a change from the rostered little frolic to Cambridge and back with Joe. At least we gave Abbots Ripton and Great Ponton a quality farewell with *Quicksilver* as the motive power. She was the second of the original four class 'A4s' built for the new Silver Jubilee streamlined trains in 1935. These were introduced to celebrate the silver jubilee of King George V and Queen Mary. These four engines entered traffic painted in a special commemorative silver colour style livery. The remaining 31 to be built entered traffic in other liveries, some with varying styles of special decorative embellishment being added for other dedicated train workings.

My first, and as it turned out, only lodge turn to York was beset with difficulties. On 16th September with Harry Wheeler we were rostered to work 714 down, the 4.30 pm express goods King's Cross Goods to York, Dringhouses. We had 'V2' No. 60903, one of the better members of this class. She was a good steamer and ran well. On the journey down we were delayed by a hot box causing us to be put in slow road to detach the offending wagon at Biggleswade. We thus lost our booked path, and were unable to recoup any of the arrears during the New England yard stop for attaching and detaching wagons. With the high level of usage over the double track section north of Grantham until south of Doncaster, losing a booked path becomes critical. We suffered diversion into goods loops to allow other booked services to run in their correct pathing, and the delays built up as the journey progressed. We were scheduled into Dringhouses yard, go LE to York Shed, and to book off at 11.55 pm - we eventually did so at 2.30 am.

We were rostered to sign on again at 9.10 am, but could not do so until 12.30 pm to comply with the minimum normal rest period of 10 hours between working trains on a lodge turn. Our booked 9.55 am departure, was delayed still further due to trouble with a damaged engine coupling on our power for the day, another 'Spaceship' No. 92168. We eventually departed at 2.00 pm, well out of course, to experience the inevitable delays once again. By Peterborough we had run out of hours. Immediately on arrival there Harry asked for relief, and we completed our two day trip by travelling home 'on the cushions' back to London. We were both very tired and thoroughly fed up - it had developed into a most frustrating two day trip together.

One could carry on describing the various turns of work, but hopefully a fair impression has been offered. This chapter has discussed a representative cross section to illustrate the variety of express work undertaken by Top Shed.

Appendix One

Engine Wheel Arrangements
and ex-LNER Designations

The 'Whyte' system (named after its creator) describes the number of wheels commencing from the front of the engine - leading support wheels, coupled wheels, and trailing support wheels. With rare exceptions, leading and trailing wheel groupings are single-axle pony trucks, or multi-axle single bogie units. It is a system used world wide. The former LNER classified the different wheel arrangements using letters as follows:

Class	Wheels	Class	Wheels	Class	Wheels	Class	Wheels
A	4-6-2	H	4-4-4	O	2-8-0	V	2-6-2
B	4-6-0	I	4-2-2	P	2-8-2	W	4-6-4 #
C	4-4-2	J	0-6-0	Q	0-8-0	X	2-2-4
D	4-4-0	K	2-6-0	R	0-8-2	Y	0-4-0
E	2-4-0	L	2-6-4	S	0-8-4	Z	0-4-2
F	2-4-2	M	0-6-4	T	4-8-0		
G	0-4-4	N	0-6-2	U	2-8-0+0-8-2		

\#   The one engine built with this wheel arrangement, No. 10000, was strictly speaking, a 4-6-2-2, as each trailing axle under the cab worked independently, not as a single bogie unit. It was officially described as a 4-6-4, with the letter 'W' used in this context.

The Beyer-Garratt engine class 'U' is in effect two separate engine chassis supporting a separate boiler support frame, and hence the double description. In America, and elsewhere, some larger engines were articulated within one integral engine and boiler chassis, e.g., 4-6-6-4, indicating a leading 4-wheel bogie, followed by two separate sets of six-coupled wheels, provided with flexible movement to accommodate curved track, followed by a trailing 4-wheel rear bogie.

In the case of tank engines, whose water and coal supplies are carried within the single chassis, the letter 'T' is added to the wheel arrangement, as in 4-6-2T. This indicates that no separate tender for coal and water is attached to the engine. Again, there were occasional exceptions to this rule, but these can be disregarded for all practical explanations. Some older engines carried their water supply in a well tank between the frames and were designated 'WT' instead of 'T' to indicate this difference.

Although the 'Whyte' notation system was, and is still, used by rail administrations worldwide, there are other description systems in use, e.g., the French Railways (SNCF), used the number of axles instead of wheels. For example a class '231' described their 4-6-2 wheel arrangement, which description prefixed the engine class letter and individual fleet number, e.g., 231 E 14.

In the final years of the Southern Railway a system using numbers to identify carrying axles and letters to identify coupled wheels, was introduced. For example, '21C' described the 4-6-2 engine, the first number indicated the 2 leading carrying axles, the second number the 1 trailing carrying axle, and the letter C, the 3 coupled-wheel axles.

For non-steam locomotives the 'Whyte' system has been adapted to indicate powered and unpowered axles, whether coupled or not coupled, and any smaller size carrying wheels. On non-steam locomotives, bogies, as distinct from the wheels, can be attached or independent, usually identified with a '+' or '-' sign respectively being included between the individual bogie descriptions. The descriptive principle is similar, but more complex! Another system uses a mix of upper and lower case letters to describe the axles, and their function, powered or unpowered.

Appendix Two

The 'Jazz' Train Workings
at Liverpool Street Station

The recast suburban train service introduced on the Liverpool St inner suburban area from 1921 when the already intensive workings were reviewed, soon became known as the 'Jazz' service. The generally accepted origin of the description is said to come from the brightly coloured post-war ladies fashions that came into vogue after the drab wartime dress styles of World War I. The rapidly gaining popularity of the new jazz style music introduced into this country from America was associated with the new female attire. To speed up passenger flows on the re-vamped services, timed with half-minute station stops, the GER had the excellent idea of painting brightly coloured cant-rail stripes on the carriages (so as to be above passenger's heads), to denote the different classes of travel accommodation. These colours were very quickly associated with the new and colourful jazz dance scene, and hence the nickname, which became universally recognized to describe these services. The legacy of this still survives today with the yellow stripe to denote first class type accommodation, inherited from BR practice by the various train operating companies, some of whom continue to use this useful visual aid.

One particular feature of the updated service, and probably the most important of the many aspects that contributed to its almost immediate success, was the absolutely crucial part played by the engine turn around procedures at Liverpool St. These were a key feature of the overall service reliability.

Before explaining these procedures, a general background description of the stage upon which this operational spectacular was enacted each day for many years with incredible success, is necessary. The main stage was platforms 1 to 4 at Liverpool St, from which the Enfield and Chingford services operated. The equally important stage 'props' were (i) the engine bays, or dead-ends, provided, one for each platform, just off the country end of each platform face, (ii) the Sykes' 'Lock & Block' signalling system, and (iii) the excellent suburban engines used to work the trains with the introduction, as a later improvement, of the 5-car articulated coaching stock sets, known as the 'Quint-Art' stock. The actors who played the 'on-stage' roles were the footplate crews, signalmen, guards and station staff. The supporting cast were the fitters, examiners, shunters and workshop staff. The production team who orchestrated this complex daily operation comprised the train planners who had written the script for it in the first place, and those headquarters members who were responsible for the overall direction, day in and day out, of the 'play'. A not inconsiderable proportion of the GER company resources were therefore involved.

To describe it as a staged production is not incorrect, for this is what it was - a very carefully orchestrated choreograph of considerable complexity, not dissimilar to any of the larger scale musical productions in London's west-end theatres today. It achieved a world-wide fame as the most intensively operated steam suburban service ever to be timetabled. Not the largest - the Southern Railway could probably make a strong claim on this account - but the most intensive, related to the limited trackwork and facilities provided. Railway managers from many countries came, over the years, to see it. They marvelled at the effectiveness of the daily transport of the many thousands of passengers and the apparent ease with which it was achieved.

The trains were equipped by the GER with the Westinghouse ('Westo') compressed air operated braking system. The newly formed LNER were to review this with the wish to convert to their recently standardised vacuum brake system, but soon realised it was impossible if the high standards of frequency and punctual operation were to be maintained. The vacuum brake could not have allowed reliable timekeeping of the intensive services which ran on two minute headways controlled by the Sykes' 'Lock and

'N7/1' class 0-6-2T No. 69663 on the 1.16 pm Enfield Town-Liverpool Street at Seven Sisters on 11th October, 1958. *K.L. Cook*

This 'N7/4', No. 69600, was the first of the class to be built (as GER No. 1000 in 1915). It is seen approaching Hackney Downs with the 2.18 pm Liverpool Street-Chingford service on 1st November, 1958. This GER-built batch of engines (BR Nos. 69600-69611) remained unique in mainland Britain as the only BR-operated passenger locomotives that were never equipped with the vacuum brake, remaining as Westinghouse brake only from building to scrapping. No. 69611 remained in service to the end of the steam 'Jazz' workings in November 1960. *R.C. Riley*

Block' system interlocked with the mechanically-operated traditional semaphore signalling equipment that was provided on all passenger tracks in the inner London area. The description 'Lock and Block' came from the lock that operated on each starting signal and on the signal box starting signal lever in the locking frame - known today as the 'section signal' - that interlocked with the block instrument providing the 'line clear' authority to permit the passage of each train. The physical passage of each train through the section was an integral component of the signalling sequence in order that the locking system could in turn be released ready for the next train to pass. It was virtually impossible for a signalman to allow a train accidentally into an already occupied section ahead of it so long as the system was operated correctly in accordance with the authorized instructions. This was a vital feature of the safety system, particularly important in adverse weather conditions when drivers' forward visibility might be restricted. With each track scheduled to carry 24 trains per hour, and sometimes more in practice, all steam hauled (which meant drifting smoke and steam) throughout the morning and evening peak rush three hours - unlike today's barely two hours with all electric services and excellent driver's forward visibility - such a safeguard was vital and of critical importance. The near perfect safety record of the 'Jazz' train services throughout the existence of the system was its own silent and adequate testimony to the effectiveness of it.

The sequence of the 'staged' operation was enacted in rotation at each individual platform, Nos. 1-4, at 10 minute intervals for each train cycle of arrival and departure at each of the four platforms, i.e., 4 cycles in total every 10 minutes throughout the operating peak rush hour periods. A single cycle was 'staged' as follows.

As the incoming train ran into the platform, the fireman stepped down from the cab just before the engine finally stopped. This positioned him directly alongside the rear engine buffers as it did so. The moment movement ceased he was in under the buffers between the engine and front coach to shut the air brake hose cocks before parting the hoses (the GE never had shunters to do this). As the air hoses were parted it was important not to have his face immediately adjacent to the air hose couplings (which could be at about face level, depending upon the fireman's physical stance) because of the *circa* 50 psi pressure being released from the hoses. After being parted the hoses were stowed behind their respective retaining bracket clips before the carriage hose cock was momentarily cracked open to ensure the train brakes were sufficiently applied before the driver buffered up against the coach to slack off the engine coupling. After stopping the driver would be reversing the engine ready to buffer up while his mate was doing the air hoses. A quick shout from the fireman the moment he was ready, the buffers were squeezed, and the engine coupling would be off the coach coupling hook in an instant.

In bringing the train to a stand the driver positioned the engine side tank water filler lid alongside the water column leather bag using a painted mark on the platform edge denoting the centre of the cab doors (positioned for the normal bunker first running direction). The fireman's next move after uncoupling saw him climbing up onto the front footplating to put the water bag in, while the driver dropped down off the engine to turn the water on. While all this was happening at the inward end, at the outward, departing end, the engine of the preceding train was dropping back out of the bay beyond the platform end to couple up and create the full train pipe brake pressure to release the train brakes. The guard, having stowed the tail lamp in the outward (or country) end brake van compartment, checked the driver's name. Before departure he placed the tail lamp from the inward (or London) end brake van compartment ready for departure.

Next, he would be checking the full train pipe pressure had been created, do a quick brake test by just cracking open his emergency brake valve and then be checking his watch for departure time and the 'Right away' tip from the platform staff. The departing engine driver would be watching for the momentary drop in the train pipe pressure on his brake gauge as confirmation of the guard's brake test. An electric plunger was provided for the platform staff to advise the signalman when the train was ready to depart, which coordinated matters. This avoided the train being given the platform starting signal (which in turn could 'lock up' the station operation) if for any reason the train wasn't ready as scheduled.

As the train began moving to depart, on the inward engine the water was immediately shut off by the driver, the fireman threw the bag out, locked the tank lid, and regained the cab, behind his driver, who then began to follow the departing train down the platform into the dead-end, or bay, as it was officially called. This was one of those authorised exceptions when there were two separate moving trains within one section with no intermediate controlling signals. The light engine driver had to exercise great care to control his speed and be prepared to stop short if the departing train should stop unexpectedly for any reason (with a green 'pea-souper smog' and hence greasy rails, this would require very careful attention). Arriving in the dead-end (with slick working by the signalman to re-set the entrance points and pull off the 'tommy-dod' shunting signal immediately the departing train had cleared the points, to authorise this movement), the water bag would again be put in, this time in the opposite side tank, to finish topping up the tanks, by which time the next train was running in. By the time the tank was sufficiently full (on the larger class 'N7' engines it didn't have to be *completely* full to the very brim, but on the older smaller engines this was required) the outlet points would be reset ready behind the incoming train as it was coming to a stand in the platform, and the outlet 'tommy-dod' shunting signal cleared to back onto the train. The engine was coupled up, the brake released ready for the 'Right away', with the driver watching his brake gauge for the pressure 'blip' caused by the guard's brake test. The train was then ready for departure exactly 10 minutes after the previous train had departed from the same platform. During these operations, the headcode discs, or the lighted oil headlamps as appropriate, and the destination board display were checked and altered as necessary by the fireman as further duties to be undertaken in an already time-filled schedule. The fire had also to be attended to as necessary and the boiler water levels checked and topped up as required. The need for a quick brake test was to confirm the airbrake hose pipe cocks had been correctly opened during the coupling-up procedure by the fireman.

In his box, the signalman would be continuously operating the signals, points and block signalling instruments seeking line clearance over the down suburban line for each departing train by sending the 'Is Line Clear' bell codes to his opposite mate at the next box, then sending the 'Train Entering Section' bell codes, and in due course receiving the 'Train Out of Section' bell codes. Alongside this he was receiving and sending the similar bell codes for trains coming to him on the up suburban line. On average, every 10 minutes he worked something like 26 point lever movements, controlling about 40 individual sets of points, about 30 signal lever movements controlling the same number of signals, and sent and received 24 bell codes - this totals about 80 actions, or one every 7½ seconds, in addition to which he was keeping a sharp lookout through the box windows to see nothing untoward was happening. And . . . he maintained this work rate for *about three hours* with little respite for the four platforms we are considering. On top of this would be the train or engine movements involving other platforms and lines as occasion required. All train and engine movements were recorded in the box register by the booking lad while this was going on. If he was lucky the lad had time to organise the kettle for a cup of tea. If any upset to the working occurred, this minor luxury would be sacrificed until later.

The train movements to platforms 1, 2, 3 and 4 operated in rotation with all trains using just the one pair of tracks, the up and down suburban, into and out of the station throat, i.e., every 10 minute cycle meant four trains over the up line and another four trains over the down line, all with manual signalling. By the time my footplate career had commenced in 1951, the scene and operational sequence above described was exactly the same procedure, but the semaphores and points had been converted to electric operation at the inner London end of the system, inwards from Bethnal Green, with semaphores outwards from Hackney Downs for most of the Enfield, Chingford & Lea Valley network. These routes were to be progressively converted to full electric signal and point operation from the later 1950s onwards, particularly in the run up to the NE London electrification scheme, although this did not fully complete the signalling modernisation at that time.

As trains ran into Liverpool St, the driver brought the train to a stand with an almost fully recharged brake system on the train, with somewhere about 55-60 psi on the clock in the train pipe (full brake release pressure was 70 psi). When the fireman uncoupled after closing the train pipe brake cocks, he then cracked a little touch of air out of the pipe, as already explained - regulations authorised this exemption from the requirement to fully discharge the train pipe that normally ensured the brake blocks were hard on. The reason for leaving a good pressure in the train pipe, meant the outgoing engine when coupled on, had only a minimum of train pipe pressure to recreate to fully release the brakes at the prescribed 70 psi pressure, ready for departure within the allotted time margin. It would have been impossible to have achieved the 10 minute cycle with vacuum working, because of the need to destroy fully and then to recreate fully the brake each time at Liverpool St, plus the longer brake cycle time - off/on/off - at each intermediate half-minute station stop. With the Westo-system the triple brake valve feature on each coach (which operated on a 3 psi differential pressure) permitted simultaneous brake release using air pressure from pre-charged air reservoirs under each coach throughout the train, unlike the vacuum system which works on a sequential release of each coach brake in turn along the length of the train. Equally, of course, in reverse, when approaching a station to stop, all brakes are simultaneously applied with the Westo-system, unlike the vacuum system, thus it provided a quicker and very positive immediate brake application over the entire train length allowing higher station approach speeds to be safely operated. Hence, the continued survival of the Westo on the 'Jazz', until the very end of steam working - the last steam-worked Westo-operated passenger trains regularly operated on BR, by very many years (except the Isle of Wight system where this small self-contained network was never altered).

The other aspect of the GE Westo-working on the 'Jazz' was that with the station stops so tightly timed with the next train tight behind, you had to arrive and depart quickly on the ½ minute (or less) stops - remember this was with steam, not electric multiple units! This was the only steam service in the UK, and possibly the world, to be so tightly timed in this manner. Trains ran into the platform at almost line running speeds, usually anything up to about 45 mph, to stop smoothly at the platform without a jolt.

It was a very slick operation, the like of which will never be seen with steam working again. Passengers were well versed in the need to alight and board promptly - they soon learned that to do otherwise meant either being over-carried, or watching the train depart before their very eyes! Guards used their whistles to good effect, and did not wait for late-comers rushing onto the platform, as the next train was never far behind.

Those hard worked class 'N7' 0-6-2 tanks in my day - supplemented by the four-coupled 'Gobbler' 2-4-2 tanks and six-coupled 'Buckjumper' 0-6-0 tanks, in the earlier days of the service - earned their corn, many, many, times over! Each peak hour train was formed of 2 x five-coach articulated close coupled sets, comprising 38 compartments each x 12 seats in each set with up to six standing - pack 'em in and pack 'em tight, was the rule! It can be readily calculated that well over 1,000 passengers per train could arrive at Liverpool St in the busiest periods, *every two minutes or so, on these four platforms alone*, quite apart from the remaining 14 platforms at this very busy terminus. It is mind boggling to understand the full logistics that surrounded the total station operation, in a predominately mechanical age of signalling, with the parallel pressure on the Underground train services that it created. The 'Jazz' engines were worked hard, usually with full regulator, particularly on the shorter lengths between closely spaced stations. To work the 10-coach heavily loaded trains demanded this if the slick schedules were to be maintained! It was often a culture shock to visitors and even professional footplate men from elsewhere, when first they observed the engine handling techniques used and if occasion dictated it, the extent to which the boiler water level and steam pressure would sometimes be sacrificed to keep time. These workings took few prisoners - crews pushed poor steaming engines with dirty fires at the end of a shift, for example, to the very limits to keep the service running.

Rostered work on these services never came my way, but 'ghost' turns on rest days were indulged/enjoyed - all very unofficial - with mates in the business, so to speak, initially firing and later driving. One had to be up to scratch to run them to time and avoid delay to other trains - run too quickly and you got checked by the train ahead causing loss of time with braking. Go too slowly and the one behind would suffer likewise. Living away from home in the Ilford hostel offered regular opportunities to go 'ghosting' on days off, and to get the full experience of such a unique operation in its final years before it disappeared for ever. If there are any regrets from my footplate years, the missed chance to work in the 'Jazz' links at Stratford has to be one of them. It required enginemanship of a high order.

Today, the last genuine steam 'Jazz' train has long since departed to the scrapman's graveyard. Liverpool Street is almost 100 per cent electric - trains, points and signals - with state of the art computers that can operate the entire rush hour service without human intervention, if required. The dead-end bays have long since disappeared, the total station layout has been significantly simplified and most platforms lengthened to accommodate longer trains. A nostalgic reference to the 'Jazz' can occasionally still be heard from an older passenger. For the vast majority it has never existed - 1960 is a long time ago!

For me, today's station has many attractions. Without doubt, the extensive re-building is excellent and imaginative . . . but, it seems incomplete without the hearty throbbing of the Westinghouse brake pumps echoing back from the walls and overall station roof.

'N7/1' class 0-6-2T No. 69670 waits with its passenger train for departure time at Liverpool Street station in July 1960.   *John C. Baker*